W9-BZB-170

FOUNDATION PRESS

PRINCIPLES OF
PRODUCTS LIABILITY

By

MARK A. GEISTFELD
Crystal Eastman Professor of Law
New York University School of Law

CONCEPTS AND INSIGHTS SERIES

FOUNDATION PRESS
New York, New York
2006

THOMSON
™
WEST

© 2006 By FOUNDATION PRESS
          395 Hudson Street
          New York, NY 10014
          Phone Toll Free 1–877–888–1330
          Fax (212) 367–6799
          fdpress.com
Printed in the United States of America

ISBN–13: 978–1–58778–974–8
ISBN–10: 1–58778–974–4

TEXT IS PRINTED ON 10% POST CONSUMER RECYCLED PAPER

For Janette and Max

*

ACKNOWLEDGEMENTS

This project began while I was a second–year law student at Columbia University. After writing a paper on product warranties and tort liability for a seminar taught by Professor Susan Rose-Ackerman, she encouraged me to continue developing my ideas. That line of inquiry resulted in my economics doctoral dissertation at Columbia and ultimately helped to propel me onto the faculty at New York University School of Law. The study of tort law had grabbed me completely. At each critical step, Susan was incredibly helpful and supportive. I can't thank her enough. My approach to the subject was then deeply influenced by my colleagues at NYU, particularly Lewis Kornhauser. I have also had the good fortune of being supported by my Dean, Ricky Revesz, both in the particulars of this project and in all other matters. Financial support was provided by the Filomen D'Agostino and Max E. Greenberg Research Fund of the New York University School of Law.

As he has done for me so many other times, Bob Rabin graciously gave helpful input on the manuscript and guidance along the way. Mike Green generously provided numerous suggestions and critiques, somehow finding the time to do so despite his commitments to the ongoing project of restating tort law. My tort colleagues in New York City—Tony Seebok, Cathy Sharkey, Martin Stone, and Ben Zipursky—provided much-needed help on the causation chapter. The most useful input has come from my students at NYU, both in Torts and Products Liability, who over the years have helped me to develop many of the ideas in this book. Two of them, Anik Guha and Jacob Kreutzer, provided invaluable research assistance.

My most deeply felt thanks go to Janette Sadik-Khan, who has been with me since those early days at Columbia. We did this project together. Our son Max let me work on summer afternoons when he really wanted me to come to the beach for a game of wave ball. He is a compelling reason why it is worth trying to make the world a safer place.

Mark A. Geistfeld

New York City
September, 2005

*

v

TABLE OF CONTENTS

A NOTE ON CITATIONS

Unlike the traditional law review article or legal brief, I have not provided citations for every legal proposition. Aside from the citations for direct quotations, I have tried to give those citations that provide a good entry into the extensive literature on products liability and the related issues in tort law. Many citations are repeated throughout the book, and for those I have relied upon the following abbreviations:

Madden & Owen on Products Liability

David G. Owen, M. Stuart Madden & Mary J. Davis, Madden & Owen on Products Liability (3d ed. 2000)

Prosser & Keeton on Torts

W. Page Keeton, Dan B. Dobbs, Robert E. Keeton, and David G. Owen, Prosser and Keeton on the Law of Torts (5th ed. 1984)

Restatement (Second)

Restatement (Second) of Torts §§ 1–503 (1965)
Restatement (Second) of Torts §§ 504A–707A (1977)
Restatement (Second) of Torts §§ 708–end (1979)

Restatement (Third)

Restatement (Third) of Torts: Products Liability (1998)

Shapo, Law of Products Liability

Marshall S. Shapo, The Law of Products Liability (4th ed. 2001)

*

PRINCIPLES OF
PRODUCTS LIABILITY

*

INTRODUCTION

Product risk is pervasive, increasingly so in the modern economy. Automobiles can crash. Drugs can cause harmful side effects. Chemicals can be carcinogens. Even seemingly benign products pose the risk of serious physical harm. Food, the most basic of all products, can be contaminated. Or a bottle of soda can explode.

The probability that a product will severely injure a particular person is typically quite low. But when millions of people use products, a low probability of individual injury translates into a vast number of product-caused injuries. According to one estimate based on government data, the annual cost of product accidents in the U.S. is roughly $100 billion.[1] This estimate may be low.[2] Automobile fatalities, for example, account for over 40,000 deaths each year. Cigarette smoking causes more than 400,000 premature deaths each year.

When a product causes physical harm, a question of tort law arises. Does the victim have a right to receive monetary compensation for the injury from the product seller? The answer is determined by the set of legal rules known as products liability. These rules are a form of tort law because they determine the civil liability of one party for causing the physical harms suffered by another, the prototypical question of tort law.[3] The extent to which well-established tort principles justify products liability rules, though, is less clear.

The origins of products liability can be traced to the ancient English laws imposing strict liability on the sellers of contaminated foods. Nevertheless, products liability was not conceptualized as a

---

1. *See* David G. Owen, John E. Montgomery & Mary J. Davis, Products Liability and Safety: Cases and Materials 2 (4th ed. 2004).

2. A study by the Rand Corporation based on survey evidence estimates that all accidents in the United States imposed direct and work-loss annual costs of $175.9 billion or 4 percent of Gross National Product in the late 1980s. Deborah R. Hensler et al., Compensation for Accidental Injuries in the United States (1991). This figure does not include latent injuries or those requiring institutionalization or resulting in death. Approximately 30 percent of the accidents covered by the survey involved product use, and another 18 percent were associated with motor-vehicle use. This study accordingly suggests that the social cost of product accidents in the 1980s substantially exceeded $80 billion per year once the study's cost estimate is adjusted to account for fatalities and latent injuries like cancer. This adjustment, coupled with an adjustment for inflation, indicates that product-caused injuries involved costs well over $100 billion per year by the mid–1990s.

3. *See generally* Kenneth S. Abraham, The Forms and Functions of Tort Law (2d ed. 2002).

field of tort law until the mid-twentieth century. The problem of product-caused injuries was deemed to be an aspect of the contract law of product warranties, except for those cases in which the product seller negligently caused physical harm to another. In the famous 1944 case *Escola v. Coca Cola Bottling Company*,[4] Justice Roger Traynor of the California Supreme Court argued that the contaminated-food cases justify a tort rule making product sellers strictly liable for physical harms caused by defective products. In 1965, this rule of strict products liability was adopted by the American Law Institute in § 402A of the *Restatement (Second) of Torts*, and then by most states within the next ten years. The dozen or so pages devoted to the problem of product defects in the *Restatement (Second)* subsequently led to a body of law requiring over 300 pages of exposition in the *Restatement (Third) of Torts: Products Liability*, which was adopted by the American Law Institute in 1998.

The growth of products liability has been astounding, particularly when compared to the slowly evolving tort rules of the common law. In light of this rapid growth, many do not find it plausible that products liability is based on well-established principles of tort law. According to one view, the growth of products liability can be attributed to "a conceptual revolution that is among the most dramatic ever witnessed in the Anglo–American legal system."[5]

The seeming departure from firmly established principles makes it possible to criticize forcefully the modern tort system. Allegations of excessive tort liability in the U.S. often are illustrated with products liability cases, such as the widely reported case involving a $2.7 million punitive damages award to an elderly woman burned by hot coffee.[6] The plaintiff became the "poster lady" for tort reform efforts in the U.S. Congress.[7] According to critics, cases like this show that unfettered jury discretion and sympathy for injury victims largely explain the rapid growth of products liability. In this view, well-established tort principles have given way to the massive redistribution of social wealth.

---

4. 150 P.2d 436 (Cal. 1944).

5. George L. Priest, *The Invention of Enterprise Liability: A Critical History of the Intellectual Foundations of Modern Tort Law*, 14 J. Legal Stud. 461, 461 (1985).

6. Liebeck v. McDonald's Restaurants, P.T.S., Inc., No. CV–93–02419, 1995 WL 360309 (D.N.M. Aug. 18,

1994). The jury awarded plaintiff a total of $2.9 million, which was subsequently reduced by the judge to $640,000. The facts of this case are described more fully in Chapter 9, section III.

7. Aric Press, *Are Lawyers Burning America?*, Newsweek, Mar. 20, 1995, at 32.

Since the 1980s, the growth of products liability has subsided.[8] Once again, the change is subject to differing interpretations. It may reflect a changing political mindset that distrusts governmental regulation in favor of market competition: The courts should not determine issues of product safety; the market should. Or the increasingly apparent limitations of tort liability may be attributable to those very same legal principles that gave rise to the modern regime of strict products liability.

Not surprisingly, the political controversy over products liability finds expression in doctrinal debates. According to the *Restatement (Second)*, the rationale for strict products liability is that a defective product frustrates consumer expectations of product safety. The *Restatement (Second)* accordingly frames the rule of strict products liability to protect consumer expectations. The rule has been enormously influential. It has largely shaped the development of products liability, having been widely adopted by states and other jurisdictions around the world, including the European Union and Japan. Despite this impressive pedigree, the *Restatement (Third)* rejects consumer expectations as the basis for liability in the most important classes of product cases, those involving defects of product design or warnings. The *Restatement (Third)* instead evaluates the defectiveness of a product design or warning in cost-benefit terms known as the *risk-utility test*. Whether this liability rule should be framed in terms of consumer expectations or cost-benefit analysis is now the most controversial doctrinal issue in products liability. A liability rule protecting consumer expectations appears to protect fairly the victims of product accidents, whereas cost-benefit analysis is the calculus of efficiency preferred by the business community. Critics of the *Restatement (Third)* claim that its cost-benefit risk-utility test is based upon a pro-business political bias, rather than the fair tort principles that gave rise to strict products liability.

This doctrinal debate is part of a wider debate regarding the appropriate purpose of tort law. Many legal scholars have argued that tort law, including products liability, is justified by moral principles for which efficiency considerations are irrelevant.[9] Others argue that tort law should efficiently minimize accident costs and

---

8. *See* James A. Henderson, Jr. & Theodore Eisenberg, *The Quiet Revolution in Products Liability: An Empirical Study of Legal Change*, 37 UCLA L. Rev. 479 (1990); Theodore Eisenberg & James A. Henderson, Jr., *Inside the Quiet Revolution in Products Liability*, 39 UCLA L. Rev. 731 (1992).

9. *E.g.*, Ernest Weinrib, The Idea of Private Law 132 (1995) (arguing that tort law is based upon a principle of corrective justice that "rules out the economic analysis of private law").

thereby maximize social wealth.[10] By adopting cost-benefit analysis as the guide to liability, the *Restatement (Third)* appears to have taken a side in this controversy. In an effort to stay neutral, the *Restatement (Third)* argues that the cost-benefit rule is fair, but these arguments do not address the concerns voiced by justice theorists.[11] Moreover, many judges apparently are not persuaded that efficient products liability rules are fair. Judicial opinions in product cases tend to rely on fairness norms when courts perceive a conflict between fairness and efficiency.[12] The debate about the appropriate roles of efficiency and fairness concerns in tort law thus appears to encompass the doctrinal debate pitting the fair, consumer expectations standard of liability in the *Restatement (Second)* against the efficient, risk-utility test in the *Restatement (Third)*.

The study of products liability thus implicates numerous foundational questions. Is products liability based on well-established tort principles, or has this area of law been largely shaped by political considerations? If there are underlying principles of products liability, are they ones of fairness or efficiency? One might even ask why these questions are relevant. Isn't it possible to understand the legal rules without worrying about underlying principles?

To address these questions, the book begins by showing how the doctrinal development of products liability has resulted in controversy over the fundamental concepts of consumer expectations and risk-utility balancing. Having shown that this dispute cannot be resolved by doctrinal analysis, the first section of the book goes on to develop further these concepts. The second section of the book, by far the longest, applies this conceptual analysis to the liability rules, often by reference to the leading cases. The analysis is not exhaustive.[13] It addresses the most important substantive doctrines of products liability: the rules for determining

---

10. *E.g.*, Richard A. Posner, The Economics of Justice (1981).

11. The issue of fairness is discussed in Chapter 2, section I.

12. *See* James A. Henderson, Jr., *Judicial Reliance on Public Policy: An Empirical Analysis of Products Liability Decisions*, 59 Geo. Wash. L. Rev. 1570 (1991). Henderson found that judicial opinions "explicitly developed and relied upon public policy reasoning in 15% of the products liability decisions." *Id.* at 1589. "[F]airness was developed 18% more frequently than efficiency, and fairness controlled in the decision 24% more frequently." *Id.* at 1595.

13. Though it covers the primary doctrines of products liability, the discussion here cannot cover every important issue in products liability. For more extensive coverage, see the multi-volume treatises, Madden & Owen on Products Liability; Shapo, Law of Products Liability. There is now an excellent one-volume treatise, which was published too recently for me to rely upon. David G. Owen, Products Liability Law (2005).

different types of defects based on construction or manufacturing flaws, product design, and hazard warnings; the requirement of causation; the determination of damages; defenses based on consumer conduct; and the rules concerning the parties who can sue and be sued. After describing the relevant black-letter rules and the corresponding majority and minority positions on these issues, the doctrinal analysis repeatedly shows how the fundamental doctrines of products liability can be understood in terms of a few basic principles.

The approach of the book thus corresponds to the approach typically taken by casebooks: The relevant concepts are first developed, followed by the important doctrines developed in terms of the leading cases. As compared to a casebook, however, the approach of this book strives for more systematic conceptual development and sustained doctrinal study. This approach does not mean the book is suitable only for the advanced study of products liability, however. The book also should be useful for a more general study of tort law. Most casebooks on tort law understandably devote considerable attention to products liability. The approach taken here locates products liability within tort law more generally, emphasizing the important similarities to and differences from other types of tort actions. By analyzing products liability in this manner, one can learn a great deal about tort law. Sustained doctrinal study also provides insights into the common-law system. The rapid development of products liability has attracted the attention of many scholars interested in the nature of legal reasoning and the processes of the common law.[14] The book develops that theme by showing how many doctrinal controversies in products liability can be attributed to the evolutionary process of the common law. Case-by-case litigation can frame issues in a manner that importantly influences doctrinal development. This dynamic of the common law is hard to capture adequately in a casebook, but is essential for understanding products liability and tort law more generally. Products liability turns out to be an extremely interesting subject of study, not merely because of its large stakes and political salience.

---

14. *E.g.*, Martin P. Golding, Legal Reasoning 112–25 (1983) (using the development of products liability doctrine culminating in the rejection of privity to illustrate legal reasoning by common-law courts and noting that this *"line* of cases ... has often been used to show the technique of case law development"); Edward H. Levi, An Introduction to Legal Reasoning 1–19 (1949).

PART ONE

CONCEPTUAL OVERVIEW

As compared to other forms of tort liability, the regime of strict products liability appears to be novel and new. The appearance is deceptive. Strict products liability is based on firmly established tort principles. The implied warranty and negligence principles each provide a sufficient, independent basis for imposing strict liability upon the seller of a product that is defective in not being able to perform its intended function, such as an exploding soda bottle.

Having two separate doctrinal bases for strict products liability may seem to be a good thing. The overlap of the doctrines, though, may not extend across all product cases. What if the product performed just as the manufacturer intended, but the plaintiff claims that the design itself is defective? Or that the warning is inadequate or defective? According to many courts and commentators, the implied warranty and negligence principles do not necessarily yield the same results for product cases involving defects of product design or warnings, the most important forms of products liability.

Any difference between these two forms of tort liability would be highly important. The liability rule in the *Restatement (Second) of Torts* is based upon the implied warranty, explaining the traditional prominence of consumer expectations in product cases. After adopting this rule, many courts became dissatisfied with the vagueness of consumer expectations, leading them to adopt the risk-utility test. On the basis of this case law, the *Restatement (Third) of Torts* rejects consumer expectations as an independent basis for liability, instead relying upon the negligence-based, risk-utility test for determining design and warning defects.

The different liability rules in the *Restatement (Second)* and the *Restatement (Third)* lend credence to the claim of an astute foreign observer that products liability law in the U.S. involves "a bewildering array of conflicting cases."[1] To make sense of the case law, we first need to address a number of fundamental questions. How did the doctrinal development of strict products liability result in differing liability rules for design and warning defects? What is the content of a liability rule based on consumer expectations? How

1. Jane Stapleton, Product Liability 5 (1994).

does that rule relate to the risk-utility test? By tackling these conceptual questions, we will significantly enhance our ability to analyze and understand doctrinal issues.

Chapter 1

THE DOCTRINAL DEVELOPMENT OF PRODUCTS LIABILITY

The modern tort regime of strict products liability evolved in response to the issues posed by the famous nineteenth century English case *Winterbottom v. Wright*.[1] The case involved a plaintiff who had been driving a coach supplied and serviced by the defendant. The plaintiff was an employee of the coach's owner and had no contractual relationship with the defendant. The coach broke down due to a latent defect, throwing the plaintiff to the ground and permanently disabling him. The plaintiff's tort suit against the defendant was dismissed by the court because there was no contractual relationship or *privity* between the parties. According to the court, unless the liability of product sellers is limited by privity, "the most absurd and outrageous consequences, to which I see no limit, would ensue."

During the nineteenth century, courts repeatedly relied upon the requirement of privity to limit a seller's liability for defective products. The seller of a defective product could be liable to the buyer but not third parties. Judges were concerned that any expansion of liability beyond the contractual relationship would expose manufacturers and other product sellers to excessive liability, thereby disrupting product markets to the detriment of society.

Today, manufacturers and other product sellers are liable in tort for physical injuries caused by product defects, regardless of privity. The buyer, other users, and bystanders can all recover from the seller of a defective product. Although this change in law appears to be quite dramatic, strict products liability evolved from two different bodies of tort law that were already established at the time when *Winterbottom* was decided in the 1840s.[2]

1. 152 Eng. Rep. 402 (Ex. 1842).

2. The historical development of products liability has been well described many times. For particularly helpful sources in addition to those cited in this section, see Richard A. Epstein, Modern Products Liability Law (1980); George L. Priest, *The Invention of Enterprise Liability: A Critical History of the Intellectual Foundations of Modern Tort Law*, 14 J. Legal Stud. 461 (1985); Robert L. Rabin, *Restating the Law: The Dilemmas of Products Liability*, 30 U. Mich. J.L. Reform 197 (1997); Gary T. Schwartz, *Foreword: Understanding Products Liability*, 67 Cal. L. Rev. 435 (1979).

I. The Evolution of Strict Products Liability from the Implied Warranty

Long before *Winterbottom* limited the liability of a product seller to those parties with whom it had a contractual relationship, courts had formulated the doctrine of the implied warranty. According to this doctrine, the nature of a sales transaction implies certain duties or responsibilities on the seller's part and a corresponding set of rights held by the buyer. Because the duties and rights spring from the sales transaction, it may seem that the implied warranty is a rule of contract law. Such a contractual understanding of the doctrine was held by courts and lawyers in the mid-nineteenth century, and a contractual conceptualization of the implied warranty fit well with the privity requirement adopted by *Winterbottom*. Understood as a rule of contract law, the implied warranty applied only to the contracting parties.[3] A seller who breached the implied warranty by selling a defective product thus incurred obligations only to the buyer. That limited obligation finds expression in the privity requirement, which also limits a seller's tort liability for defective products to the buyer. The implied warranty seemed to be comfortably accommodated by *Winterbottom*.

A more detailed examination of the implied warranty shows otherwise. The doctrine has a tort rationale sufficient to justify the modern regime of strict products liability. This rationale was obscured by its contractual counterpart for almost a century after the *Winterbottom* decision, but once the tort rationale for the implied warranty was widely recognized, courts and commentators quickly relied upon it to justify the rule of strict products liability. The logic of the implied warranty not only overturned the *Winterbottom* privity requirement, it also supported the rule of strict liability.

The implied warranty was originally based on tort principles. By 1700, a product seller was strictly liable in tort for innocent misrepresentations regarding the title of ownership.[4] The wrong involved the buyer's injury caused by detrimentally relying upon the seller's misrepresentation. By agreeing to sell the product, the seller impliedly affirms the validity of title and the concomitant right to convey ownership. The buyer who has paid money for the product reasonably expected the title to be valid. If the title is not valid, the buyer was injured by reasonably relying on the seller's

---

3. "[L]ate nineteenth century contract law adopted an inflexible notion of privity—an idea that it was somehow contrary to the nature of contract that it should be capable of conferring enforce- able rights on third parties." Jane Stapleton, Products Liability 15 (1994).

4. William L. Prosser, *The Implied Warranty of Merchantable Quality*, 27 Minn. L. Rev. 117, 119 (1943).

misrepresentation of a material fact, the required elements for the tort of deceit or misrepresentation. The seller's liability is not based upon any express contractual terms or upon fraud or negligence. The seller may have honestly, though mistakenly believed that the title was valid. The seller's liability is based entirely on the fact that the invalid title frustrated the buyer's reasonable expectation of ownership. The liability is firmly grounded in tort law.

Depending upon the nature of the market transaction, the buyer's reasonable expectations can also justify the implied warranty of quality or merchantability. Prior to the industrial revolution, the product seller typically was also the maker or producer of the product. The sales transaction involved face-to-face bargaining. The buyer could inspect the goods or demand a quality assurance from the seller. In these circumstances, the sales transaction did not generate any other reasonable expectation of quality. The buyer could only reasonably expect the quality he observed or expressly demanded from the seller. The nature of market transactions was profoundly changed by the industrial revolution and the growth of mass markets. Increasingly, products were distributed from the manufacturer to middlemen to retailers and finally to consumers. Lacking the opportunity or ability to inspect the goods, a purchaser could have a reasonable expectation of quality that was implied by the sales transaction. This reasonable expectation provides the foundation for the implied warranty of quality.

The industrial revolution in England occurred roughly between 1760 and 1830, and during this period the English courts recognized the implied warranty of quality. One of the early, influential cases involved a sales transaction of "waste silk."[5] The seller delivered something that was unfit for the purposes of waste silk. The contract had no express terms making the seller liable in these circumstances, but the court nevertheless found the seller liable for breaching the implied warranty of merchantable quality. A buyer who pays money for something the seller describes as "waste silk" reasonably expects to receive goods fitting that description. The frustration of that reasonable expectation is sufficient to make the seller legally responsible for the resultant harm, despite the absence of an express contractual provision holding the seller liable in these circumstances. The reasoning is no different from that which justifies tort liability for the sale of a product with a defective title.

To see why, suppose the sale involved a can of beans. Unbeknownst to both the retail grocer and the consumer, the beans were contaminated, causing the consumer to suffer bodily injury after

5. Gardiner v. Gray, 4 Camp. 144, 171 Eng. Rep. 46 (1815).

eating the beans. How are the requirements for tort liability satisfied in these circumstances? How can the grocer be affirming the quality of the beans, given his inability to inspect the contents of a concealed can? And how can the buyer reasonably rely upon that affirmation? As William Prosser explains:

> Even on this basis, and on the assumption that the buyer is aware that the seller does not know what is in the can, it is at least arguable that reliance upon the seller's "skill or judgment," as distinct from his information, may be found. Certainly the buyer is relying upon something when he buys; he cannot be thought willing to buy a pig in a poke and accept the can with whatever is in it, for better or for worse. Certainly he is not relying upon any information of his own as to its contents. The "reliance" required in a cause of action for any form of misrepresentation need not be sole reliance, or the only inducement to act; it is enough that it plays a material part in the inducement. The plaintiff may rely upon two or more elements making up the sum total. This is true of warranties. When the buyer goes to a dealer, he knows that the man is in the business of selling goods of the kind to be purchased; that he has selected the particular goods and is offering them to his trade for the uses for which they are made; that he buys from manufacturers and wholesalers and has information as to which of them are reliable; and that he has had past experience with similar goods; and usually with the particular brand. Is not this both "skill" and "judgment" ...? And is there not enough, in the usual case, to permit a jury to find that reliance upon it has played some important part in inducing the purchase? How many women buy of one corner grocer rather than another, without the belief that he is a competent grocer?[6]

The rationale for tort liability ultimately requires only one of the varied reasons identified by Prosser: "Certainly the buyer is relying upon something when he buys; he cannot be thought willing to buy a pig in a poke and accept the can with whatever is in it, for better or worse." The same type of reliance underlies the implied warranty of title. A sales transaction minimally implies certain

---

6. Prosser, *supra* note 4, at 148–49 (citations and paragraph structure omitted). Prosser says that this reasoning appears to be "beside the point," because it is addressed to the implied warranty of fitness for a particular purpose, whereas the implied warranty of quality does not "rest[] upon misrepresentation, with its tort theories, but upon contract." *Id*. at 149. The reasoning in this passage is not "beside the point," however, since it depicts the way in which the implied warranty of quality protects the consumer's interest in physical security, a core concern of tort law and not contract law. Prosser subsequently recognized the tort rationale for the implied warranty. In his role as Reporter, he drafted the rule of strict products liability in the *Restatement (Second)*.

things about the product, including a valid title and the product's ability to perform safely its intended function. These implied representations create reasonable expectations concerning material facts—the buyer reasonably expects to own a can of edible beans. The seller frustrates these reasonable expectations either by not conveying valid title to the beans (defect of title) or by conveying a can of beans not fit for human consumption (defect of quality). When either type of defect causes injury to the buyer, the seller has completed a tort. The buyer was foreseeably injured by reasonably relying on the seller's misrepresentation of a material fact. This reasoning explains why "[t]he warranty of title stood anciently upon the same footing as the warranty of quality."[7] The footing was in tort.

The tort rationale for the implied warranty can be clearly identified today, but the matter was murky when *Winterbottom* was decided. The implied warranty is created by the contract governing the sales transaction, and there is an obvious contractual rationale for the doctrine. In a contract governing the sale of "waste silk," presumably the parties mutually intended to exchange waste silk. An exchange of something else frustrates the parties' mutual intent and provides a basis for voiding the contract. Since the mutual intention of the parties regarding product quality is implied by the nature of virtually any product transaction, there is a clear contractual basis for the implied warranty of merchantable quality. Consequently, the contractual rationale for the implied warranty dominated legal thinking in the nineteenth century. By the 1800s, the English courts had already recognized contract actions for breach of an express warranty, a contractual doctrine holding sellers responsible for express representations of product quality. When English courts adopted the implied warranty of product quality in the ensuing decades, "a whole generation of lawyers had been taught to regard any warranty as a contract."[8] When *Winterbottom* was decided in the 1840s, the implied warranty was firmly entrenched as a doctrine of contract law.

The jurisprudence of the time also made it natural to conceptualize the implied warranty as an exclusive doctrine of contract law. "The early common law was traditionally hostile to double remedies," which meant that tort and contract were treated as "disconnected spheres, not co-arising actions."[9] Under this jurisprudential approach, the contractual rationale for the implied warranty ren-

7. James Barr Ames, *The History of Assumpsit*, 2 Harv. L. Rev. 1, 10 (1888).

8. Prosser, *supra* note 4, at 120.

9. Vernon Palmer, *Why Privity Entered Tort—An Historical Reexamination of* Winterbottom v. Wright, 27 Am. J. Legal Hist. 85, 89 (1983).

dered the tort rationale irrelevant. "In the 19th century, however, the mutual exclusivity of remedies began to break down, even as the clarification of tort and contract differences occurred."[10] The change in jurisprudence meant that the implied warranty no longer had to be limited to contract law, but would anyone remember its tort origins?

The tort rationale for the implied warranty remained obscure until U.S. courts relied upon the concept to devise liability rules governing contaminated food, an issue of pressing national concern in the early twentieth century. In addressing this issue, the U.S. courts looked to the ancient English rule that obligated sellers to supply "wholesome" food. This doctrine had existed for centuries before the time when *Winterbottom* was decided, but the doctrine had only been applied to cases involving buyers and sellers and appeared to fit comfortably with the *Winterbottom* privity requirement. However, the nature of the food cases makes it easier to conceptualize the implied warranty as a matter of tort law. Contaminated food ordinarily causes bodily injury, and protecting the individual interest in physical security is the core concern of tort law.[11] Not surprisingly, "[t]he early American decisions [in the first decades of the twentieth century] thought that 'warranty' was the name for [the liability rule], and imposed strict liability upon the seller of food, in favor of his purchaser, as 'a principle, not only salutary, but necessary to the preservation of health and life.' "[12] By coupling the legal concept of warranty with the tort rule of strict liability, the food cases helped to reinvigorate the tort rationale for the implied warranty.

The food cases also helped to overturn the *Winterbottom* privity requirement. The logic of these cases does not depend on privity for the simple reason that one who is not the purchaser can reasonably rely upon a seller's provision of wholesome food. Someone who eats canned beans reasonably expects the food to be safe for consumption, even if someone else in the family purchased the can. The product seller can also foresee that the food will be eaten by someone other than the purchaser. The victim of the contaminated food therefore was foreseeably injured by reasonably relying upon the seller's misrepresentation of a material fact, satisfying the elements of the tort even though the seller lacked contractual privity with the victim. As a logical matter, the contaminated-food

---

10. *Id.* at 90.

11. *See* Chapter 2, section 1.

12. William L. Prosser, *The Assault Upon the Citadel (Strict Liability to the*

Consumer), 69 Yale L.J. 1099, 1104 (1960) (citations omitted).

cases do not require privity, a conclusion reached by an increasing number of courts as the twentieth century progressed.[13]

Once the courts began applying strict tort liability to defective foods, the question naturally arose whether strict liability should apply to other defective products. Unless food requires a special rule, the contaminated-food cases could not be harmonized with the privity requirement in *Winterbottom*. The doctrinal development of strict products liability importantly depended on whether the courts could draw a persuasive distinction between food and other products.

When evaluated in terms of the tort rationale for the implied warranty, there is no reason to distinguish food from other products. In the transaction involving the can of contaminated beans, tort principles are implicated for reasons that do not depend upon any unique characteristics of food. Tort liability finds justification in the fact that the product defect (contaminated food) harms the consumer's interest in physical security, the core concern of tort law. By offering any product for sale, the seller implicitly affirms that the product is safe for its intended use. The implicit affirmation makes it reasonable for the consumer to expect that the product is safe. The affirmation is false for defective products, and if the misrepresentation (defect) frustrates the consumer's reasonable safety expectations by causing physical harm, the requirements for tort liability have been satisfied. Any product defect that causes physical harm implicates the tort version of the implied warranty. There is no persuasive reason to limit the rule of strict liability to unwholesome or defective foods, a conclusion famously reached by Professor Karl Llewellyn in the 1930s: "This is not a question of food. This is a question of consumer. Of helpless consumer.... [A] gathering of some hundred cases, from 1850 to [1937] ... demonstrate that food and drink, in part, were only typical of a general trend."[14]

Thus, the implied warranty of wholesome food embodied the necessary tort principles for the rule of strict products liability. The implied warranty shows that tort liability does not depend upon privity or any special qualities of food. Tort liability depends solely upon the way in which the product defect frustrates the consumer's reasonable expectations of safety. By causing the consumer to suffer injury, the defect alone triggers liability. The seller's conduct

---

13. *See id.* at 1110–14.

14. Karl N. Llewellyn, *On Warranty of Quality, and Society: II*, 37 Colum. L. Rev. 341, 404–05 (1937) (sentence and paragraph structure omitted).

is not otherwise relevant. The seller is strictly liable for the injuries caused by the defective product.

This rationale for strict products liability first received judicial recognition in the concurring opinion of Justice Roger Traynor of the California Supreme Court in *Escola v. Coca Cola Bottling Company*.[15] That case was decided in 1944, almost 100 years after *Winterbottom* had been decided. The case involved a food product (soda), and Traynor relied upon the rule of strict liability for contaminated foods as an important justification for reconceptualizing the implied warranty in tort terms. Traynor's argument, however, applied to all defective products and not merely food. Traynor's 1944 *Escola* concurrence helped set in motion the forces that would lead to the widespread adoption of strict products liability.

In 1961, the American Law Institute adopted a draft rule imposing strict liability on sellers of food products, leaving open the question whether the rule should apply to other products. In 1962, the draft extended strict liability to both food and products for "intimate bodily use," and again the draft was approved by the Institute. In 1963, the California Supreme Court accepted Traynor's argument for strict products liability in the landmark case *Greenman v. Yuba Power Products*,[16] a case not involving contaminated food. In 1964, the American Law Institute approved yet another draft, § 402A of the *Restatement (Second) of Torts*, imposing strict liability on the sellers of defective products.[17]

By 1971, 28 states had adopted the rule of strict liability for product defects; by 1976, 41 states had adopted it. In adopting the rule, courts frequently cited *Greenman* as a seminal or landmark case, often noting the widespread influence of Traynor's argument for strict products liability in *Escola*. Legal scholars also jumped on the bandwagon, arguing that sellers should be strictly liable for product defects.

The resultant regime of strict products liability was based on the implied warranty. In describing the historical support for strict products liability, the *Restatement (Second)* explains how the contaminated-food cases were gradually extended to other products.[18] Consequently, "[t]he basis for the rule is the ancient one of the special responsibility for the safety of the public undertaken by one who enters into the business of supplying human beings with products which may endanger the safety of their persons and property, and the forced reliance upon that undertaking on the part

15. 150 P.2d 436 (Cal. 1944).

16. 377 P.2d 897 (Cal. 1963).

17. Restatement (Second) § 402A.

18. *Id.* cmt. b.

of those who purchase such goods."[19] The emphasis on physical injuries caused by forced reliance or frustrated safety expectations essentially restates the tort version of the implied warranty. The implied warranty accordingly frames the doctrinal basis for the rule of strict products liability in the *Restatement (Second)*, as it effectively acknowledges:

> A number of courts, seeking a theoretical basis for the liability, have resorted to a "warranty".... In some instances this theory has proved to be an unfortunate one. Although warranty was in its origin a matter of tort liability, and it is generally agreed that a tort action will still lie for its breach, it has become so identified in practice with a contract of sale between the plaintiff and defendant that the warranty theory has become something of an obstacle to the recognition of the strict liability where there is no such contract. There is nothing in this Section which would prevent any court from treating the [tort] rule stated as a matter of "warranty" to the user or consumer.[20]

In acknowledging the warranty rationale for strict products liability, the *Restatement (Second)* distinguishes the tort version of the implied warranty from its contractual version: "[I]t should be recognized and understood that the 'warranty' [justifying strict products liability] is a very different kind of warranty from those usually found in the sale of goods, and that it is not subject to the various contract rules which have grown up to surround such sales."[21]

By relying on the warranty rationale for strict products liability, the *Restatement (Second)* makes the liability rule dependent on consumer expectations. Strict liability under the *Restatement (Second)* "applies only where the [defective] product is, at the time it leaves the seller's hands, in a condition not contemplated by the ultimate consumer, which will be unreasonably dangerous to him."[22] To satisfy this requirement, "The article sold must be dangerous to an extent beyond that which would be contemplated by the ordinary consumer who purchases it, with the ordinary knowledge common to the community as to its characteristics."[23] This inquiry—the *consumer expectations test*—bases tort liability on the fact that a defective product frustrates the ordinary consumer's reasonable expectations of product safety.

---

19. *Id.* cmt. f.
20. *Id.* cmt. m.
21. *Id.*

22. *Id.* cmt. g.
23. *Id.* cmt. i.

Due to the warranty rationale for strict products liability, the *Restatement (Second)* also "expresses no opinion" whether strict products liability applies "to harm to persons other than users or consumers."[24] As a tort concept, the implied warranty depends on reasonable reliance. Consumers reasonably expect the seller to provide a nondefective product, but in what way do bystanders rely on any implied representations made by the seller? As this question suggests, the injuries suffered by bystanders may be governed by tort principles different than those governing the injuries suffered by consumers, which is why we will defer discussion of bystander injuries for later.[25] Until then, we will focus on the injuries suffered by consumers.

The influence of the warranty rationale for strict products liability is now global in scope. The products liability regimes in a number of countries rely on liability standards substantively similar to those in the *Restatement (Second)*. The European Economic Community Directive on Liability for Defective Products states that "[t]he producer shall be liable for damage caused by a defect in his product."[26] A product is defective if it "does not provide the safety which a person is entitled to expect, taking all circumstances into account."[27] This Directive has influenced products liability legislation in other countries, including Japan.

The objective of protecting the reasonable expectations of consumers is also shared by other important bodies of law. Protecting the reasonable expectations of insurance consumers (policyholders) is a "regulative ideal" of insurance law.[28] Promoting consumer welfare is the fundamental standard for evaluating antitrust issues.[29]

An important contrast is provided by the *Restatement (Third) of Torts: Products Liability*, which maintains that consumer expectations are not determinative of tort liability for design and warning defects.[30] The *Restatement (Third)* provides various rationales

---

24. *Id.* caveat (1).

25. *See* Chapter 12.

26. Council Directive 85/374/EEC of July 25, 1985 on the Approximation of the Laws, Regulations and Administrative Provisions of the Member States Concerning Liability for Defective Products, art. 1, 1985 O.J. (L 210) 29.

27. *Id.* art. 6.

28. *See* Kenneth S. Abraham, *The Expectations Principle as a Regulative Ideal*, 5 Conn. Ins. L.J. 59 (1998).

29. *See, e.g.*, Reiter v. Sonotone Corp., 442 U.S. 330, 343 (1979) ("Congress designed the Sherman Act as a 'consumer welfare prescription.' "); Robert H. Bork, The Antitrust Paradox: A Policy at War with Itself 51 (1978) ("The only legitimate goal of American antitrust law is the maximization of consumer welfare.").

30. Restatement (Third) § 2 cmt. g.

for these liability rules, none of which expressly reference consumer expectations.[31] The concept of consumer expectations is based upon the implied warranty, so the *Restatement (Third)* apparently relies upon some other doctrinal basis for strict products liability. That basis is one of ordinary negligence liability.

II. The Evolution of Strict Products Liability from Negligence Principles

Return again to the 1840s when the privity requirement was adopted in *Winterbottom*. Consider how that rule fares against the tort principles embodied in negligence liability. There is no contractual relationship or privity between a pedestrian and coach driver, yet the pedestrian can recover for her injuries caused by the driver's negligence. Why did *Winterbottom* require privity in order for the victim of a product defect to recover from a negligent product seller?

In the 1840s, the courts had not expressly recognized negligence as an independent basis of liability. The common law had developed within the writ system, and negligence was only an element of various writs, rather than a tort unto itself. The resolution of *Winterbottom*, therefore, importantly depended upon whether the plaintiff's claim fit within a recognized writ or cause of action. On the alleged facts, "[t]here simply were no precedents authorizing recovery in tort."[32] The plaintiff had to argue that the contract itself provided the basis for recovery, and the *Winterbottom* court merely concluded that one must be a party to the contract in order to have any contractually based rights. Hence, *Winterbottom* did not stand "for the proposition that the background existence of a contract in the facts operated as a broad shield against tort duties to third parties," particularly since the "common law was against this proposition, having asserted from the earliest times that wrongs require no privity because they are essentially actions between strangers."[33]

The courts at this time had already recognized a legal duty involving the delivery of dangerous chattels, which enabled them to make exceptions to the privity requirement. Shortly after *Winterbottom* was decided, the New York Court of Appeals affirmed that a defendant could be liable in tort for selling a bottle of mislabeled poison that "put human life in imminent danger," despite the

---

31. *See id.* cmt. a; *see also id.* cmt. g (stating that consumer expectations are relevant only insofar as they "affect how risks are perceived and relate to foresee-ability and frequency of the risks of harm").

32. Palmer, *supra* note 9, at 94.

33. *Id.* at 92–93.

absence of privity between the parties.[34] The courts then developed another exception for cases involving "inherently dangerous" products. These cases were consistent with *Winterbottom*, since the liability was based upon a previously established legal duty and not the contract alone.

The *Winterbottom* court also justified the privity requirement by reasoning that a more expansive duty would expose product sellers to excessive liability. Even today, courts will limit the duty of a negligent product seller for precisely this reason: Too much liability can disrupt product markets and create collateral social costs that may justify a limitation of duty.[35] Presumably an "exception" to the general requirement of privity would not lead to excessive liability. Exceptions would be most appropriate for those cases of greatest concern to the tort system, those involving "imminent threats to human life" or "inherently dangerous products." By departing from the privity requirement in these limited circumstances, the courts applied a liability rule that seemed to accommodate the *Winterbottom* concern about excessive liability.

After the writ system was abolished, the courts in the latter half of the nineteenth century developed the tort of negligence. The abolition of the writ system did not render the prior case law irrelevant, and courts continued to require privity in a negligence action unless the case fell into one of the previously recognized exceptions.

This inquiry forced the courts to confront a difficult question. Why were some defective products "imminently or inherently dangerous" and subject to the tort duty, while other defective products, like the coach in *Winterbottom*, were not excepted from the privity requirement? The difficulty of answering this question is reflected in the case law as summarized by a court in 1915:

> One who manufactures articles inherently dangerous, e.g., poisons, dynamite, gunpowder, torpedoes, bottles of water under gas pressure, is liable in tort to third parties which they injure, unless he proves that he has exercised reasonable care with reference to the articles manufactured. . . . On the other hand,

34. Thomas v. Winchester, 6 N.Y. 397, 409 (1852). For support of the proposition that one owed a legal duty with respect to the delivery of dangerous chattels, see Longmeid v. Holliday, 6 Ex. 761 (1851).

35. *E.g.*, Strauss v. Belle Realty Co., 482 N.E.2d 34, 38 (N.Y. 1985) (retaining privity requirement for actions against electric utility due to concern that the ordinary tort duty would create collateral social costs involving "the obvious impact of a city-wide deprivation of electric power, or . . . the impossibility of fixing a rational boundary once beyond the contractual relationship, or . . . the societal consequences of rampant liability").

one who manufactures articles dangerous only if defectively made, or installed, e.g., tables, chairs, pictures or mirrors hung on the walls, carriages, automobiles, and so on, is not liable to third parties for injuries caused by them, except in case of willful injury or fraud.[36]

On what basis could courts conclude that defective bottles of water under gas pressure are inherently more dangerous than defective automobiles? As the question suggests, the courts were unable to identify a defensible distinction between an "imminently or inherently dangerous" defective product and other defective products.

The distinction was finally demolished by Judge Benjamin Cardozo in the 1916 landmark opinion *MacPherson v. Buick Motor Company*.[37] According to Cardozo, "If the nature of a thing is such that it is reasonably certain to place life and limb in peril when negligently made, it is then a thing of danger [and subject to a tort duty]." By making the tort duty dependent on the risk of physical harm posed by the defect, Cardozo turned the "imminently or inherently dangerous" exception to the privity requirement into a general rule of negligence liability. The tort claim seeks compensation for the injuries caused by the allegedly defective product, and the fact of physical harm would seem to establish conclusively that the alleged defect was a "thing of danger" subject to the tort duty. The particular characteristics of the product—whether it was "imminently or inherently dangerous"—no longer matter, eliminating the associated requirement of privity.

Prior to *MacPherson*, the gradual erosion of the privity requirement had also showed that the resultant expansion in tort liability would not lead to "the most absurd and outrageous consequences" as feared by the court in *Winterbottom*. Once the concern of excessive liability was practically eliminated, *MacPherson* could rely on the principles of negligence law to hold product sellers accountable for the physical harms foreseeably caused by their negligence. Privity is not required, just as it is not required when a driver negligently injures a pedestrian.

In the following years "this decision swept the country" and was "extended by degrees" until it became "in short, a general rule imposing negligence liability upon any supplier, for remuneration, of any chattel."[38]

36. Cadillac v. Johnson, 221 F. 801, 803 (2d Cir. 1915).

37. 111 N.E. 1050 (N.Y. 1916).

38. Prosser, *supra* note 12, at 1100–1103. Perhaps surprisingly, New York courts continued to "talk the language of 'inherent danger'" in the years following the *MacPherson* decision. *Id.* at 1102.

As the courts were adopting this general rule, they faced mounting pressure to apply strict liability rather than negligence.[39] The movement toward strict liability originated with the contaminated-food cases and the implied warranty. The *MacPherson* case greatly facilitated that movement. By basing tort liability on the risk posed by the defect rather than the type of product ("inherently dangerous"), the logic of *MacPherson* implies that there is no persuasive reason to distinguish contaminated foods from other defective products. Like contaminated foods, any defective product can create a risk which makes it a "thing of danger" that is properly governed by a tort duty according to *MacPherson*. If there is no persuasive distinction between contaminated foods and other defective products, then there is no persuasive reason to apply different liability rules to these products. Strict liability had long applied to the sellers of contaminated foods. Assuming the validity of that rule, strict liability should also apply to the seller of any other type of defective product.

The contaminated-food cases and the implied warranty thus facilitated the adoption of strict products liability, but that development would have occurred even if there had been no doctrine of the implied warranty. Strict products liability could have evolved solely from the principles of negligence liability.

After *MacPherson*, the plaintiff in a tort suit had to show that the defect was attributable to negligence by the defendant seller. To establish negligence, plaintiffs frequently relied upon the evidentiary doctrine of *res ipsa loquitur* or "the thing speaks for itself." In effect, the plaintiff argued that the mere existence of the defect establishes negligence on someone's part. The plaintiff then had to show that the defendant, rather than someone else, was responsible for the defect. This argument was extraordinarily successful. "[O]nce the cause of the injury is proved to lie with the defendant, once it is brought home to his plant, the jury finds for the plaintiff."[40]

By allowing plaintiffs to establish negligence liability on this basis, the courts had turned the doctrine of *res ipsa loquitur* into a rule of strict liability. A good example is provided by the landmark case *Escola v. Coca Cola Bottling Company*, which involved an exploding soda bottle that physically injured the plaintiff.[41] The evidence at trial showed that the defect was most likely attributable

---

39. *Id.* at 1103–1110.

40. *Id.* at 1115.

41. 150 P.2d 436 (Cal. 1944). For an extensive discussion of the case, see Mark Geistfeld, Escola v. Coca Cola Bottling Co.: *Strict Products Liability Unbound* in Torts Stories (Robert L. Rabin & Stephen D. Sugarman eds., 2003).

to a hairline fracture in the bottle, causing it to explode when lifted out of the case by the plaintiff. The evidence also showed that the fracture most likely occurred while the bottle was in the possession of the defendant—the bottler and distributor of the soda. In deciding that the plaintiff had properly established *res ipsa loquitur*, the California Supreme Court held, as a matter of law, that soda bottles should not be reused without a "commercially practicable" test that completely eliminated the risk of the bottles incurring hairline fractures. In effect, the court ruled that reasonable care requires the elimination of defects (hairline fractures) in reused bottles. This ruling misapplies negligence principles, because reasonable care does not ordinarily involve the total elimination of risk. Coca Cola could have reasonably used soda bottles over and over again, even if doing so created some risk of a hairline fracture. The issue depends on a balancing of the relevant risks and burdens of precaution, an inquiry absent in *Escola*. The court's finding of negligence was based entirely on conjecture rather than evidence. The court—like others at the time—had improperly applied *res ipsa loquitur* by presuming that the existence of a defect is sufficient evidence of negligence. Once the defendant invariably incurs negligence liability for a defect caused by its manufacture or distribution of the product, from its perspective the outcome is no different than that produced by the rule of strict liability.

The misapplication of *res ipsa loquitur* does not persuasively justify strict liability, however. The courts could have instead tried to apply res ipsa properly by requiring plaintiffs to provide the requisite proof that the defect in question, more likely than not, was caused by the defendant's negligence. But as Justice Traynor observed in *Escola*, this rule, if properly applied, would involve insurmountable problems of proof. "An injured person ... is not ordinarily in a position to refute [the manufacturer's evidence of reasonable care] or identify the cause of the defect, for he can hardly be familiar with the manufacturing process as the manufacturer himself is."[42] To establish *res ipsa loquitur*, the plaintiff in *Escola* would have needed to show that the cost of testing for hairline fractures in recycled bottles could be justified by the resultant reduction in the risk of such defects. The plaintiff quite likely would have been unable to satisfy this onerous evidentiary requirement.

This evidentiary problem can justify strict liability. The amount of product safety effectively induced by negligence liability depends upon the available evidence concerning the range of safety

---

42. 150 P.2d at 441.

investments that could be made by the manufacturer. If a particular safety investment is required by the standard of reasonable care but the plaintiff is unable to prove as much, a manufacturer that fails to make the investment will avoid negligence liability.[43] Evidentiary problems therefore can impair the manufacturer's incentive to incur the costly safety investments required by the negligence standard of reasonable care. In these circumstances, strict liability restores the safety incentive. Once the manufacturer becomes strictly liable for injuries caused by a defective product, the court no longer needs to evaluate the manufacturer's safety decisions on the basis of the plaintiff's proof. Strict liability takes the safety decision from the court and gives it to the manufacturer. To maximize profits, a strictly liable manufacturer must minimize the sum of its safety expenditures and liability costs, giving it an incentive to make any safety investment that reduces liability (and injuries) in a cost-effective manner. Insofar as the manufacturer would have foregone any of these safety investments in a negligence regime due to problems of proof, the shift to strict liability will increase manufacturer investments in product safety and reduce product risk.[44] The evidentiary difficulties inherent in negligence liability therefore can justify strict liability as a means of enforcing the requirements of reasonable care, particularly since this form of liability is not unfair to the defendant in any given case.[45]

The evidentiary rationale for strict liability was an important justification for the statutory schemes of workers' compensation that were widely adopted by the states in the early 1900s. Prior to workers' compensation, an employee ordinarily could recover for workplace injuries only by proving that the injury was caused by the employer's negligence. In light of the staggering toll of workplace injuries that occurred in the late nineteenth and early twentieth centuries, it became increasingly evident that the threat of negligence liability did not give employers a sufficient safety incen-

---

43. As one court observed:

It is not doubted that due care might require the defendant to adopt some device that would afford [reasonable protection against the injury suffered by plaintiff.] Such a device, if it exists, is not disclosed by the record. The burden was upon the plaintiff to show its practicability. Since the burden was not sustained, a verdict should have been directed for the defendant.

Cooley v. Public Serv. Co., 10 A.2d 673, 677 (N.H. 1940).

44. *See* Steven Shavell, *Strict Liability Versus Negligence*, 9 J. Legal Stud. 1 (1980) (showing how strict liability can reduce risk by reducing "activity" levels, where "activity" is any aspect of risky behavior that is outside the ambit of negligence liability due to evidentiary limitations).

45. *See* Chapter 2, footnote 14 and accompanying text.

tive. Management engineers and other observers began to understand that workplace injuries were largely attributable to system design rather than individual instances of malfeasance.[46] Tort law was not giving employers an incentive to adopt costly system changes, because a physically injured workman could rarely, if ever, prove that his employer's system was unreasonably dangerous. The problem of system design could be effectively addressed only by strict liability. To make the workplace safer while giving workers a guarantee of compensation for their injuries, the states enacted workers' compensation statutes. This legislation removed cases of negligence liability from the tort system in favor of a statutory scheme of strict liability.[47]

The dynamic created by the workers' compensation statutes would have produced the modern regime of strict products liability, even if courts had never recognized the implied warranty. After all, if negligence liability did not effectively regulate systems of worker safety, then presumably negligence liability was also ineffective in regulating systems of product safety. Just as strict liability would reduce workplace injuries by giving employers an incentive to adopt safer systems of production, strict liability would reduce product injuries by giving product manufacturers an incentive to adopt safer systems of quality control. For an astute observer of the tort system like Justice Traynor, the connection was obvious.[48]

Following Traynor's lead in *Escola*, the courts often justified strict liability in evidentiary terms. Based upon this case law, the *Restatement (Third)* justifies strict liability as a means of avoiding the evidentiary problems associated with proving negligence liability for construction or manufacturing defects, such as that which causes a soda bottle to explode.[49] Negligence principles justify the *Restatement (Third)* rule of strict liability.

Once strict liability is justified as a method for enforcing the duty of care, there is no fundamental inconsistency between strict liability and negligence liability. Strict liability applies when evidentiary problems impair negligence liability, and negligence liability

46. A particularly influential work in this regard was authored by the namesake of the endowed chair I now hold. *See* Crystal Eastman, Work–Accidents and the Law (1910).

47. For a more detailed and illuminating exposition of this range of issues, see John Fabian Witt, The Accidental Republic: Crippled Workingmen, Destitute Widows, and the Remaking of American Law (2004).

48. Traynor greatly benefited from the insights of tort scholars who sought to determine whether workers' compensation justified other tort reforms. This effort resulted in the influential theory of enterprise liability, a theory Traynor clearly relied upon in *Escola*. *See* Geistfeld, *supra* note 41, at 252–58.

49. *See* Chapter 4.

governs all other cases. Hence the *Restatement (Third)* can consistently adopt a rule of strict liability for construction or manufacturing defects and rules of negligence liability for the remaining types of product defects, those involving product designs and warnings.[50]

III. Controversy over the Standard of Liability

Today there is widespread consensus that product sellers should be liable for the physical harms caused by defective products. However, the two doctrinal bases for strict products liability have created controversy over the appropriate definition of defect.

The *Restatement (Second)* adopts the warranty rationale for strict products liability and defines defect in terms of frustrated consumer expectations. The *Restatement (Third)* relies on negligence principles, and so "[c]onsumer expectations do not play a determinative role in determining defectiveness" of product designs or warnings.[51] The two doctrinal bases for strict products liability may have yielded inconsistent liability rules for design and warning defects, a possibility that underlies many of the doctrinal disputes now confronting the courts.

Courts have rejected the consumer expectations test because of its well-known problems. As a leading treatise describes the test:

> The meaning is ambiguous and the test is very difficult of application to discrete problems. What does the reasonable purchaser contemplate? In one sense, he does not "expect" to be adversely affected by a risk or hazard unknown to him. In another sense, he does contemplate the "possibility" of unknown "side effects." In a sense the ordinary purchaser cannot reasonably expect anything more than that reasonable care in the exercise of the skill and knowledge available to design engineers has been exercised. The test can be utilized to explain most any result that a court or jury chooses to reach. The application of such a vague concept in many situations does not provide much guidance for a jury.[52]

The vagueness of consumer expectations caused many courts to reject it in favor of the risk-utility test, the rule adopted by the *Restatement (Third)*. In cases involving design or warning defects, the plaintiff ordinarily must show that her injury would have been prevented if the manufacturer had adopted a reasonable alternative design or warning, one passing the risk-utility test.[53] This proof is

50. Restatement (Third) § 2.
51. *Id.* cmt. g.
52. Prosser & Keeton on Torts § 99, at 699 (footnote omitted).

53. *See* Chapter 6, section II (design defects); Chapter 7, section III (warning defects).

no different than the proof required by ordinary negligence liability. In the typical negligence case, proof that the defendant failed to take a reasonable precaution establishes the unreasonableness of the defendant's actual conduct. So, too, the manufacturer's failure to take a reasonable precaution—the adoption of the reasonable alternative design or warning—establishes the unreasonableness or defectiveness of the existing design or product warning. Such evidence is not required in all product cases, however, for the same reasons that it is not required in all negligence cases. In the typical tort case, negligence can be established by circumstantial evidence, violation of a statute, or proof that the activity itself is unreasonable, regardless of the amount of care otherwise exercised by the defendant. Under the *Restatement (Third)*, each form of proof can establish defect.[54] For defective designs or warnings, the *Restatement (Third)* adopts the same set of evidentiary requirements faced by plaintiffs in other negligence cases.

By adopting the risk-utility test and its associated evidentiary requirements, the *Restatement (Third)* has generated substantial controversy among courts and commentators.[55] Some courts have been persuaded by the *Restatement (Third)*, concluding that design claims ought to be governed by the risk-utility test rather than consumer expectations. Others disagree. The proof of defect by reference to a reasonable alternative design is not obviously required by the consumer expectations test, which defines a product as being defective (the trigger of strict liability) if it frustrates the reasonable safety expectations of the ordinary consumer. Proponents of consumer expectations accordingly reject the risk-utility test in the *Restatement (Third)* for the reason that it unduly circumscribes the role of strict liability in favor of negligence principles.[56]

In the first major case to address these issues, the Connecticut Supreme Court rejected the risk-utility test in the *Restatement (Third)* and decided to "continue to adhere to [its] long-standing rule that a product's defectiveness is to be determined by the expectations of an ordinary consumer."[57] The court adopted the risk-utility test as a complement to consumer expectations for cases in which ordinary consumers may not have sufficiently formed

---

54. *See* Restatement (Third) § 3 (circumstantial proof); *id.* § 4 (noncompliance with product safety statutes or regulations); *id.* § 2 cmt. e (manifestly unreasonable design).

55. *See, e.g.*, Potter v. Chicago Pneumatic Tool Co., 694 A.2d 1319 (Conn. 1997) (describing controversy).

56. *E.g.*, John F. Vargo, Caveat Emptor: *Will the A.L.I. Erode Strict Liability in the Restatement (Third) for Products Liability?*, 10 Touro L. Rev. 21 (1993).

57. *Potter*, 694 A.2d at 1333.

expectations, but "emphasiz[ed] that our adoption of a risk-utility balancing component to our consumer expectation test does not signal a retreat from strict tort liability."[58]

Similar concerns have been voiced by other state supreme courts that have considered whether consumer expectations should be supplanted by the risk-utility test in the *Restatement (Third)*. The Kansas Supreme Court remains "convinced that in products liability cases, consumer expectations play a dominant role in the determination of defectiveness."[59] The court rejected the *Restatement (Third)* requirement that design defects must ordinarily be proven by reference to a reasonable alternative design. The manufacturer's failure to adopt a reasonable alternative design is proof of negligence, and strict products liability does not depend upon such proof.[60] The court apparently believed that consumer expectations sanction a role for strict liability that is eliminated by the risk-utility test. Other courts have also affirmed the continued vitality of consumer expectations despite its rejection in the *Restatement (Third)*.[61]

Another aspect of the controversy involves the issue of foreseeability. In accordance with established negligence principles, the risk-utility test in the *Restatement (Third)* limits liability to "foreseeable risks of harm."[62] For this reason, the Wisconsin Supreme Court concluded that the risk-utility test is inconsistent with the strict liability dimensions of consumer expectations. "Foreseeability of harm is an element of negligence," whereas "strict products liability imposes liability without regard to negligence and its attendant factors of duty of care and foreseeability."[63] A similar conclusion was reached by the Montana Supreme Court.[64]

The entire controversy has been succinctly summarized by the Maryland Court of Appeals:

> The concept of strict liability, especially as formulated in § 402A of *Restatement (Second)*, was regarded as an important pro-consumer advance; relieving persons injured by products from the requirement of proving negligence on the part of

---

58. *Id.* at 1334.

59. Delaney v. Deere and Co., 999 P.2d 930, 945 (Kan. 2000).

60. *Id.* at 946 (observing that Kansas law, prior to its adoption of strict products liability, found proof of negligent design to be insufficient when plaintiff merely asserted that a different design would have prevented the injury).

61. *See, e.g.,* Jackson v. GMC, 60 S.W.3d 800, 802 (Tenn. 2001); Vautour v. Body Masters Sports Indus., 784 A.2d 1178 (N.H. 2001).

62. Restatement (Third) § 2(b).

63. Green v. Smith & Nephew AHP, Inc., 629 N.W.2d 727, 745, 746 (Wis. 2001).

64. Sternhagen v. Dow Co., 935 P.2d 1139, 1143 (Mont. 1997).

manufacturers or others in the distribution chain and focusing, instead, on the product itself, made it easier to obtain a recovery for a defectively designed or manufactured product. Substitution of a risk-utility analysis, however, especially as formulated in the *Restatement (Third)*, has attracted considerable criticism and has been viewed by many as a retrogression, as returning to negligence concepts and placing a very difficult burden on plaintiffs.[65]

The court decided to retain the consumer expectations test. "Given the controversy that continues to surround the risk-utility standard in ... the *Restatement (Third)*, we are reluctant at this point to cast aside our existing jurisprudence in favor of such an approach on any broad, general basis."[66] As this case illustrates, the controversy engendered by the *Restatement (Third)* will not necessarily spur further evolution in the law.

IV. The Source of Controversy: The Doctrinal Ambiguity of Consumer Expectations

The controversy over the liability standard for design and warning defects centers on the appropriate roles of negligence and strict liability. The risk-utility test is based upon negligence principles, and many courts and commentators claim that consumer expectations sanction a more expansive role for strict liability. To evaluate the controversy, we need to understand why consumer expectations may allow for broader application of strict liability, and what limit, if any, consumer expectations place on the reach of strict liability.

After all, the two tests may be fundamentally equivalent, which is the interpretation offered by the Reporters of the *Restatement (Third)*, Professors James Henderson, Jr. and Aaron Twerski. In their view, the current controversy is merely an unfortunate by-product of the confusion engendered by the vague conception of consumer expectations.[67]

The vagueness of consumer expectations, though, provides reasons for believing that the liability rule is not necessarily coextensive with negligence liability. The consumer expectations test is based on the warranty rationale for strict products liability. The implied warranty first applied to contaminated food and other products with defects that escaped detection by quality-control

---

65. Halliday v. Sturm, Ruger & Co., 792 A.2d 1145, 1154 (Md. 2002).

66. *Id.* at 1159.

67. James A. Henderson, Jr. & Aaron D. Twerski, *Achieving Consensus on Defective Product Design*, 83 Cornell L. Rev. 867, 871 (1998).

measures. As a result of such a defect, the product (like an exploding soda bottle) could not perform its intended function and frustrated consumer expectations, subjecting the seller to strict liability for breach of the implied warranty. But why does the exploding bottle frustrate consumer expectations? Consumers know that perfect quality control is not ordinarily attainable or even desirable. Despite the best inspection or manufacturing procedures, some defective products will enter the market. Consumers cannot reasonably expect perfection, a conclusion that makes it possible to interpret consumer expectations in different ways with different implications for the appropriate scope of liability.

Rather than expect perfect quality control and the complete absence of defective products, consumers may only expect the seller to guarantee that the product has passed reasonable, though imperfect methods of quality control. For the expectation of reasonable quality to be frustrated, the product defect must be attributable to the seller's failure to exercise reasonable care in quality control. This form of consumer expectation yields a liability rule no different than ordinary negligence liability.

But consumers can expect something else, a possibility expressed by the implied warranty. Even though consumers do not reasonably expect perfection and understand that some defective products are inevitable, they can still expect sellers to provide a guaranteed remedy for defective products. This expectation yields the implied warranty, which gives consumers a guaranteed remedy for defective products, regardless of whether the defect stems from reasonable or unreasonable methods of quality control. An expectation of remedy, however, has two alternative interpretations, each with a different implication for the liability rule.

Consumers may expect a guaranteed remedy only because the guarantee of reasonable quality is too costly or difficult to enforce as a practical matter. To prove that a defective product breaches a guarantee of quality, the consumer must establish the unreasonableness of the seller's quality-control measures, an issue of considerable complexity for many mass-manufacturing processes. To avoid this evidentiary burden, consumers may instead prefer a guaranteed remedy. A guaranteed remedy effectively guarantees product quality, because it gives the seller an incentive to reduce the incidence of defects by adopting reasonable quality-control measures.[68] This form of consumer expectation readily explains why

---

68. For demonstration of how a guarantee of compensation in the product warranty serves as a signal (and guarantee) of product quality to imperfectly informed consumers, see Sanford J. Grossman, *The Informational Role of*

the implied warranty is limited to defective products, while also conforming to negligence principles for reasons described earlier.[69]

But there is another way to interpret the form of consumer expectation that is protected by the implied warranty. Even though consumers know that perfection is not attainable and defects occur under the best manufacturing conditions, this unavoidable risk subjects the seller to strict liability. The implied warranty therefore supports the conclusion that consumers reasonably expect a guaranteed remedy for injuries caused by at least some unavoidable risks. This form of consumer expectation can sanction a broader application of strict liability than is justified by negligence principles.

For example, risks that are truly unforeseeable at the time of sale are also unavoidable. Without knowledge of the risk, the manufacturer cannot take steps to avoid or eliminate it. When an unexpected risk materializes and causes injury, the product can frustrate the consumer's reasonable expectations of safety. This form of consumer expectation justifies seller liability for unforeseeable risks under the implied warranty, even though negligence liability is limited to foreseeable risks.

Indeed, this form of consumer expectation can justify liability rules that are not limited to defective products. If the unavoidable risks regarding quality control can frustrate consumer expectations, then the unavoidable risks posed by nondefective products might also frustrate consumer expectations. The ordinary consumer may reasonably expect a remedy simply because she was injured by the product.[70]

The reasonableness of such an expectation was implicitly recognized by Justice Traynor in his influential *Escola* concurrence:

> It is evident that the manufacturer can anticipate some hazards and guard against the recurrence of others, as the public cannot. Those who suffer injury from [ ] products are unpre-

Warranties and Private Disclosure About Product Quality, 24 J. L. & Econ. 461 (1981).

69. *See supra* section II (explaining how strict liability can be justified by the evidentiary difficulty of proving negligence).

70. *Cf.* John E. Montgomery & David G. Owen, *Reflections on the Theory and Administration of Strict Tort Liability for Defective Products*, 27 S.C. L. Rev. 803, 823 (1976) ("the consumer may have at most only a generalized expectancy—perhaps more accurately only an unconscious hope—that the product will not harm him if he treats it with a reasonable amount of care"); William C. Powers, Jr., *The Persistence of Fault in Products Liability*, 61 Tex. L. Rev. 777, 796–97 (1983) ("The vague expectations of consumers probably oscillate between never expecting a product to injure them ... and actually expecting some products to be 'lemons.' ").

pared to meet its consequences. The cost of an injury and the loss of time and health may be an overwhelming misfortune to the person injured, and a needless one, for the risk of injury can be insured by the manufacturer and distributed among the public as a cost of doing business.[71]

The bracketed term in this quote deletes the qualifier "defective," but doing so does not alter the logic of Traynor's argument. The injury itself frustrates consumer expectations, leaving the consumer "unprepared to meet its consequences."

That consumer expectations can be frustrated by the mere fact of injury finds further support in the *Restatement (Second)* formulation of the rationale for strict products liability:

> [P]ublic policy demands that the burden of accidental injuries caused by products intended for consumption be placed upon those who market them, and be treated as a cost of production against which liability insurance can be obtained; and that the consumer of such products is entitled to the maximum protection at the hands of someone, and the proper persons to afford it are those who market the products.[72]

Again, the rationale for tort liability stems from the fact of injury and not the defectiveness of the product.

A similar rationale for strict products liability appears in the *Restatement (Third)*:

> An often-cited rationale for holding wholesalers or retailers strictly liable for harm caused by manufacturing defects is that, as between them and innocent victims who suffer harm because of defective products, the product sellers as business entities are in a better position than are individual users and consumers to insure against such losses.[73]

Once again, the fact of accidental injury is providing the true rationale for tort liability, not the defectiveness of the product. If public policy demands that sellers must bear the burden of accidental product injuries, and if business entities are better positioned than consumers to insure against physical harms, then consumers can reasonably expect a remedy for their injuries. The reasonableness of the expectation has nothing to do with defects, but instead depends on the simple premise that injury insurance is best provided by product sellers.

---

71. Escola v. Coca Cola Bottling Co., 150 P.2d 436 (Cal.1944) (Traynor, J., concurring).

72. Restatement (Second) § 402A cmt. c.

73. Restatement (Third) § 2 cmt. a.

This proposition finds further support in the widely held view that the purpose of tort law is one of compensation. It "was well established by the 1950s" that "tort law had become primarily a compensation system designed to distribute the costs of injuries throughout society efficiently and fairly...."[74] According to the *Restatement (Second)*, the first purpose for which tort actions are maintainable is "to give compensation, indemnity or restitution for harms."[75] This compensatory rationale for tort liability, though often summarily dismissed today, deserves serious consideration. It can explain the important substantive tort doctrines, including the important limitations of tort liability.[76] If the primary purpose of tort liability is to compensate physical injuries, then consumers may reasonably expect product sellers to guarantee compensation for product-caused injuries, regardless of defect.

The case law therefore does not yield a clear conception of consumer expectations. In order to ensure reasonable product quality, consumers may expect either a guarantee of reasonable product quality or a guaranteed remedy for defective products. Each expectation is framed in terms of *reasonable* product quality, justifying liability rules that depend upon negligence principles. The implied warranty, though, also plausibly protects consumer expectations with respect to at least some unavoidable risks. Such an expectation can justify seller liability for unforeseeable risks or even for injuries caused by nondefective products. These possibilities support the claim that the consumer expectations test sanctions more liability than is permitted by negligence principles and the risk-utility test. The form of consumer expectation accordingly determines the relevant liability rule, but the case law has not clearly identified the relevant form of expectation. Each one has doctrinal support. Unless the concept of consumer expectations can be further developed and clarified, its inherent vagueness will continue to be a source of controversy and confusion.

---

74. G. Edward White, Tort Law in America: An Intellectual History 150 (1985).

75. Restatement (Second) § 901.

76. *See* Mark Geistfeld, *Negligence, Compensation, and the Coherence of Tort Law*, 91 Geo. L.J. 585 (2003).

Chapter 2

CONSUMER EXPECTATIONS

The choice between consumer expectations and the risk-utility test should not be controversial if the two liability standards are based upon the same principles or rationale for tort liability. Any overlap of the two would merely provide different methods for reaching the same substantive outcome. The two liability standards could be inconsistent, though, if there is some underlying inconsistency between the implied warranty and negligence liability. In that event, the choice between consumer expectations and the risk-utility test could involve a controversial, substantive choice about the appropriate principles or rationale for tort liability.

The possibility that different tort doctrines can depend upon inconsistent rationales is supported by modern torts scholarship. Many scholars believe that tort law lacks a unitary or single justification.[1] According to this conception, tort law has multiple purposes, each depending upon differing justifications. Some tort doctrines might further a principle of fairness, whereas others might promote economic efficiency even when doing so would be unfair. If this conception of tort law is correct, different tort doctrines like the implied warranty and negligence liability could depend on conflicting justifications. The choice of a single doctrinal basis for strict products liability would then involve a basic choice about the appropriate purpose of products liability.

Such a fundamental decision may be implicated by the choice between consumer expectations and the risk-utility test. Liability rules formulated to protect consumer expectations can fairly protect the consumer interest in avoiding product-caused injury. The risk-utility test, by contrast, allocates scarce resources according to the criterion of allocative efficiency. The test finds a product design

---

1. *See, e.g.*, Prosser & Keeton on Torts § 2, at 6 (concluding that "it is not easy to find any single guiding principle which determines when [tort] compensation is to be paid"); Fowler V. Harper et al., 3 The Law of Torts § 11.5, at 98–99 (2d ed. 1986) (listing six different possible objectives of tort law in accident cases); *see also* Kenneth S. Abraham, The Forms and Functions of Tort Law 14 (2d ed. 2002) ("The functions of tort law are 'mixed': they co-exist, sometimes in tension with each other, with one or more dominating in some contexts and others coming to the forefront at other times."); Gary T. Schwartz, *Mixed Theories of Tort Law: Affirming Both Deterrence and Corrective Justice*, 75 Tex. L. Rev. 1801, 1826 (1997) (noting the difficulty of deriving a theory of tort law and observing that "[i]t is certainly possible that tort law has developed haphazardly over time").

or warning to be defective if the benefit of a safety improvement (the reduced *risk*) exceeds its cost (the decreased *utility* of the change). By requiring only those safety improvements that pass a cost-benefit test, this liability rule promotes allocative efficiency. The pursuit of this form of economic efficiency may come at the expense of fairly protecting consumers, however. As one court observed, the risk-utility test has been criticized for "representing an unwanted ascendancy of corporate interests under the guise of tort reform."[2] The risk-utility test could only produce an "unwanted ascendancy of corporate interests" if it did not fairly protect consumer interests. The choice between consumer expectations and the risk-utility test therefore may involve a hard choice between a fair products liability system and an efficient one.

There is, however, no necessary conflict between fairness and efficiency in product cases. The different doctrinal bases of strict products liability could rest upon consistent principles or the same rationale. Perhaps consumers reasonably expect product sellers to supply products that satisfy the risk-utility test, eliminating any conflict between the fair and efficient liability rule.

To address these issues, we need to develop the concept of consumer expectations. The current conception is vague and subject to differing interpretations. The case law does not sufficiently clarify matters. Once the concept has been developed, we can determine the relation between consumer expectations and the risk-utility test.

I. Consumer Expectations and Tort Principles (The Fairness of Efficient Products Liability Rules)

To identify the issue of fairness that must be addressed by tort law, we can first consider how a tort rule governs risky interactions between strangers, like automobile drivers and pedestrians. Having identified the issue of fairness, we can then consider how it translates into cases involving parties with a preexisting relationship, like product sellers and consumers.

An automobile driver typically desires the transportation to pursue various economic or liberty interests. As an unwanted byproduct of that activity, the driver exposes pedestrians to a risk of bodily injury. A pedestrian also transports herself in furtherance of her economic and liberty interests. In the event of a crash that physically harms the pedestrian, by definition, the pedestrian's interest in physical security has been injured. The pedestrian also suffers emotional harm (pain and suffering) and economic harm

2. Halliday v. Sturm, Ruger & Co., 792 A.2d 1145, 1154–55 (Md. 2002).

(like medical expenses). If the driver were obligated to compensate those harms, the monetary damages would be detrimental to her economic interests. Any precautionary obligations that tort law imposes on the driver, such as a duty to drive slowly, are also detrimental to her liberty interests. Similarly, any precautionary obligations that tort law imposes on the pedestrian (no jaywalking) restrict her liberty. The way in which tort law regulates the risky interaction therefore means at least one party's interests will be burdened or harmed: Either the pedestrian's interests in liberty and physical security; the driver's liberty interests, including the economic interest; or the interests of both parties. How these conflicting interests should be mediated is the basic question of fairness that must be addressed by tort law.

Tort law mediates the conflicting driver-pedestrian interests by impartially considering the interests of each party. Impartiality requires equal treatment of identical interests, such as the liberty interests of the driver and pedestrian. Impartiality need not require equal treatment of different interests.

Tort law traditionally has distinguished between liberty and security interests, giving "peculiar importance" to the nature of these interests and their social value.[3] By distinguishing these interests, tort law can give one a different weight or priority than the other. For example, "the law has always placed a higher value upon human safety than upon mere rights in property."[4]

Due to the priority of the security interest, the core concern of tort law is to protect individuals from *physical harm*, a category encompassing harm to the individual interests in bodily integrity, land and chattels.[5] To protect individuals from physical harm is to make them physically secure with respect to these interests. The priority of the security interest accordingly explains why tort law is primarily concerned about physical harm.

The priority of the security interest can be justified by autonomy, an ideal that individuals should be able to live the life of their

---

3. Restatement (Second) § 77 cmt. i.

4. Prosser & Keeton on Torts § 21, at 132.

5. The initial conceptualization of torts as a distinct field of law was largely accomplished by Oliver Wendell Holmes. "Above all, his approach centered tort doctrine around its emerging primary source of litigation, accidental personal injuries." Thomas C. Grey, *Accidental Torts*, 54 Vand. L. Rev. 1225, 1282 (2001). Today "the problem of accidental personal injury and property damage" remains at "the core of tort law." Restatement (Third) of Torts: General Principles, Reporter's Introductory Note (Council Draft No. 1, Sept. 25, 1998). Because physical harm is the core concern of tort law, most jurisdictions recognize the tort claim only if the product defect caused or perhaps threatens bodily injury or property damage. *See* Chapter 9, section I (discussing the division between tort and contract law with respect to economic loss).

own choosing. To be autonomous agents, individuals must have both liberty and physical security, a requirement vividly expressed by the New Hampshire state motto, "Live free or die." Without liberty, physical security may not be worth having. But liberty depends on security. Unless our bodies and physical possessions are adequately secure, the threat of physical harm severely compromises our ability to make plans and live the life of our choosing. The aftermath of September 11, 2001 provides a sobering illustration. Individuals must be adequately protected from the threat of physical harm before they can meaningfully exercise their liberty. Consequently, leading justice theorists maintain that fair tort rules prioritize the individual interest in physical security over the conflicting liberty and economic interests of others.[6]

This principle of fairness justifies the consumer expectations test, which requires the amount of product safety that is reasonably expected by the ordinary consumer. This liability rule clearly prioritizes the consumer's security interest or safety expectations over the competing economic interest of the product seller.

By contrast, there is no apparent priority of the security interest in the risk-utility test or any other liability rule formulated in cost-benefit terms. If a precaution yields a safety benefit of $1 and costs $1.01, then the precaution fails the risk-utility test and is not required by the tort duty. A cost-benefit test does not give any added weight to the safety benefit of protecting physical security.

For this reason, there can be a conflict between fairness and efficiency in the driver-pedestrian setting. The fair liability rule can prioritize the pedestrian's security interest over the driver's liberty interest, whereas the efficient liability rule treats these interests equally in the cost-benefit calculus. Relative to the efficient rule, the fair tort rule can require more safety to protect the prioritized security interest of the pedestrian.

This principle of fairness has different implications in most product cases. The driver-pedestrian interaction creates an *interpersonal* conflict of the liberty and security interests, and that conflict is absent from the manufacturer-consumer interaction. Like the driver, the manufacturer creates the risk of physical harm. The similarities between the driver and manufacturer end there. Any costly tort obligations incurred by the driver are not passed onto the pedestrian, whereas any tort burdens incurred by the manufac-

---

6. *See generally* Richard W. Wright, *Justice and Reasonable Care in Negligence Law*, 47 Amer. J. Juris. 143 (2002) (showing that leading justice theorists recognize that the principles of justice prioritize the security interest and do not countenance a risk-utility test that always gives equal weight to the security and liberty interests).

turer—the cost of safety precautions and injury compensation—are passed onto the consumer in the form of higher prices. Products liability rules largely implicate only consumer interests, which is why "it is not a factor ... that the imposition of liability would have a negative effect on corporate earnings or would reduce employment in a given industry."[7] To the extent that the manufacturer-consumer interaction only implicates an *intrapersonal* conflict of the consumer's interests in security and liberty, the fair balance of interests becomes altered.

In comparing her own security and liberty interests, the consumer gives no special priority to either one. The consumer prefers to pay for product safety only if the benefit of risk reduction (borne by the consumer) exceeds the cost of the safety investment (also borne by the consumer). Consumers therefore reasonably expect product safety decisions to be governed by a cost-benefit calculus, because that decision rule maximizes consumer well-being or welfare. The fair liability rule, which provides for the best protection of consumer interests, is no different than the cost-benefit rule.

Of course, a cost-benefit rule like the risk-utility test will not fully satisfy the preferences of each consumer. Individuals have different preferences for product safety and other aspects of quality, making it ordinarily infeasible for product sellers to satisfy completely the preferences of everyone (as you undoubtedly have experienced). Product sellers in competitive markets respond to aggregate consumer demand. Consumer expectations are formed by the *market* transaction, and each consumer should understand that the

---

7. Restatement (Third) § 2 cmt. f at 23. To be sure, tort liability will increase costs, which in turn will affect price, aggregate demand and the net profits of product sellers. These impacts on the interests of product sellers are not relevant to the analysis, however. The equilibrium price must cover all of the seller's costs, including liability costs. At this baseline, the consumer pays for the full cost of tort liability. Another baseline could alter the conclusion. Given a baseline of no liability, the adoption of tort liability would increase cost and price, which in turn could decrease aggregate demand and thereby reduce price. The price reduction induced by the reduction in demand means that from a baseline of no liability, consumers need not bear the full cost of tort liability, depending on the relevant elasticities. *See* Richard Craswell, *Passing On the Costs of Legal Rules: Efficiency* *and Distribution in Buyer–Seller Relationships*, 43 Stan. L. Rev. 361 (1991). The appropriate baseline accordingly determines whether or not consumers incur the full cost of tort liability. The appropriate baseline cannot be determined by economic analysis, since cost-benefit analysis depends on prices which in turn depend on the initial allocation of property rights. *See* Lewis A. Kornhauser, *Wealth Maximization* in 3 The New Palgrave Dictionary of Economics and the Law 679 (Peter Newman ed., 1998). The initial allocation of property rights must instead depend upon normative justification, and so the normatively justified tort rule defines the appropriate baseline for evaluating the distributive impact of tort liability. At this baseline, the consumer pays for the full cost of tort liability, since the equilibrium price must cover all of the seller's costs, including its liability costs.

market contains other buyers with differing preferences. As long as the product satisfies the reasonable expectations of the ordinary consumer, any individual consumer usually has no reasonable basis for expecting otherwise.[8]

For these purposes, the consumer includes the buyer and other users of the product. The buyer pays for the safety precautions and guarantees of injury compensation via the associated price increases. One who buys a product frequently contemplates that it will be used by others, typically family members, friends or employees. In making the purchase decision, the buyer presumably gives equal consideration to the welfare of these other users, including employees.[9] The buyer does not have to give greater consideration to the interests of other users, since they can only reasonably expect the amount of product safety that is acceptable to the buyer. The interests of these parties coincide, making it defensible to conceptualize the consumer as including both the buyer and any reasonably foreseeable user of the product.[10]

The consumer does not necessarily consider bystanders when making the purchase decision, nor is there any reason to assume

---

8. *Cf.* William L. Prosser, *The Implied Warranty of Merchantible Quality*, 27 Minn. L. Rev. 117, 125–30 (1943) (explaining how the implied warranty depends on "usages of the trade" and is defined by reference to goods "of the kind or quality commonly sold in the market"). When the individual consumer has expectations that differ from those of other participants in the market, and the transaction proceeds on that basis, seller liability is governed by the implied warranty of fitness for the buyer's particular purpose. *See generally id.*

9. In a well-functioning labor market, the employer must compensate the employee for any job-related risks. Rather than paying the employee a higher wage to face a particular risk, the employer could instead pay for a safety precaution that eliminates the risk. The employer's decision accordingly involves a comparison of the cost posed by the risk with the cost of the safety precaution that would eliminate the risk, the same comparison made by the product purchaser. *See infra* section II.A.

10. The courts conceptualize the consumer in this manner. *E.g.*, Henningsen v. Bloomfield Motors, 161 A.2d 69, 80–81 (N.J. 1960) (observing that

"the connotation of 'consumer' [is] broader than that of 'buyer.' He signifie[s] such a person who, in the reasonable contemplation of the parties to the sale, might be expected to use the product."). Similarly, welfare economists typically evaluate consumer behavior in terms of households rather than individuals. *See, e.g.*, Robin Boadway & Neil Bruce, Welfare Economics (1984). To see why this conceptualization is defensible for tort purposes, consider the duty landowners owe to social guests or "licensees" in most jurisdictions. "Licensees are those on the land by the landowner's express or implied consent but who are there for their own purposes." Dan B. Dobbs, The Law of Torts § 233, at 596 (2000). "In the absence of special circumstances, courts do not regard the landowner's permission to enter or even his invitation to a social guest as an assurance that the premises will be made safe.... This means, subject to [exceptions], that the landowner need not inspect the land or correct unsafe conditions for the licensee." *Id.* at 597. In essence, the exceptions involve situations in which the safety conditions faced by the landowner differ from those faced by the guest. *Cf. id.* (describing rule that landowners must warn guests

that the liability rule must treat the two parties identically. The bystander is someone like a pedestrian who faces the risk of being injured by another person's use of a product (the car), suggesting that the driver-pedestrian interaction provides the appropriate way to consider bystander injuries. For this reason, even though the efficient rule is fair for consumers, it may be unfair for bystanders. The appropriate treatment of bystander interests requires separate analysis, providing another reason why we will leave that issue for a later chapter.[11] Until then, we will assume that a product risks injury only to consumers.

In addition to this important caveat, there is one more reason why the fair products liability rule might not always correspond to the efficient rule. Tort rules are defined in terms of the plaintiff's individual tort right and the correlative tort duty of the defendant. As a matter of fairness, tort liability requires that the defendant must have breached a duty owed to the plaintiff in violation of the plaintiff's right. Since a fair tort rule must satisfy the requirements of the right-duty nexus running between the plaintiff and defendant, liability cannot be justified for the sole reason that it efficiently promotes product safety. The required right-duty nexus can limit or constrain the ability of a fair tort rule to pursue efficiency.[12]

Subject to these qualifications, the fair liability rule corresponds to the efficient rule in product cases, even if the two otherwise conflict in other types of tort cases, like those involving drivers and pedestrians. Due to this correspondence, the fair liability rule of consumer expectations can be developed by economic analysis.

II. The Economics of Consumer Expectations

Economic analysis assumes that decision makers strive to make the best possible choices to further their desired goals or objectives.

of concealed dangers). The basic tort principle, then, is that the licensee or guest deserves no greater protection from risk than the landowner, the same principle justifying the conception of consumer expectations that encompasses both purchasers (landowners) and users (licensees).

11. Recall that bystanders also require separate analysis because they do not have the reliance interest required for the tort version of the implied warranty. *See* Chapter 1, section 1. The issue of bystander injuries is the subject of Chapter 12.

12. The requirement of the right-duty nexus was famously articulated by Judge Cardozo in a case holding that a tort plaintiff can recover only by showing that the defendant's breach of duty constitutes a " 'wrong' to herself, i.e., a violation of her own right, and not merely a wrong to someone else, nor conduct 'wrongful' because unsocial." Palsgraf v. Long Island R.R., 162 N.E. 99 (N.Y. 1928). For a good example of how this fairness requirement can constrain the ability of the tort system to promote product safety, see Chapter 8, section I.B. (discussing market-share liability).

Manufacturers make product decisions in order to maximize profits, while consumers make these decisions in order to maximize their well-being or welfare. The objective of consumer decision making—consumer expectations—therefore can be readily analyzed with economic methodology.

There are two different types of consumer expectations, one objective and the other subjective. By distinguishing objective or *reasonable* expectations from subjective or *actual* expectations, we can eliminate the ambiguity that has plagued the concept of consumer expectations.

A.   Reasonable Consumer Expectations: A Rationale for the Risk–Utility Test

Under ideal decision-making conditions, everyone knows everything necessary to make the right choices. There is no cost to acquire or process information. No matter how much information is required, no matter how complicated the issue, everyone is fully informed and able to make decisions that best promote or protect their well-being or welfare. A perfectly informed consumer chooses the amount of product safety that makes her as well off as possible, given the cost and technological constraints faced by product sellers.

The safety expectations of perfectly informed consumers accordingly determine the conditions under which there should be no tort liability. These expectations determine the product-safety configuration that best promotes consumer welfare, and no individual consumer can reasonably expect more from a product seller.

To determine the content of reasonable consumer expectations, we need to rely upon a few basic principles of microeconomics, each of which is highly intuitive:

  ● All else being equal, a manufacturer will lose sales to competitors offering lower prices. Each consumer of the higher priced product would increase her welfare by purchasing the same product at a lower price from another seller (and using the savings to buy other goods).

  ● The price a manufacturer charges for a product must at least cover the manufacturer's costs; otherwise, the manufacturer would lose money on each sale and could save money (maximize profits) by no longer selling the product.

Based on your own experience, you probably know that consumers prefer lower prices and that manufacturers and other product sellers must cover their costs. Those are the only economic principles you need to know.

To see why, consider the purchase decision of a consumer who is going to buy a car. In deciding which brand to choose, the consumer obviously cares about the purchase price. She also cares about the overall quality of the car (smooth ride, appealing style, and so on). The operating expenses also matter. A fuel-efficient car costs less than a gas hog, all else being equal. The expected maintenance costs also matter, as does the expected life of the car. And then there is the cost of car insurance, which covers various expenses the consumer might incur in the event of an accident: repair costs, the cost of personal injury, including medical costs, and perhaps liability costs for the injuries suffered by others. All of these expenses may not be covered by car insurance, so the consumer will also consider any uninsured accident costs she can expect to incur by using the car. The sum total of these varied costs yields the product's *full price*, an amount that can be significantly higher than the purchase price.

The total impact of the car purchase on consumer welfare depends upon the full price of the product and not merely the purchase price. A perfectly informed consumer is fully cognizant of this fact and acts accordingly. *All else being equal, consumers prefer the product configuration that yields the lowest full price, even if it involves a higher purchase price than others available on the market (with higher full prices).*

For our purposes, every component of the product's full price is not relevant. Products liability addresses issues pertaining to product safety and the compensation of product-caused injuries. To focus on these issues, we can simplify matters. Assume the consumer has already decided to purchase a particular type of car. The only remaining decision involves an airbag, an important safety precaution with an interesting history.[13] Suppose that the standard version of the car comes without an airbag, but for an additional price, the consumer can have an airbag installed. The consumer's decision whether to purchase the airbag depends on her expectations of safety and the cost of the airbag or safety precaution, the issues of relevance for products liability.

---

13. Many aspects of automobile safety design are regulated by the National Highway Traffic Safety Administration, which promulgated regulations in 1976 requiring manufacturers either to install lap and shoulder belts, airbags, or both restraint systems. As of 1989, only a few manufacturers were installing airbags as standard equipment, and there were an increasing number of tort claims alleging that cars without airbags were defectively designed. Many state courts allowed these claims to proceed, but eventually the U.S. Supreme Court ruled that the airbag claims were preempted by the federal regulation. *See* Geier v. American Honda Motor Co., 529 U.S. 861 (2000). Today, all newly manufactured cars must have airbags. *See* 49 U.S.C. § 30127.

In determining whether the airbag increases or decreases the full price of the car, the consumer needs to account for more than the amount by which the airbag increases the purchase price. The airbag might also impose other costs on the consumer, such as replacement or maintenance costs. The consumer adds up all of these costs to determine the total cost or the burden (denoted B) she would incur as a result of the airbag. The consumer must also determine the safety benefit that she would derive from the airbag. Without the protection provided by an airbag, the consumer faces a higher probability of being injured in a crash and incurring the associated costs. Multiplying this probability (denoted P) by the cost of injury or loss (L) yields the expected injury costs (PL) of not having an airbag.[14] To decide whether she should purchase the airbag, the consumer must compare the total cost or burden B of the airbag with the expected injury costs PL she would otherwise incur by foregoing the airbag. If the airbag increases the full price, the consumer would buy the standard version of the car without an airbag. The consumer would find it worthwhile to purchase the airbag only if doing so decreases the full price of the car:

full price with airbag < full price without airbag

total cost of airbag < expected injury costs

$$B < PL$$

14. The way in which the consumer determines the cost of nonmonetary injuries, like pain and suffering, is discussed in Chapter 9, section II.B. To see why the consumer rationally determines the expected injury costs by multiplying the probability of injury by the magnitude of loss in the event of injury, suppose there is a 1 in 100 monthly chance of a crash causing $100 injury. The consumer does not know whether the crash will occur, so she will necessarily make mistakes in estimating the outcome. The best decision rule for the consumer therefore is to minimize the cost of errors she will undoubtedly make. The consumer might optimistically decide she will never crash and estimate the injury cost at zero. If she drives the car for 100 months, then her estimate probably will be correct 99 times. The error costs for these months are zero. But the odds are that 100 months of driving will result in one crash, so in that month the consumer estimates zero injury costs but incurs $100 of costs. Over the course of 100 months, then, the consumer's error costs are $100. At the other extreme, the consumer might pessimistically assume she will crash each month. Over the course of 100 months, she is likely to be correct once (zero error costs) but wrong for those 99 months without a crash (error costs of $9,900). Now consider a decision rule based on the expected or average value of injury. A 1 percent chance of incurring a $100 injury in any month yields an expected injury cost of $1 per month. Under this decision rule, the consumer's estimate is wrong in each month. She never suffers a $1 loss in any given month. For the 99 months without a crash, she overestimates her injury costs by $99. For the one month with a crash, she underestimates her injury costs by $99. The total estimate over the course of 100 months, however, She estimated $100 in total injury costs (100 months at $1 per month) and experienced $100 in injury costs. A decision rule based on the expected value of loss therefore minimizes the consumer's error costs, making it the rational rule.

By decreasing the total cost or full price of the product for the consumer, the airbag increases consumer welfare. It would cost the consumer less to purchase the airbag (B) than to forego the airbag and face the added risk and expense of injury (PL). Thus, *consumers prefer or reasonably expect only those safety investments that cost less than the safety benefit or reduction in expected injury costs.*

This formulation of reasonable consumer expectations conforms to the well-known negligence standard articulated by Judge Learned Hand, commonly called the Hand formula.[15]

Reasonable consumer expectations also conform to the risk-utility test. The *risk* of the car design without an airbag refers to the increased risk the consumer will suffer injury due to the absence of the airbag. This measure corresponds to the risk term PL or the increased injury costs the consumer expects to incur if the car does not have an airbag. The *utility* of the design without an airbag involves any savings the consumer experiences by not having the airbag, an amount equal to the burden B or total cost of the airbag. Under the risk-utility test, the car is defective for not having an airbag if the *utility* of the existing design is less than the increased *risk* posed by the design:

added utility of design w/o airbag < added risk of design w/o airbag

total cost of airbag < expected injury costs

$$B < PL$$

The concept of reasonable consumer expectations therefore justifies a liability rule formulated in terms of the risk-utility test, or its equivalent, the Hand formula. By providing the amount of product safety required by the risk-utility test, a product seller maximizes consumer welfare. The ordinary consumer could not reasonably expect more from the product seller, resulting in the satisfaction of consumer expectations.

Since the risk-utility test finds justification in the reasonable safety expectations of the ordinary consumer, it follows that the risk-utility test is not necessarily a "technocratic" exercise that somehow departs from the way in which consumers evaluate products, contrary to the claims of some tort scholars.[16] Costs and

---

15. United States v. Carroll Towing Co., 159 F.2d 169, 173 (2d Cir. 1947) (concluding that "if the probability [of injury] be called P; the injury, L, and the burden, B; liability depends upon whether B is less than L multiplied by P: i.e., whether $B < PL$").

16. *See* Douglas A. Kysar, *The Expectations of Consumers*, 103 Colum. L. Rev. 1700 (2003) (arguing that the risk-utility test embodies a preference for the

benefits are evaluated from the ordinary consumer's perspective. The consumer's valuation of the risk and safety benefits necessarily depends on all factors she deems to be of importance in making that decision. When framed in terms of reasonable consumer expectations, the risk-utility test depends only upon the appropriate consumer interests.

B. Actual Consumer Expectations: The Duty Question

When consumers are not well informed, they make mistakes and have frustrated expectations. The disappointment of *actual* consumer expectations therefore justifies a tort duty in order to protect consumers from the adverse safety consequences that would otherwise be produced by their poorly informed product decisions. The substantive content of the tort duty—the safety requirements that tort law imposes on product sellers—is then determined by *reasonable* consumer expectations or the risk-utility test. To trigger tort liability, the product must frustrate both actual expectations, establishing the duty, and reasonable expectations, establishing the breach of duty.

Of course, consumers do not have to be uninformed. A consumer can learn about product risk, presumably in the hope of making fewer mistaken product choices. The increased knowledge, however, typically comes at a cost—the additional time and effort the consumer must expend to acquire and process the information. These *information costs* make the consumer less willing to learn about product risk. The consumer might not have enough time to collect all the information, or the available information can take too much time to evaluate. The benefit of learning about a one in 10,000 risk of being injured by a particular configuration of a car's steering wheel, for example, is likely to be lower than the cost the consumer would incur to become informed of the risk. For such risks, the ordinary consumer would rationally decide to remain uninformed. Information costs explain why consumers are not completely informed about product risk.

Since consumers are often imperfectly informed, we need to understand how imperfect information affects actual consumer expectations of product safety. To evaluate this issue, we can return

technical expertise of engineers over the populist beliefs of consumers); Marshall S. Shapo, Tort Law and Culture 225 (2003) (equating the risk-utility test with "an exercise in balance sheets" and the consumer expectations test "with a more psychologically oriented view of law [tied] closely to the wellsprings of human behavior"). If the risk-utility test is not framed in terms of reasonable consumer expectations, then its implementation in the courtroom may be problematic. *See* Chapter 6, section II.C.

to the airbag example. Recall that the consumer prefers the airbag if the total cost or burden B of the airbag is less than the expected injury costs PL created by the absence of an airbag, or $B < PL$. An imperfectly informed consumer does not know the product risk PL and must estimate these expected injury costs. The estimate $E(PL)$ can be wrong, resulting in product choices that frustrate the consumer's actual expectations of product safety.

Suppose the consumer estimate of the risk is too low, $E(PL) < PL$. When the consumer underestimates risk, the following possibility arises:

$$E(PL) < B < PL$$

By underestimating the risk, the consumer underestimates the safety benefit of the airbag (the reduction in expected injury costs PL). This error can cause the consumer to conclude that such a small safety benefit does not justify the cost of the airbag ($E(PL) < B$), even though the safety benefit in fact does justify the airbag ($B < PL$). The consumer's choice to forego the airbag actually increases the product's full price and decreases her welfare, contrary to her expectations. The product is more risky than the consumer expected.

Consumers can make mistakes of another type. Suppose the safety benefit of the airbag does not justify its cost, $PL < B$, so that a well-informed consumer would not purchase the airbag. If an imperfectly informed consumer overestimates risk, $PL < E(PL)$, the following possibility arises:

$$PL < B < E(PL)$$

By overestimating risk and the safety benefit of the airbag, the consumer may decide to purchase the airbag ($B < E(PL)$), even though the safety benefit does not actually justify the cost of the airbag ($PL < B$). Once again, the consumer has frustrated safety expectations. The consumer pays for the airbag on the mistaken expectation that there is sufficient risk to merit the safety expenditure. This time, the mistake involves the consumer's decision to purchase too much product safety, not too little.

When consumers mistakenly purchase too much safety, their frustrated expectations do not justify tort liability. Product sellers have no duty to decrease product safety by increasing product risk. Among other problems, such a duty would undermine protection of the security interest, the core concern of tort law. The appropriateness of the tort duty accordingly depends on whether consumers tend to underestimate risk (and purchase too little safety) or overestimate risk (and purchase too much safety).

The way in which individuals evaluate risk has been extensively studied by psychologists. These studies have found that imperfectly informed consumers frequently rely on rules-of-thumb or heuristics to make decisions about risk.[17] In attempting to identify the nature of these heuristics, the studies have found that individuals tend to overestimate risks that are brought to their attention. Many product risks, though, are not salient to the consumer. Typically, one learns about a product risk after it has caused injury, and most individuals have experienced or otherwise learned about only a few of the vast number of potential injuries. Most consumers infer from the more common or representative experience of safe product use that risk is not present or worth worrying about. Consumers who make safety decisions by relying on rules-of-thumb therefore frequently underestimate risk.

Market competition also forces sellers to portray their products in a manner that causes consumers to underestimate risk. To do so, the seller need not commit fraud. Rather than misrepresenting risk, the seller can emphasize those product attributes that are likely to trigger consumer heuristics resulting in the underestimation of risk. By inducing consumers to underestimate risk, the seller can reduce consumer estimates of the product's full price, thereby increasing sales. The dynamics of market competition predictably lead sellers to exploit consumer heuristics in the very manner that justifies tort liability.[18]

Hence there is ample support for the conclusion that consumers underestimate product risk, resulting in the frustration of actual safety expectations. This rationale for the tort duty, however, assumes that the ordinary consumer spends the time and effort to evaluate product risk. Upon inspection, this assumption turns out to be highly problematic for reasons providing a more general rationale for the tort duty.

A consumer who faces information costs may rationally decide not to evaluate product risk. Suppose there are two types of consumers. One type is completely uninformed of product risk. The

---

17. See, e.g., Judgment Under Uncertainty: Heuristics and Biases (Daniel Kahneman et al. eds., 1982); Heuristics and Biases: The Psychology of Intuitive Judgment (Thomas Gilovich et al. eds., 2002); Howard Latin, "Good" Warnings, Bad Products, and Cognitive Limitations, 41 UCLA L. Rev. 1193 (1994) (summarizing and evaluating empirical studies of how individuals make risky decisions).

18. See Jon D. Hanson & Douglas A. Kysar, Taking Behavioralism Seriously: The Problem of Market Manipulation, 74 N.Y.U. L. Rev. 630 (1999); Jon D. Hanson & Douglas A. Kysar, Taking Behavioralism Seriously: Some Evidence of Market Manipulation, 112 Harv. L. Rev. 1420 (1999).

other type is well informed, having incurred the necessary information costs. If there are enough well-informed buyers in the market, their aggregate demand for product quality will induce sellers to supply reasonably safe products.[19] The information held by some consumers can benefit others who are not well informed of product risk. But since the information is costly to acquire and process, any consumer may rationally decide to "free ride" on the informed choices of others, thereby saving the information costs. The consumer can get the benefits of information (safe products) without incurring the information costs. Reasoning similarly, other consumers will make the same choice. The "free rider" problem may result in no consumer incurring the information costs necessary for making decisions about product safety.

Even if the market does not suffer from this problem, information costs can force each consumer to forego the evaluation of numerous product risks. Consider again the one in 10,000 risk of being injured by a particular configuration of a car's steering wheel. Just as information costs can prevent consumers from finding it worthwhile to learn of this risk, information costs can prevent consumers from evaluating it. Consumers face a bewildering array of product choices. Over 30,000 items are available in the typical supermarket.[20] Experience with a brand may provide the consumer with some knowledge, but even that is short-lived. For U.S. manufacturing firms that remain in operation over a manufacturing census period (every five years), almost two-thirds of the firms change their product mixes, with the product switches involving almost half of existing products.[21] The consumer's ability to evaluate risk is then made even more difficult by the increased complexity of products. Who has the time, energy and desire to evaluate each and every one of these product risks, particularly given the range of other decisions we face on a daily basis?[22]

Rather than attempting to evaluate all product risks, consumers can rely upon a tort duty. By making the manufacturer responsible for the safety decision, the tort duty can reduce information

19. *See* Alan Schwartz & Louis L. Wilde, *Imperfect Information in Markets for Contract Terms: The Examples of Warranties and Security Interests*, 69 Va. L. Rev. 1387 (1983); Louis L. Wilde & Alan Schwartz, *Equilibrium Comparison Shopping*, 46 Rev. Econ. Stud. 543 (1979).

20. G. Cross, An All–Consuming Century: Why Commercialism Won in Modern America (2000).

21. *See* Andrew B. Bernard et al., Product Choice and Product Switching (Nat'l Bureau of Econ. Research, Working Paper No. 9789, 2003).

22. *See* Xavier Gabaix et al., The Allocation of Attention: Theory and Evidence (M.I.T. Dep't of Econ., Working Paper No. 03–31, 2003) (analyzing attention as a scarce resource allocated by cost-benefit principles and providing empirical support that individuals act in this manner).

costs and increase the amount of information about product risks.[23] This outcome would increase consumer welfare, and so consumers could rationally conclude that the best method of making safety decisions is via a tort duty requiring product sellers to guarantee reasonable product safety.

This rationale for the tort duty can be assessed with some available data. From 1987 through 1993, the cost of products liability in the U.S. ranged from 13.5 cents to 25.9 cents per $100 of retail sales.[24] In effect, by paying 25 cents per $100 of sales, a consumer can rely on the safety guarantee supplied by the tort system and avoid the information and error costs she otherwise would incur when evaluating product safety on her own. The payment also gives the consumer a right to compensation for physical injuries caused by defective products. In exchange for these benefits, would you be willing to pay 25 cents for each $100 of product purchases?

Of course, the answer to this question does not determine whether the products liability system is desirable. But as the

23. By making the seller responsible for defective products, the tort guarantee effectively requires sellers to acquire the relevant information. The guarantee is likely to reduce total information costs. The manufacturer has greater technical expertise and can make one thorough investigation of the product, spreading that information cost among all consumers via a price increase. The associated cost per consumer will often be less than the average amount that each consumer otherwise would incur to investigate product safety on her own. And since information acquisition depends on a comparison of costs and benefits incurred by the decision maker, a reduction in costs should increase the total amount of information acquired, assuming there is no change in the benefits of the information.

A tort duty, moreover, is likely to increase the benefits of information for the decision maker. A seller owing a duty to all consumers considers the benefit of added information in terms of that group, whereas the individual consumer acquiring information only considers her private benefit. The benefit for the group will typically exceed the benefit for the individual consumer, particularly for markets plagued by the free-rider problem discussed earlier. Since information acquisition depends on the decision maker's comparison of costs with benefits, an increase in benefits should increase the amount of information acquired, all else being equal.

For other reasons why a tort duty would improve safety decisions in situations of high information costs, see Steven P. Croley & Jon D. Hanson, *Rescuing the Revolution: The Revived Case for Enterprise Liability*, 91 Mich. L. Rev. 683 (1993).

24. Marc Galanter, *Real World Torts: An Antidote to Anecdote*, 55 Md. L. Rev. 1093, 1145 (1996) (citing J. Robert Hunter, Product Liability Insurance Experience 1984–93: A Report of the Insurance Group of the Consumer Federation of America (1995)). The figure is based on insurance premiums paid by sellers for products liability and thus needs to be adjusted to account for self-insurance. *Id.* A different study found that the total liability risk faced by U.S. corporations, not confined to products liability, was 25.5 cents for every $100 of revenue in the mid–1990s. *Id.* (citing Tillinghast–Towers Perrin Risk Management Publications & Risk and Insurance Management Soc'y, 1995 Cost of Risk Survey (1995)).

question reveals, the justification for the tort duty importantly depends on information costs. When information costs are low, consumers presumably have enough information to evaluate product risk and make the correct product choices. Actual consumer expectations are not disappointed, and a tort duty is neither necessary nor beneficial for consumers. When information costs are high, consumers are likely to make heuristic-based decisions or rationally disregard the evaluation of product risk. Actual consumer expectations can be disappointed, justifying a tort duty that requires the amount of product safety that best promotes consumer welfare.

As an implication of this reasoning, consumer expectations are not necessarily satisfied merely because the danger in question is open or obvious. Many believe that "the expectancy test plainly precludes liability in such cases."[25] This belief does not adequately account for information costs. Even though the ordinary consumer might be aware of danger, information costs can prevent her from making a good risk-utility decision. A consumer who is merely aware of danger must estimate the risk. Due to information costs, the consumer can underestimate the risk and make an erroneous risk-utility decision. Information costs may also induce the consumer to forego the risk-utility evaluation altogether. In order for consumer expectations to be satisfied, the consumer must have made the safety decision on the basis of good information about all of the risk-utility factors, not merely the potential for danger.[26]

Economic analysis of actual consumer expectations thus provides a way to conceptualize duty in products liability. *A tort duty is most defensible when the ordinary consumer would incur high information costs to evaluate a product choice involving a risk of physical harm.* As information costs go down, the tort duty becomes harder to justify with consumer expectations. In the extreme case of no information costs, the tort duty is unnecessary. Consumers can fully evaluate all product risks on the basis of perfect information. These perfectly informed consumers never have frustrated expectations, because they make whatever product choices maximize their welfare.

---

25. 1 Madden & Owen on Products Liability § 5:6, at 299.

26. For further discussion of why the seller's tort duty includes open and obvious risks, see Chapter 6, section I.A. For discussion of how duty is limited when the consumer knows the risk and has appropriately evaluated it, see Chapter 6, section III (discussing categorical liability); Chapter 7, section II (discussing duty to warn); and Chapter 10, section II (discussing assumption of risk).

Chapter 3

THE REQUIREMENT OF DEFECT

Even though the ordinary consumer reasonably expects the amount of product safety required by the risk-utility test, these two liability rules are not necessarily coextensive. The risk-utility test limits liability to defective products, whereas consumer expectations need not limit liability in this manner. The ordinary consumer could expect to be compensated for a product-caused injury, regardless of defect.

This expectation yields the insurance rationale for tort liability, which maintains that tort compensation is a desirable form of insurance. If the ordinary consumer finds tort compensation to be a desirable form of insurance, then tort compensation can be justified by the fact of injury and the associated need for insurance. There is no reason to limit compensation to the injuries caused by defective products. The insurance rationale has been an important justification for the rule of strict products liability, providing doctrinal support for the claim that consumer expectations justify a more expansive role for tort liability than the risk-utility test.[1]

To complete our analysis of consumer expectations, we need to determine whether the concept supports a rule of strict liability not limited by the requirement of defect. The inquiry is particularly important because the requirement of defect is the most significant limitation of liability in product cases. Unless the seller otherwise incurs tort obligations (by making fraudulent statements, for example), its duty is limited to the provision of a nondefective product. This limitation of liability can be squared with consumer expectations only if the ordinary consumer does not reasonably expect to receive tort compensation—a form of insurance—merely because she suffered a product-caused injury.

I. Consumer Expectations of Insurance

The insurance dimension of product cases does not encompass safety concerns. Lacking any safety rationale, tort compensation serves the sole purpose of compensating injury, the role of insurance.

---

1. *See* Chapter 1, section IV (discussing the reasons why consumers might reasonably expect compensation for injuries caused by nondefective products and showing the doctrinal importance of this rationale for strict products liability).

51

Tort law promotes safety by giving product sellers an incentive to provide nondefective products. A product that is not defective still poses a risk of injury whenever the cost of eliminating any particular risk is too high: $B > PL$. If the product seller were liable for these *residual risks*, it would minimize costs (and product price) by paying tort damages for these injuries (with expected costs PL) rather than by adopting a more costly safety precaution (costing $B > PL$) to eliminate the risk of injury (and liability). The insurance dimension of product cases thus involves injury compensation for the residual risks posed by nondefective products

The cost of all residual risks factors into the full price or total cost of the product for the consumer:

full price = expected cost of residual risks + total remaining cost

The consumer could insure against residual risks by purchasing from the seller a guaranteed right to compensation for the injuries caused by the product. This guarantee would increase product price by an amount equaling the seller's expected liability costs for the residual risks. Due to this price increase, the consumer implicitly pays an insurance premium for the guarantee of compensation in the event a residual risk causes injury. In effect, the product sale is a bundled transaction in which the consumer purchases from the seller both the product and an insurance policy.

The consumer would prefer the bundled transaction if it reduced the total cost or full price of the product as compared to the next-best alternative (an unbundled transaction in which the insurance for residual risks is provided by another source). In these circumstances, consumer expectations would justify a tort rule holding the product seller liable for the injuries proximately caused by a nondefective product. Otherwise, consumer expectations justify the limitation of liability to defective products.

By framing the issue in these terms, the rationale for the requirement of defect might seem obvious. At the time of purchase, the consumer can readily determine that the seller is not guaranteeing a remedy for the injuries caused by a nondefective product. How could the obvious absence of the insurance guarantee for residual risks frustrate the actual expectations of the ordinary consumer?

As previously discussed, consumer expectations can be frustrated by open and obvious risks.[2] The consumer can be aware of some attribute of the product, whether a patent danger or the absence of an insurance guarantee, without being able to make a good decision

---

2. *See* Chapter 2, section II.B.

about the matter. The consumer might not have sufficient information—mere awareness is not the same as adequate knowledge—or she might not evaluate the issue properly. Individuals are aware of many things, but they do not fully evaluate each and every one of them. The time and hassle of doing so makes that impossible. Consequently, the ordinary consumer can know that the seller is not guaranteeing compensation for injuries caused by nondefective products without having made a well-informed choice. To have satisfied expectations, the ordinary consumer must make an informed decision of whether to forego the seller's guarantee of tort compensation for injuries caused by a nondefective product.

For example, suppose the product seller, in exchange for a higher price, offered to compensate the consumer for all injuries proximately caused by the product, whether defective or not. Knowing that she could purchase the same insurance elsewhere for a lower price, the consumer declined the offer and bought the product without that guarantee, paying a lower price. The consumer had all of the information required to make a well-informed choice, so the transaction presumptively satisfies actual consumer expectations regarding insurance. In these circumstances, consumer expectations do not justify tort liability for all product-caused injuries. The seller's tort duty is appropriately limited by the requirement of defect.[3]

To analyze the requirement of defect, we accordingly need to evaluate the insurance decisions actually faced by consumers. The analysis depends upon historical context. Consumers have not always been able to choose among insurance options, an historical fact that importantly affects the issue of whether tort liability should be limited by the requirement of defect or instead be extended to cover all product-caused injuries as per the insurance rationale for tort liability.

II. The Historical Contingency of the Insurance Rationale for Tort Liability

Health insurance was not widely available in the U.S. until the 1950s.[4] Before then, consumers who purchased products without the bundled tort insurance were not necessarily choosing a lower

---

3. In making the insurance choice, the consumer did not know whether the product was defective, and so the seller's provision of a defective product would frustrate consumer safety expectations.

4. *See* Rashi Fein, Medical Care, Medical Costs: The Search for a Health Insurance Policy 21–24 (1986); Paul Starr, The Social Transformation of American Medicine 240, 327–28 (1982).

priced alternative. The choice for most consumers was between seller-provided tort insurance and little or no insurance.

During this period, consumer expectations supported the insurance rationale for tort liability. For the ordinary consumer, some insurance is better than no insurance.[5] Accidental injuries were often financially ruinous for individuals in this era, making it even more doubtful that consumers actually preferred to be uninsured or underinsured.[6] Moreover, the very same consumer informational problem that justifies the tort duty also explains why product sellers were unwilling to provide the tort insurance for nondefective products.[7] The fact that consumers knew they were buying products without a guarantee of injury compensation therefore did not mean that the ordinary consumer had made an informed *choice* to do so. Product sellers were not offering guaranteed compensation for injuries caused by nondefective products, but the ordinary consumer presumably preferred to have this insurance. The resultant frustration of actual consumer expectations is sufficient to justify a tort duty, and reasonable consumer expectations can then justify a liability rule forcing sellers to provide insurance or tort compensation for the injuries caused by nondefective products.

Consistently with this conclusion, many tort scholars in the first half of the twentieth century argued that tort compensation can be justified as a mode of insurance.[8] When the courts adopted strict products liability in the middle of the century, they often justified the liability rule with the insurance rationale.[9] The insur-

---

5. As established by the economic analysis of insurance, anyone with a diminishing marginal utility of money prefers insurance priced at the actuarially fair premium. Presumably most individuals have this trait, since the marginal utility that a wealthy person derives from a dollar is presumably much less than the marginal utility derived by a poor person. For further elaboration of the economic analysis of insurance, see Chapter 9, section II.A.

6. For a particularly influential study reaching this conclusion, see Committee to Study Compensation of Automobile Accidents, Report to the Columbia University Council for Research in the Social Science (1932).

7. The tort duty assumes that consumers underestimate or are unaware of the relevant risk. *See* Chapter 2, section II.B. Consumer estimates of the prod-

uct's full price would be increased if the seller guaranteed compensation for all injuries, because the purchase price of the product would incorporate the residual-risk costs that had previously been underestimated by consumers. The increase in full price would decrease consumer demand, so product sellers would prefer not to provide guaranteed compensation for all injuries.

8. For extensive discussions of the development of enterprise liability, see Virginia E. Nolan & Edmund Ursin, Understanding Enterprise Liability: Rethinking Tort Reform for the Twenty-first Century (1995); George L. Priest, *The Invention of Enterprise Liability: A Critical History of the Intellectual Foundations of Modern Tort Law*, 14 J. Legal Stud. 461 (1985); Mark C. Rahdert, Covering Accident Costs: Insurance, Liability, and Tort Reform (1995).

9. *See* Chapter 1, section IV.

ance rationale for tort liability therefore was formulated at a time when consumers faced limited insurance options.

The insurance market has dramatically changed, however. Since the mid-twentieth century, health insurance has become widely available. This market grew rapidly during World War II when employers began offering health insurance as an employee benefit which was not subject to wage controls, making it an important form of employee remuneration in a tight labor market. The insurance provided by employers also had tax advantages, further promoting its growth. By the 1960s, a sizable portion of the population had health insurance, such insurance was widely available, and government-funded social insurance programs had expanded substantially.[10] Today the vast majority of accident victims receive some injury compensation from their own insurance policies and government programs.[11]

The consumer's insurance choice is no longer limited to manufacturer-provided tort insurance as opposed to no insurance. It now involves a range of insurance options. The historical conditions that gave rise to the insurance rationale no longer exist. In light of these changed conditions, we need to reconsider the expectations of the ordinary consumer who purchases a product without full tort insurance covering injuries caused by nondefective products.

III. The High Cost of Tort Insurance: A Rationale for the Requirement of Defect

Consumer expectations of insurance depend on the relative cost of seller-provided tort insurance as compared to other forms of insurance, which usually are *first-party* insurance arrangements because the policyholder (consumer) is also the party suffering the underlying injury. The tort insurance provided by product sellers has different structural features than first-party insurance, creating a significant cost differential.

The cost differential between the two forms of insurance is largely attributable to the trigger and scope of coverage.[12] The coverage supplied by a first-party insurance policy is triggered by

10. *See* Fein, *supra* note 4; Starr, *supra* note 4.

11. *See* Deborah R. Hensler et al., Compensation for Accidental Injuries in the United States 108 (1991) (summarizing study which found that 85 percent of all accident victims received some compensation from their own insurance and public programs).

12. First-party insurance may also be cheaper due to its comparative advantage in minimizing the costs of moral hazard and adverse selection. *See* Richard A. Epstein, *Products Liability as an Insurance Market*, 14 J. Legal Stud. 645 (1985); George L. Priest, *The Current Insurance Crisis and Modern Tort Law*, 96 Yale L.J. 1521 (1987).

the fact of loss (like medical expenses for health insurance). The cause of loss ordinarily is not relevant. The fact of injury or loss usually is easy to prove (submitting bills), so policyholders typically do not need a lawyer to receive insurance proceeds. By contrast, the trigger of coverage for seller-provided tort insurance involves the cause of loss—the seller's product must have proximately caused the injury. To establish the requisite causal link in order to recover the insurance or tort proceeds, the consumer typically needs a lawyer. Often, many products are causally implicated in an accident, and a potentially contentious and costly factual inquiry may be required to resolve the liability question.[13] These litigation expenses increase the cost of tort insurance, as do other litigation expenses.[14] An insurance trigger based on the *fact* of loss therefore is less costly to implement than a trigger based on the *cause* of loss, creating a significant cost differential between first-party insurance and the tort insurance provided by product sellers.

The seller-provided tort insurance also has a limited scope of coverage that creates additional costs for the consumer. The tort insurance does not cover losses unrelated to product use. To cover these contingencies (like medical expenses due to illness), individuals must purchase other insurance. But since first-party insurance coverage typically is triggered by the fact of loss rather than its cause, individuals who have such insurance might receive double compensation when injured by products. The health insurer, for example, is obligated to pay whenever the policyholder suffered an insured-against loss (medical expenses), and the manufacturer is obligated to pay tort damages for such loss (due to the collateral-source rule), even though the consumer has already received health insurance proceeds. Double recovery can be avoided if the health insurer exercises a contractual or statutory right to indemnification out of the tort recovery received by the policyholder, known as *subrogation*. The separate legal proceeding, however, often is complicated and costly due to the need to determine which part of the

13. *See* Mark Geistfeld, *Implementing Enterprise Liability: A Comment on Henderson and Twerski*, 67 N.Y.U. L. Rev. 1157 (1992). Rather than merely raising transaction costs, some argue that the problem of multiple causes would render unworkable a system of products liability not limited by the requirement of defect. *See* James A. Henderson, Jr. & Aaron D. Twerski, *Closing the American Products Liability Frontier: The Rejection of Liability Without Defect*, 66 N.Y.U. L. Rev. 1263 (1991).

14. Many items of tort damages are difficult and costly to prove. And even though this form of tort liability does not require proof of defect, these cases frequently would involve litigation regarding the defendant's conduct or degree or risk posed by the product. The plaintiff might introduce evidence regarding the manufacturer's fault or the egregiousness of its conduct in an effort to gain the jury's sympathy so that it decides contested issues, such as the amount of pain-and-suffering damages, in the plaintiff's favor.

tort award or settlement is covered by the insurance policy. Consequently, insurers do not always exercise this right. The tort insurance provided by product sellers therefore may be an inefficient form of double insurance or otherwise increase the administrative cost of first-party insurance policies by necessitating subrogation actions, providing another reason why consumers are likely to have lower total insurance costs if the tort liability of product sellers were limited to defective products.

A variety of factors thus strongly indicate that the cost of seller-provided tort insurance per dollar of coverage significantly exceeds the cost of first-party insurance. This conclusion finds support in the available data.[15]

Of course, consumers do not always have first-party insurance. As a practical matter, tort insurance often would provide some insurance to individuals who otherwise would be uninsured.[16] If consumers would be better off with the mandatory, but relatively expensive tort insurance, then insurance costs do not persuasively justify the limitation of a seller's duty to defective products.

Although the problem of underinsurance must be addressed by an expansion of insurance coverage, the problem does not justify the expansion of tort liability. Even if consumers were compensated for all product-caused injuries, underinsurance would continue to be a substantial problem since individuals are injured for various reasons unrelated to product use. Moreover, the problem of underinsurance would be better addressed by other means. Due to the relatively high cost of tort insurance, more extensive coverage could be provided for the same total cost by other insurance mechanisms. The government could legislatively mandate minimum levels of first-party insurance coverage, similar to the governmentally mandated insurance regarding motor-vehicle accidents and social security. Those who are unable to afford this insurance could be subsidized through the tax system, which is a more efficient way to redistribute wealth than the tort system.[17] The government also could provide the insurance, subsidized if necessary, much like it

---

15. *See* Mark Geistfeld, *Should Enterprise Liability Replace the Rule of Strict Liability for Abnormally Dangerous Activities?*, 45 UCLA L. Rev. 611, 625–33, 639–46 (1998) (relying on empirical data and a heuristic assessment to conclude that for each $1 of injury compensation, consumers would have to spend roughly 40 cents more for the tort insurance provided by manufacturers as compared to the insurance consumers could otherwise purchase on their own).

16. The lack of widespread health-insurance coverage in the U.S. is widely known. Less well known is the absence of widespread insurance coverage for disability.

17. *See* Louis Kaplow & Steven Shavell, *Why the Legal System is Less Efficient Than the Income Tax in Redistributing Income*, 23 J. Legal Stud. 667 (1994).

already does in a variety of situations. Not only are these forms of insurance less costly, they can avoid the way in which tort insurance regressively redistributes wealth from the poor to the rich.[18] To be sure, the government has not yet solved the problem of underinsurance, but consideration of the underlying political dynamics also suggests that the government would never adopt tort rules extending strict liability to nondefective products or would enact legislation eliminating such a common-law rule of liability.[19] Underinsurance is undoubtedly a significant social problem, but an expansion of tort liability is neither the appropriate nor most feasible solution.

These considerations explain why "[d]espite wide variations in judicial definitions of 'defect,' there is universal agreement on this requirement and a general fear that eliminating it would foster liability on an 'insurance' basis."[20] Tort compensation for nondefective products would increase total insurance costs for consumers, thereby decreasing consumer welfare. The ordinary consumer therefore does not reasonably expect to receive tort compensation on an "insurance basis," but instead expects only those forms of liability that increase consumer welfare by promoting product safety. Consumer expectations justify the requirement of defect.

---

18. In paying the same price for a product, consumers pay the same premium for tort insurance. Those who earn more will receive higher tort damages for lost wages than those who earn less, even though each pays the same premium. Tort damages are thus regressive in the sense that they redistribute wealth from the poor to the rich. *See* George L. Priest, *The Current Insurance Crisis and Modern Tort Law*, 96 Yale L.J. 1521 (1987).

19. *Cf.* Mark Geistfeld, *The Political Economy of Neocontractual Proposals for*

Products Liability Reform, 72 Tex. L. Rev. 803, 836–42 (1994) (describing how interest-group politics create a bias for legislative reforms that reduce the scope of tort liability for product-caused injuries).

20. Shapo, 1 Law of Products Liability ¶ 8.01 at 4003–04. *See also* Rahdert, *supra* note 8, at 59 ("Where courts (and sometimes legislatures) have embraced the insurance rationale, they usually have done so in a cautious, qualified manner.").

Chapter 4

THE COMPLEMENTARY ROLES OF CONSUMER EXPECTATIONS AND THE RISK-UTILITY TEST

Having developed the concept of consumer expectations, we can now reassess the ongoing controversy over the appropriate liability rule for design and warning defects. The dispute, long simmering in the courts, has been brought to a boil by the *Restatement (Third)*. For decades, courts have disagreed about the appropriate roles of consumer expectations and the risk-utility test. Any effort to restate this body of law—the project of the *Restatement (Third)*—would appear to be destined for controversy. And the *Restatement (Third)* has been controversial.

In the first major case addressing these issues, the Connecticut Supreme Court in *Potter v. Chicago Pneumatic Tool Company* rejected the risk-utility test in the *Restatement (Third)* in favor of consumer expectations.[1] The court also adopted the risk-utility test as a complement to consumer expectations for cases in which consumers do not have sufficiently formed expectations of product safety. The resulting liability rule, according to the *Restatement (Third)*, "is, in actuality, perfectly consistent with this Restatement."[2] The Connecticut Supreme Court, though, insisted that "our adoption of a risk-utility balancing component to our consumer expectation test does not signal a retreat from strict tort liability."[3] The court was not concerned about the substantive content of the risk-utility test, but instead was apparently troubled by the *Restatement (Third)*'s treatment of consumer expectations and the associated role of strict liability. Of the various rationales for the risk-utility test in the *Restatement (Third)*, none expressly reference consumer expectations.[4] In order to adhere to consumer expectations, the court had to reject the risk-utility test in the *Restatement (Third)*. After confirming that consumer expectations provide the foundation for liability, the court was not foreclosed from adopting a liability rule that otherwise is "perfectly consistent" with the risk-utility test in the *Restatement (Third)*. As this case

---

1. 694 A.2d 1319 (Conn. 1997).

2. Restatement (Third) § 2 Rptrs' Note at 72.

3. *Potter*, 694 A.2d at 1334.

4. *See* Restatement (Third), § 2 cmt. a; *see also id.* cmt. g (stating that consumer expectations are relevant only insofar as they "affect how risks are perceived and relate to foreseeability and frequency of the risks of harm").

shows, the *Restatement (Third)* controversially fails to recognize the way in which the risk-utility test depends upon, and is complemented by, consumer expectations.[5]

Tort law justifiably regulates product transactions when consumers make poorly informed contractual decisions in the product market, resulting in overly unsafe products that frustrate the actual safety expectations of the ordinary consumer. The existence of the tort duty—the reason for subjecting product sellers to the prospect of tort liability under the risk-utility test—is predicated upon the frustration of consumer expectations. In this respect, the risk-utility test necessarily depends upon consumer expectations.

Why, then, did the *Restatement (Third)* fail to make this connection? To capture the appropriate relation between consumer expectations and the risk-utility test, actual consumer expectations (the duty question) must be distinguished from reasonable consumer expectations (the risk-utility test). That distinction has not been adequately drawn by the courts, and so it does not appear in a restatement of the case law.

The source of the problem resides in the nature of the cases that were restated into the rule of strict products liability in the *Restatement (Second)*. When the *Restatement (Second)* was promulgated in the 1960s, the case law involved products with defects that caused them to malfunction, like the exploding bottle of soda. In these cases, the defect can be identified or defined by the product malfunction. The defect does not have to be defined in terms of reasonable consumer expectations, nor is there any reason to distinguish actual expectations from reasonable expectations. To be sure, the liability rule could be formulated in this manner: A

---

5. Tort scholars have voiced similar concerns. Consider the views of Professor Shapo, who has sharply criticized the *Restatement (Third)* for its rejection of consumer expectations. *E.g.*, Marshall S. Shapo, *In Search of the Law of Products Liability: The ALI Restatement Project*, 48 Vand. L. Rev. 631 (1995). Shapo's views on consumer expectations are nuanced, but his basic thesis is that a manufacturer's portrayal of its product should be the "initial" and "principal" factor determining the manufacturer's liability. Marshall S. Shapo, *A Representational Theory of Consumer Protection: Doctrine, Function, and Legal Liability for Product Disappointment*, 60 Va. L. Rev. 1109, 1115 (1974). As previously discussed, the seller's ability to influence consumer perceptions of product risk provides a compelling justification for the tort duty—the "initial" element of the liability claim. *See* Chapter 2, section II.B. With respect to the liability rule, Shapo's consumerist concerns are presumably satisfied if sellers are required to provide the amount of product safety that is reasonably expected by consumers. These reasonable consumer expectations justify the risk-utility test. *See* Chapter 2, section II.A. Consequently, Shapo can defensibly claim that consumer expectations are the "principal" factor for liability purposes, even though the risk-utility test is the appropriate liability rule for design and warning defects.

60

malfunctioning product frustrates both actual consumer expectations (establishing duty) and reasonable consumer expectations (establishing defect).[6] But why make the liability rule depend upon reasonable expectations when the product defect is obviously defined by the product malfunction? Any reference to reasonable consumer expectations would seem to be superfluous, if not misguided. A self-defeating product malfunction was the only type of defect extensively considered by those who drafted the rule of strict products liability in the *Restatement (Second)*.[7] The focus on these defects was natural in light of the case law being restated, explaining why the *Restatement (Second)* rule of strict products liability does not distinguish actual consumer expectations from reasonable expectations.

After the courts had adopted the *Restatement (Second)* rule of strict products liability, plaintiffs began to file tort claims alleging defects in products that did not malfunction. These allegations of defect involved the design of the product or the content of the product warning. Unable to evaluate these claims by reference to a product malfunction, the courts had to develop another definition of defect. In struggling with this issue, many courts understandably relied upon the *Restatement (Second)* liability rule.

The *Restatement (Second)* rule was bound to create confusion in design and warning cases. A liability rule defined solely in terms of actual consumer expectations conflates the element of duty with the separate requirement of defect. Actual consumer expectations cannot simultaneously determine both duty and defect, for otherwise a court's recognition of the tort duty implies that the product was defective.

This conflation-of-elements can be illustrated by *Denny v. Ford Motor Company*, in which the jury concluded that the design of a Sports Utility Vehicle (SUV) passed the risk-utility test but was nevertheless defective for creating a risk of rollover that breached the implied warranty.[8] *Denny* has provoked a fair amount of contro-

---

6. *See* Chapter 1, section IV (explaining why evidentiary concerns regarding quality-control measures cause the ordinary consumer to reasonably expect the seller to guarantee the nondefectiveness of the product).

7. *See* David G. Owen, *The Graying of Products Liability Law: Paths Taken and Untaken in the New Restatement*, 61 Tenn. L. Rev. 1241, 1243 (1994) (observing that § 402A was drafted at a time when "the defect concept was only roughly understood and was conceived

of quite naively as a *unitary* concept"). Others have argued that the drafters of the *Restatement (Second)* failed to consider design defects. *See, e.g.*, George L. Priest, *Strict Products Liability: The Original Intent*, 10 Cardozo L. Rev. 2301 (1989). Some design defects, however, can cause the product to malfunction, and so this type of design defect was contemplated by the drafters of the *Restatement (Second)*.

8. 662 N.E.2d 730 (N.Y. 1995).

versy, although its critics have not recognized how the outcome logically follows from the way in which the implied-warranty claim conflated the elements of duty and defect. Actual consumer expectations are frustrated when the ordinary consumer underestimates the product risk posed by the SUV design, thereby justifying the tort duty.[9] The ordinary consumer who underestimates design risks will also underestimate the risk that a well-designed SUV will rollover. The ordinary consumer will be surprised to learn the true risk of rollover, resulting in frustrated expectations. When defect is defined in these terms, the same fact that establishes duty (the underestimation of risk) also establishes defect (the unexpectedly high risk of rollover), enabling the jury to conclude that the design passed the risk-utility test and still frustrated consumer expectations in violation of the implied warranty.

This result is exceptional only because the underlying problem is not apparent in the vast majority of design and warning cases. Ordinarily, the plaintiff's proof addresses the safety features of the product, such as the absence of an airbag in an automobile or the absence of a hazard disclosure in the product warning.[10] This proof focuses the jury's attention on the safety precaution. Once the jury frames consumer expectations in terms of a safety precaution instead of the associated risk, it will treat consumer expectations as a floor or less demanding liability standard than the risk-utility test. Consumers who underestimate risk also expect insufficient amounts of product safety.[11] The ordinary consumer does not have sufficiently demanding expectations with respect to safety precautions, and so the jury can find that the actual safety expectations of the ordinary consumer are satisfied by a product that does not have a safety precaution required by the risk-utility test. For this reason, courts have assumed that consumer expectations are less demanding than the risk-utility test, which is why the opposite result in *Denny* has been so controversial.

The exceptional feature of *Denny* involved the form of the plaintiff's proof. Rather than address the safety features of the design, the plaintiff's proof with respect to the implied warranty focused entirely on the risk of rollover. Once the jury thinks about risk rather than a particular safety feature, the plaintiff has a much easier time persuading the jury that the design frustrates consumer expectations. The existence of the tort duty implies that the ordi-

---

9. *See* Chapter 2, section II.B.

10. This is the conventional method of proving defect. Lacking proof of a safety feature that should have been incorporated into the design or warning, the claim would involve categorical lia-

bility, a form of liability that has been rejected by virtually every court. *See* Chapter 6, section III.

11. *See* Chapter 2, section II.B.

nary consumer underestimates or is unaware of product risk. The ordinary consumer will expect the product to be less risky than it actually is, even if the product otherwise passes the risk-utility test. Consumer expectations are now the more demanding liability standard only because of the distinctive form of the plaintiff's proof.

The logic of liability in *Denny*, however, is not unique to that case. A liability rule formulated exclusively in terms of actual consumer expectations conflates the element of duty with the requirement of defect. The recognition of the tort duty implies the existence of a defect. Any effort to avoid this outcome by keeping the two elements separate necessarily relies upon logical errors, much like those permeating *Denny*.[12]

Other courts have tried to formulate the defect test for design and warnings in terms of actual consumer expectations, and they, too, have produced confusing opinions. By the time the *Restatement (Third)* was drafted in the 1990s, the confusion caused most courts and virtually all commentators to conclude that consumer expectations should not determine defects of product design and warnings.[13]

---

12. According to the court, the SUV design passed the risk-utility test because the risk of rollover was less than the utility of off-road driving. The court then held that for purposes of the implied warranty, the utility factor is determined by the SUV's "ordinary purpose" of "suburban driving and everyday road travel." The utility of off-road driving is no longer relevant, resulting in an unreasonable risk of rollover that breached the implied warranty. The court believed that these were "distinctive" facts, leading to the "unusual circumstances" in which a design passes the risk-utility test and violates the implied warranty. For this reason, it thought that the distinction between the two claims "may have little or no effect in most cases."

Contrary to what the court has said, *Denny* actually supports exceptionally wide swaths of liability. The implied warranty is not limited by the requirement of privity in New York, so it can govern cases involving crashes between passenger vehicles and SUVs. In these crashes, "SUVs impose excessive collision damage because the height differen-tial creates a mismatch between their structures and the protective structures of vehicles with lower ride-heights." Howard Latin & Bobby Kasolas, *Bad Designs, Lethal Profits: The Duty to Protect Other Motorists Against SUV Collision Risks*, 82 B.U. L. Rev. 1161, 1201 (2002). According to *Denny*, the utility afforded by the SUV's height differential is entirely irrelevant to the implied warranty insofar as the differential is only required for off-road driving. Lacking that form of utility, the height differential of the SUV design does not create significant utility on the highway that offsets the substantial risk created for passenger vehicles. The design is not fit for the intended purpose of highway driving, resulting in a violation of the implied warranty for cases in which the occupants of passenger vehicles were injured by the increased height differential of the SUV. The logic of *Denny* accordingly implies that large numbers of SUVs operated on the public roadways of New York are defective, an outcome clearly different than what the court had contemplated.

13. *See* Chapter 1, section III.

Over the years, the issue of duty had also receded in importance, much like in other areas of tort law.[14] Once duty ceases to be of concern, the actual safety expectations of the ordinary consumer no longer seem so significant, particularly in an era when the prominent and controversial product cases involved allegations of design or warning defects. A focus on these cases highlights the importance of risk-utility considerations, leading the *Restatement (Third)* to emphasize the risk-utility test while downplaying consumer expectations.

Historical reasons therefore explain why the *Restatement (Second)* and the *Restatement (Third)* give different emphasis to consumer expectations and the risk-utility test. At a time when the case law involved malfunctioning products, the *Restatement (Second)* understandably defined the liability rule exclusively in terms of actual consumer expectations. After courts adopted the *Restatement (Second)* rule of strict products liability, the mix of cases changed. The courts increasingly became aware that actual consumer expectations do not provide a good liability rule for design and warning defects, leading them to adopt the risk-utility test. These cases enabled the *Restatement (Third)* to emphasize the risk-utility test rather than consumer expectations.

The different emphases do not imply a fundamental difference of approach, however. One is strictly liable under the *Restatement (Second)* for selling "any product in a defective condition unreasonably dangerous to the user or consumer ...."[15] The "unreasonably dangerous" requirement can be interpreted to mean that the product must frustrate the reasonable safety expectations of the ordinary consumer, yielding the risk-utility test as the appropriate method for evaluating defects of design and warnings. So understood, the rule of strict products liability in the *Restatement (Second)* is consistent with the risk-utility test in the *Restatement (Third)*.

A different conclusion is reached by the *Restatement (Third)*, which claims that "in contrast to [the rule of strict liability for] manufacturing defects, design defects and defects based on inadequate instructions or warnings are predicated on a different concept of responsibility."[16] If this claim is correct, the *Restatement (Second)* rule of strict products liability, formulated in terms of consumer expectations, is substantively different than the *Restate-*

---

14. *See* John C.P. Goldberg & Benjamin C. Zipursky, *The Moral of* MacPherson, 146 U. Pa. L. Rev. 1733 (1998) (describing the decline of duty in torts

jurisprudence over the course of the twentieth century).

15. Restatement (Second) § 402A.

16. Restatement (Third) § 2 cmt. a.

ment (Third) risk-utility test, formulated in terms of negligence principles. Consumer expectations and the rule of strict liability purportedly involve a "different concept of responsibility" than the risk-utility test.

To evaluate this claim, we need to assess the seven different rationales for strict liability in the *Restatement (Third)*. Of these varied rationales, only one expressly invokes consumer expectations. The concept of consumer expectations, however, can account for four of the other *Restatement (Third)* rationales for strict liability.[17] Only two rationales require separate analysis.

According to the *Restatement (Third)*, strict liability can be justified because manufacturers choose quality-control levels which "entail[] an element of deliberation about the amount of injury that will result from their activity." This rationale for strict liability cannot be justified by consumer expectations, nor does it withstand scrutiny. Manufacturers deliberately choose risk levels in designing products and formulating warnings. By not installing the airbag, the car manufacturer has chosen to increase the level of risk posed by the automobile. If the manufacturer's deliberate risk choices justify strict liability for manufacturing defects, then its deliberate risk choices should also justify strict liability for design and warning cases. The *Restatement (Third)* and the case law reject such an expansive role for strict liability, implying that strict liability is not justified merely because manufacturers deliberately choose risk levels.[18]

---

17. The *Restatement (Third)* justifies strict liability, in part, because products with manufacturing defects "disappoint reasonable expectations of product performance." *Id.* As previously discussed, negligence liability could protect the reasonable safety expectations of the ordinary consumer, but that protection is lacking whenever product sellers can escape liability due to problems of proof. Strict liability therefore serves an "instrumental function of creating safety incentives" greater than those in a negligence regime "under which, as a practical matter, sellers may escape their appropriate share of liability." *Id.* "And by eliminating the issue of manufacturer fault from plaintiff's case, strict liability reduces the transaction costs in litigating that issue." *Id.* The reduced litigation costs make it easier for consumers to enforce the tort duty. As previously discussed, the tort duty assumes that consumers underestimate product risk

and the associated cost of product accidents. Consequently, strict liability also "discourages the consumption of defective products by causing the purchase price of products to reflect, more than would a rule of negligence, the cost of defects." *Id.* Our prior analysis of consumer expectations therefore accounts for these five rationales for strict liability in the *Restatement (Third)*.

18. The *Restatement (Third)* tries to distinguish design and warning cases: "The implications of deliberately drawing lines with respect to product design safety are different. A reasonably designed product still carries with it elements of risk that must be protected against by the user or consumer since some risks cannot be designed out of the product at reasonable cost." *Id.* The distinction is unpersuasive. The risk of manufacturing defects cannot be eliminated at reasonable cost, since perfect

The remaining rationale for strict liability in the *Restatement (Third)* is that "consumers who benefit from products without suffering harm should share [through increased prices] the burden of unavoidable injury costs that result from manufacturing defects." Presumably, the unavoidable nature of these injury costs somehow makes it appropriate to share them among consumers. But if consumers should share unavoidable injury costs for manufacturing defects, then consumers also should share the unavoidable injury costs created by nondefective product design. The requirement of defect forecloses any sharing of these accident costs among consumers, rendering invalid this remaining rationale for strict liability.

The other rationales for the rule of strict liability in the *Restatement (Third)* can all be derived from the concept of consumer expectations. This concept also justifies the risk-utility test for design and warning defects.[19] Contrary to what the *Restatement (Third)* has claimed, the liability rules in the *Restatement (Second)* and the *Restatement (Third)* do not depend upon "a different concept of responsibility."

This conclusion should not be surprising. The *Restatement (Second)* rule of strict products liability is the source of modern products liability law. The rule has evolved over time as courts have applied it to different sets of circumstances, resulting in a larger number of distinct doctrines addressed by the *Restatement (Third)*. As the common origin of the varied doctrines, the *Restatement (Second)* rule of strict products liability ought to be substantively compatible with the case law that has been restated by the *Restatement (Third)*.

By viewing the two *Restatements* in this way, we can more clearly identify the fault lines that have emerged in the debate over the *Restatement (Third)*. Proponents of the *Restatement (Second)* defensibly emphasize the importance of consumer expectations. To ignore consumer expectations is to ignore the purpose of this body of law. Others understandably emphasize the importance of well-defined liability rules. As the *Denny* case illustrates, a liability rule defined in terms of actual consumer expectations is bound to produce confusion in design and warning cases. The proponents of

quality control ordinarily is not feasible. The inherent residual risk posed by quality control and product design also cannot be distinguished on the ground that the design risks "must be protected against by the consumer or user." One can exercise extreme care while driving and still get into a crash. An airbag, not the consumer's driving skills, is the only way to protect the consumer from these residual risks, just as the manufacturer's quality-control measures can provide the only protection from construction or manufacturing defects.

19. *See* Chapter 2, section II.A.

the *Restatement (Third)* have ample reasons for criticizing consumer expectations. The debate appears to be at an impasse.

To move forward, we need to distinguish *actual* consumer expectations from *reasonable* consumer expectations. In evaluating how consumers actually behave, we found that consumer safety decisions are plagued by informational problems, information costs, and heuristics or rules-of-thumb.[20] In these circumstances, the choice of product safety can defensibly be made by some other decision maker. Tort law gives the decision to the jury, based upon application of the relevant liability rules to the facts at hand. What sort of decision should the jury make for consumers? If the jury tried to replicate the decision making of actual consumers, tort law would merely reproduce the safety problem created by uninformed consumer choice. To address the safety problem, the jury must instead make the safety decisions that the consumer *should* make. The jury needs to determine the amount of product safety that the ordinary consumer would reasonably expect. The tort inquiry must invoke the concept of reasonableness, making it necessary to distinguish the frustration of actual consumer expectations—the rationale for the tort duty—from reasonable consumer expectations— the method for determining the amount of safety required by the tort duty.

The concept of reasonable consumer expectations, in turn, unites the liability rules the *Restatement (Second)* and the *Restatement (Third)*. The concept is normative, one that depends upon the reason or rationale for tort liability. The tort duty protects consumers only because they are unable to make informed product choices, and so the tort duty can require the amount of product safety that would be chosen by consumers if they were adequately informed. By applying a liability rule of this type, the jury tries to make the safety choices that would be made by the ordinary consumer who had good information about the relevant factors. The proper application of this liability rule substitutes informed consumer decision making by the jury for the uninformed decisions actually made by consumers. A well-informed consumer chooses the amount of product safety that best promotes her interests or well-being. The ordinary consumer therefore reasonably expects the amount of product safety that maximizes consumer welfare. So understood, the concept of reasonable expectations yields the risk-utility test for design and warning defects, providing the link between the concept of consumer expectations in the *Restatement (Second)* and the risk-utility test in the *Restatement (Third)*.

---

20. *See* Chapter 2, section II.B.

Since the distinction between actual consumer expectations and reasonable consumer expectations unites the liability rules in the *Restatement (Second)* and *Restatement (Third)*, it follows that this distinction should also help to clarify the associated doctrinal disputes among the courts. Instead of being competing conceptions of responsibility, consumer expectations and the risk-utility test turn out to be complementary. Each is necessary for a complete conception of products liability.

*

PART TWO

DOCTRINAL ANALYSIS

We have now identified a number of concepts that are central to the understanding of products liability.

- Strict products liability can be justified by the implied warranty, which yields the consumer expectations test for liability.

- Strict products liability can be justified by negligence principles, which yield the rule of strict liability for construction or manufacturing defects and the risk-utility test for design and warning defects.

- Doctrinal analysis is not sufficient for developing an adequate conception of consumer expectations. The case law supports different forms of expectations having differing implications for the appropriate liability rule, which in turn has created conflicting interpretations of the relation between consumer expectations and the risk-utility test.

- This controversy must be resolved by reference to fundamental tort principles, which identify the need to protect adequately the consumer interest in physical security as the rationale for products liability (leaving aside the issue of bystander injuries for later discussion).

- The tort duty can be justified when the actual safety expectations of the ordinary consumer are frustrated. Consumers facing high information costs typically are unable to make well-informed safety decisions, even with respect to risks of which they are aware, resulting in disappointed safety expectations requiring protection by tort law.

- A seller fulfills its tort obligations by providing products that satisfy the reasonable expectations of the ordinary consumer. As revealed by the product choices of well-informed consumers, products passing the risk-utility test maximize consumer welfare. The ordinary consumer could not reasonably expect more from a product seller. Products passing the risk-utility test therefore satisfy reasonable consumer expectations.

- Consumer expectations do not justify the insurance rationale for tort liability, implying that tort liability can be justified only on grounds of risk reduction or deterrence. Such liability

69

utilizes tort damages only as a means of giving product sellers an incentive to supply nondefective products.

• The implied warranty and negligence principles yield a unified conception of products liability. Due to that conceptual unity, the rule of strict products liability in the *Restatement (Second)* should be consistent with the liability rules in the *Restatement (Third)*, including the risk-utility test.

Having developed these concepts, we can now use them to analyze the important doctrines of products liability. As illustrated by the ongoing debate over the risk-utility test and consumer expectations, our understanding of the issues can be greatly improved by the relevant concepts.

Doctrinal analysis also provides further opportunity to understand the important concepts of products liability. The same concepts find repeated application in varied doctrinal issues, enabling one to better understand the concept and its implications. Indeed, the repeated application of the same concepts across doctrinal issues helps to establish them as the principles of products liability.

Chapter 5

CONSTRUCTION OR MANUFACTURING DEFECTS

By now, the concept of a construction or manufacturing defect should be familiar. Contaminated food, exploding soda bottles, and similar product malfunctions comprise this category of defect. Something can go awry in the construction or manufacturing process, generating a product that does not conform to the manufacturer's design specifications. Too much carbonated gas can be injected into a soda bottle, causing it to explode and physically injure the consumer.

Construction defects are governed by a rule of strict liability in the vast majority of states. To recover, the plaintiff must prove that the product was in a defective condition when sold by the defendant, and that the defect proximately caused a compensable injury for which the plaintiff seeks recovery.[1] The plaintiff also can pursue a negligence claim or a warranty claim under the Uniform Commercial Code.[2] Indeed, plaintiffs frequently make all three claims in the complaint, although a "separate and more difficult question arises as to whether a case should be submitted to a jury on multiple theories of recovery."[3]

---

1. Restatement (Third) § 1.

2. Even if the plaintiff could recover under strict products liability, a negligence claim makes relevant evidence regarding the manufacturer's conduct, which may then influence the jury's decision regarding other contested issues like the amount of nonmonetary damages. *Cf.* Richard L. Cupp, Jr. & Danielle Polage, *The Rhetoric of Strict Products Liability Versus Negligence: An Empirical Analysis*, 77 N.Y.U. L. Rev. 874 (2002) (summarizing results of an empirical study finding that plaintiffs have a higher likelihood of success and are likely to have larger verdicts when the claim is based on negligence rather than strict liability). *See also* 1 Madden & Owen on Products Liability § 4.1 (describing substantial overlap between strict products liability and warranty claims while also identifying important differences).

3. Restatement (Third) § 2 cmt. n (taking position that the plaintiff should not be able to present two "factually identical" defect claims to the jury due to the possibility of juror confusion and inconsistent verdicts). The problem of juror confusion and inconsistent verdicts is most acute for design and warning defects. The warranty claim is based on consumer expectations, and in most jurisdictions the tort claim is based on the risk-utility test. If jurors receive separate instructions on these two claims, they could understandably conclude that consumer expectations and the risk-utility test are substantively different liability standards. *Compare* Chapter 4 (discussing the problems that arise when consumer expectations is treated as a liability standard different from the risk-utility test). This problem would not arise if only one of the substantively equivalent liability theories were submitted to the jury

Having already considered negligence liability and the implied warranty, we can now address some of the issues raised by the rule of strict liability.[4]

I. Proof of Defect

A construction or manufacturing defect occurs "when the product departs from its intended design even though all possible care was exercised in the preparation and marketing of the product."[5] These defects can take various forms. Materials or component parts of the product can be flawed or contaminated; the product can be improperly assembled or constructed; or the product can be improperly packaged. These defects can also occur after the product has been constructed or manufactured. Delivery of the product can create the defect, as when soda bottles are mishandled during delivery and incur hairline fractures that unduly weaken the bottle, causing it to explode when lifted by the consumer.

To prove that the product departed from its blueprint or design specifications, usually the plaintiff only needs to compare the product to the design. That comparison may require expert testimony.[6]

For this purpose, the relevant blueprint or design specifications must be of a certain type. A manufacturer could claim that the design of a soda bottle includes its method of production, so that a bottle does not depart from its design as long as its characteristics are within the expected parameters of the production process. Since the manufacturer expects that the production process will yield a certain number of bottles with manufacturing defects, it could argue that an exploding soda bottle was contemplated by the design of the production process and is not defective in this respect. In order for the soda bottle to be defective for departing from its intended design, the design must pertain to the product itself, and not the process of production. Insofar as the manufacturing process produces products of differing quality or characteristics, a product is defective for departing from the quality or characteristics that the manufacturer tried or intended to achieve in making the product. The manufacturer did not have the objective of producing soda bottles that explode, and so these bottles are defective for departing from this particular aspect of the product design.

---

4. *See* Chapter 1, section I (warranty) and section II (negligence).

5. Restatement (Third) § 2(a) (defining "manufacturing defects").

6. *E.g.*, Pouncey v. Ford Motor Co., 464 F.2d 957 (5th Cir. 1972) (involving both parties proffering expert testimony on issue of whether the plaintiff's car had a fan blade with an excessive number of metallic impurities in the steel which weakened the metal).

In some cases, the plaintiff may not be able to identify the specific defect. The product can be destroyed in the accident, making it impossible to determine whether the product had a manufacturing defect. Lacking direct evidence of the defect, the plaintiff may still be able to prove that the product was defective by relying on the *malfunction doctrine*:

> Under the malfunction doctrine ... a product defect may be inferred by circumstantial evidence that (1) the product malfunctioned, (2) the malfunction occurred during proper use, and (3) the product had not been altered or misused in a manner that probably caused the malfunction.[7]

As a doctrine of circumstantial evidence, the malfunction doctrine is analogous to the evidentiary doctrine of *res ipsa loquitur* in negligence cases. A "self-defeating malfunction of [the] most basic sort .... 'speaks for itself' on the issue of defectiveness."[8]

To rely upon the malfunction doctrine, the plaintiff must prove, by a preponderance of the evidence, that the accident was caused by a product malfunction and not some other cause, such as the plaintiff's own conduct or ordinary deterioration of the product. The plaintiff does not have to provide any other evidence of defect, nor must the plaintiff identify a specific defect. The self-defeating malfunction provides a sufficient basis for making the seller liable. As one court explains:

> [T]here are those kinds of conditions which, whether caused by design or manufacture, can never be said to involve a reasonable risk. For example, the steering mechanism of a new automobile should not cause the car to swerve off the road; the drive shaft of a new automobile should not separate from the vehicle when it is driven in a normal manner; the brakes of a new automobile should not suddenly fail; and the accelerator of a new automobile should not stick without warning, causing the vehicle suddenly to accelerate. Conditions like these, even if resulting from the design of the products, are defective and unreasonably dangerous without the necessity of weighing and balancing the various factors involved.[9]

The malfunction doctrine does not reduce the plaintiff's evidentiary burden. "[T]he law reports brim with decisions that recite

7. David G. Owen, *Manufacturing Defects*, 53 S.C. L. Rev. 851, 873 (2002). *See also* Restatement (Third) § 3 (describing elements plaintiffs must establish to create an inference of product defect by circumstantial evidence).

8. James A. Henderson, Jr. & Aaron D. Twerski, *Achieving Consensus on Defective Product Design*, 83 Cornell L. Rev. 867, 874 (1998).

9. Phipps v. General Motors Corp., 363 A.2d 955, 959 (Md. 1976) (citations omitted).

the propriety of the doctrine as a general proposition but hold it inapplicable to the facts. The opinions in such cases frequently note that ... the law will not allow plaintiffs or juries to rely on guess, conjecture, or speculation."[10]

This aspect of the malfunction doctrine has important implications. The rule of strict liability for manufacturing defects can be justified on the ground that negligence liability is largely ineffective because of its onerous evidentiary requirements for plaintiffs.[11] As the malfunction doctrine shows, evidentiary difficulties are not a sufficient reason for altering the plaintiff's burden of proving that the product was defective. For cases in which the accident destroys the product, the malfunction doctrine can provide the only means of recovery for the plaintiff. Without any product to examine, the plaintiff faces obvious difficulties in proving that the product was defectively constructed or manufactured. The malfunction doctrine permits proof by circumstantial evidence, but it does not reduce the plaintiff's burden of proving that the accident was caused by a self-defeating malfunction. The malfunction doctrine accordingly requires the plaintiff to prove defect (the malfunction) even when the circumstances make it exceedingly difficult or impossible to do so. As applied to these cases, the malfunction doctrine shows that *the rationale for reducing the plaintiff's evidentiary burden applies only when the evidence otherwise sufficiently shows that the product was defective.*

This limitation of the evidentiary rationale for strict liability can be defended. If a liability rule does not require sufficient proof that the product was defective, there is an increased likelihood that the sellers of nondefective products will incur liability. Such liability presumably goes beyond the amount required to give product sellers an adequate incentive to supply nondefective products, turning them into "insurers" of their products. The insurance rationale for tort liability cannot be justified by reasonable consumer expectations.[12] The mere existence of evidentiary difficulties, like those created by accidents in which the product is destroyed, does not justify tort liability.

II. "Unavoidably Unsafe" Products

Pursuant to comment *k* of the *Restatement (Second)*, strict liability does not apply to "unavoidably unsafe products":

10. Owen, *supra* note 7, at 878 (citations omitted).

11. *See* Chapter 1, section II.

12. *See* Chapter 3, section III.

There are some products which, in the present state of human knowledge, are quite incapable of being made safe for their intended and ordinary use. These are especially common in the field of drugs. An outstanding example is the vaccine for the Pasteur treatment of rabies, which not uncommonly leads to very serious and damaging consequences when it is injected. Since the disease itself invariably leads to a dreadful death, both the marketing and the use of the vaccine are fully justified, notwithstanding the unavoidable high degree of risk which they involve. Such a product, properly prepared, and accompanied by proper direction and warning, is not defective, nor is it *unreasonably* dangerous. The same is true in particular of many other drugs, vaccines, and the like, many of which for this very reason cannot legally be sold except to physicians, or under the prescription of a physician. It is also true of many new or experimental drugs as to which, because of lack of time and opportunity for sufficient medical experience, there can be no assurance of safety, or perhaps even of purity of ingredients, but such experience as there is justifies the marketing and use of the drug notwithstanding a medically recognizable risk. The seller of such products, again with the qualification that they are properly prepared and marketed, and proper warning is given, where the situation calls for it, is not to be held to strict liability for unfortunate consequences attending their use, merely because he has undertaken to supply the public with an apparently useful and desirable product, attended with a known but apparently reasonable risk.[13]

To understand comment *k*, we can consider the "outstanding example" of an "unavoidably unsafe" product—the Pasteur rabies vaccine. Even when the manufacturer has "properly prepared" the vaccine, it can be contaminated with brain tissue, creating dangerous side-effects for the user.[14] Consequently, the rabies vaccine can have "no assurance ... of purity of ingredients," because these "products ... in the present state of human knowledge, are quite incapable of being made safe for their intended and ordinary use." Impurities, like those in contaminated food, are a common form of construction or manufacturing defect subject to strict liability, but the seller of "properly prepared" rabies vaccine accompanied by a "proper warning" is not subject to liability for injuries caused by contaminated vaccine. The vaccine treats a disease that "invariably leads to a dreadful death," so the seller should not incur liability

---

13. Restatement (Second) § 402A cmt. k.

14. Rogers v. Miles Lab., 802 P.2d 1346, 1350–51 (Wash. 1991).

for supplying "the public with an apparently useful and desirable product, attended with a known but apparently reasonable risk."

The limitation of tort liability to improper preparation (unreasonable manufacturing processes) or inadequate (and unreasonable) warnings seems sensible enough when applied to the Pasteur rabies vaccine. The express rationale for doing so, however, would seem to apply to numerous other products. The "present state of human knowledge" does not make it possible to have perfect quality-control measures in the construction of automobiles. These products are "useful and desirable" while being "attended with a known and apparently reasonable risk." Automobiles would appear to satisfy all of the express requirements for an "unavoidably unsafe" product, but the limitation of strict liability no longer seems so sensible.

The courts have not exempted automobile sellers from strict liability. "While comment *k* could be read to apply to other products, it does not really give us any examples or suggest other areas where the policy balancing is precisely the same. For this reason, the courts and most commentators have assumed that comment *k* relates to pharmaceuticals . . . ."[15] The practical effect of this interpretation has been enormous. A "great majority" of courts have relied upon comment *k* to exempt from strict liability the manufacturers of pharmaceutical products.[16]

This interpretation of comment *k* is problematic. Comment *k* uses pharmaceutical products to illustrate the relevant characteristics of an "unavoidably unsafe" product; it does not define an "unavoidably unsafe" product as a pharmaceutical product. Perhaps the relevant characteristics of an "unavoidably unsafe" product effectively limit comment *k* to pharmaceutical products. That conclusion, though, should be based upon analysis rather than being assumed. To interpret comment *k*, we need to identify the reasons why some products like the rabies vaccine ought to be exempt from strict liability.

A particularly instructive example involves blood and blood products. "A nation's blood supply is a unique, life-giving resource and an expression of its sense of community. However, the characteristic that makes donated blood an expression of the highest motives also makes it a threat to health."[17] Donated blood, whether

---

15. Victor E. Schwartz, *Unavoidably Unsafe Products: Clarifying the Meaning and Policy Behind Comment k*, 42 Wash. & Lee L. Rev. 1139, 1141 (1985).

16. 2 Madden & Owen on Products Liability § 22:3, at 558.

17. Institute of Medicine, HIV and the Blood Supply: An Analysis of Crisis Decision-Making 1 (1995).

used in transfusions or blood products, has been responsible for the transmission of diseases such as AIDS, hepatitis and perhaps the variant Creutzfeldt–Jacob (or mad cow) disease, causing extensive injuries among hemophiliacs and others who have received contaminated blood.[18] The specifications or "design" for blood or blood products does not include contaminants capable of causing blood-borne diseases, and blood suppliers have adopted various measures to enhance the purity or safety of the blood supply. Contaminated blood departs from the product specifications, much like contaminated food departs from its specifications and is defective for that reason. Without the exemption afforded by comment *k*, the sellers of contaminated blood would face strict liability under the *Restatement (Second)*.

Most courts have exempted blood suppliers from strict liability, with many relying upon comment *k*. The exemption from strict liability is legislatively enshrined in "blood shield" statutes. Virtually all states now have statutes protecting hospitals and blood banks from strict liability for the sale of contaminated blood. The widespread support for some type of rule exempting blood suppliers from strict liability indicates that blood is a prototypical product that should not be subjected to strict liability.

In justifying the exemption, courts and legislatures have often expressed concern about the way in which strict liability could have a potentially disruptive effect on the supply of blood. As the Connecticut Supreme Court concluded, the blood shield statutes "reflect a legislative judgment that to require providers to serve as insurers of the safety of these materials might impose such an overwhelming burden as to discourage the gathering and distribution of blood."[19]

As compared to most products, the incidence of construction or manufacturing defects in blood products can be substantially higher. In large part, the increased risk stems from new blood-borne diseases that cannot be detected at the time of sale. HIV entered the blood supply in the 1970s. The test for detecting HIV in blood was not available until 1985. At that time, "the rate of infection among donors in San Francisco was found to be 1 in 2,632."[20] By

---

18. An excellent description of the factual context and litigation history regarding HIV-contaminated blood is provided by Eric A. Feldman, *Blood Justice: Courts, Conflict, and Compensation in Japan, France, and the United States*, 34 Law & Soc'y Rev. 651 (2000). Unless otherwise noted, this article provides support for the factual descriptions in the ensuing discussion.

19. Zichichi v. Middlesex Memorial Hospital, 528 A.2d 805, 810 (Conn. 1987).

20. Michael J. Miller, *Note, Strict Liability, Negligence and the Standard of Care for Transfusion–Transmitted Dis-*

the late 1980s, almost half of America's 20,000 hemophiliacs were HIV-positive and there were about 29,000 other individuals who were HIV-positive because of blood transfusions. The rate and number of injuries caused by contaminated blood is far greater than the rate and number of injuries caused by construction defects in most product lines. Moreover, the risk posed by contaminated blood cannot necessarily be reduced to more ordinary levels once tests become available for detecting contaminants. Almost 10 years after the development of a test for detecting the presence of HIV in blood, the "chance of being infected by HIV through blood products [was about] 1 in 68,000 units transfused," causing an estimated "90 cases of transfusion transmitted AIDS a year."[21]

Due to the high number of injuries caused by contaminated blood, strict liability would have a potentially devastating effect on the financial viability of the blood-products industry. In a class-action lawsuit filed by hemophiliacs infected with HIV, Judge Richard Posner concluded that defendant manufacturers might easily have been "facing $25 billion in potential liability (conceivably more)." Such liability would "hurl the industry into bankruptcy," and with it "a major segment of the international pharmaceutical industry."[22]

The bankruptcy of blood suppliers and other pharmaceutical manufacturers would create social problems qualitatively different than those created by the bankruptcy of other product manufacturers, like 'the suppliers of automobiles and soda. Blood and other pharmaceutical products are necessary for public health and safety. Blood products save lives. By significantly increasing the risk of bankruptcy for the manufacturers of such products, strict liability can have a pernicious effect, despite the beneficial safety incentive it otherwise gives product sellers with respect to the adoption of quality-control measures.[23]

This same reasoning explains why comment *k* uses the Pasteur rabies vaccine as an "outstanding example" of an "unavoidably unsafe" product. The vaccine "not uncommonly leads to very serious and damaging consequences when it is injected." The vaccine, in other words, poses an abnormally high risk of construction or manufacturing defect even when the seller uses reasonable quality-control measures. However, "[s]ince the disease itself invar-

ease, 36 Ariz. L. Rev. 473, 480 (1994) (citation omitted).

21. *Id.* at 479–80 (citations omitted).

22. In the Matter of Rhone–Poulenc Rorer Inc., 51 F.3d 1293 (7th Cir. 1995).

23. For a description of the safety benefits that can be attained by strict liability and not negligence liability, see Chapter 1, section II.

iably leads to a dreadful death, both the marketing and use of the vaccine are fully justified, notwithstanding the unavoidable high degree of risk which they involve." The justification is one of public health and safety. The vaccine saves lives, just like blood products. By potentially disrupting the supply of the vaccine, strict liability can harm public health.

A higher risk of injury, coupled with a social concern for bankruptcy rooted in the requirements of public health and safety, differentiates blood and other pharmaceutical products from the vast majority of other products. These characteristics justify the exemption of a product from strict liability under comment *k* of the *Restatement (Second)*, much like a highly risky activity with significant social value is exempted from the *Restatement (Second)* rule of strict liability for abnormally dangerous activities.[24]

By contrast, the *Restatement (Third)* has no similar exemption: the seller of any prescription drug or medical device containing a manufacturing defect is subject to strict liability.[25] In support of its rule, the *Restatement (Third)* relies upon a confused interpretation of comment *k* based exclusively on cases decided prior to the adoption of the *Restatement (Second)*, most of which are inapposite to the issue of whether pharmaceutical products should be exempted from strict liability.[26] With respect to blood products, the *Restate-*

---

24. Restatement (Second) § 520(f).

25. Restatement (Third) §§ 6(b)(1), 6(e)(1).

26. In support of its rule that prescription drug manufacturers are strictly liable for manufacturing defects, the *Restatement (Third)* cites four cases. See Restatement (Third) § 6 cmt. c Rptrs' Note. One case involves an action for fraud and negligence based upon an ordinary manufacturing defect distinguishable from the extraordinary type of defects involved in the contaminated blood cases: Hruska v. Parke, Davis & Co., 6 F.2d 536 (8th Cir. 1925) (holding that manufacturer of a medicinal preparation can be liable for using mineral oil rather than vegetable or animal oil). Two cases involve negligence liability: Abbott Labs. v. Lapp, 78 F.2d 170 (7th Cir. 1935); Randall v. Goodrich–Gamble Co., 70 N.W.2d 261 (Minn. 1955). The remaining case exempts the defendant from liability for the sale of blood contaminated by hepatitis virus that could not have been detected by the exercise of reasonable care, a holding consistent with comment *k* although based on the statutory meaning of "filthy" under the Tennessee Food, Drug and Cosmetic Act: Merck & Co. v. Kidd, 242 F.2d 592 (6th Cir.), *cert. denied*, 355 U.S. 814 (1957). The *Restatement (Third)* then assumes that comment *k* does not apply to manufacturing defects because products with such defects are not "properly prepared." As discussed in the text, this interpretation is inconsistent with the express language of comment *k* and its reliance on the Pasteur rabies vaccine as an "outstanding example" of an "unavoidably unsafe" product. The interpretation is also inconsistent with another provision in the *Restatement (Third)* acknowledging that the contaminated-blood cases involve manufacturing defects that would be subject to strict liability absent a "special rule" exempting the seller from strict liability. *See Restatement (Third)* § 19 cmt. c. Such a special rule is supplied by comment *k* as many courts have held. Hence the treatment of comment *k* in the *Restatement (Third)* is confusing at best.

ment (Third) maintains that the sale of blood is a *service* not subject to strict *products* liability.[27] Perhaps blood products should be exempted from strict liability, but not because blood is a service. "If blood is considered a service, drugs would appear to be too ...."[28] A blood bank can exist for the sole purpose of selling blood for a profit, just like a manufacturer can have the sole purpose of selling drugs for a profit. And like drugs, blood products can be self-administered by patients, as illustrated by the clotting factor used by hemophiliacs. The drug manufacturers have not been exempted from strict liability on the ground that they are selling a service rather than a product, so the product/service distinction does not persuasively explain why blood suppliers should be exempted from strict liability. Overall, the *Restatement (Third)* has taken a puzzling approach to blood products and the more general problem of identifying the reasons why a product should be exempted from the rule of strict products liability.

Nevertheless, the *Restatement (Third)* rule is not necessarily worse than a rule exempting all pharmaceutical products from strict liability, the rule that has been adopted by most jurisdictions. A drug does not have a manufacturing defect merely because it poses an unavoidable risk of causing an injurious side-effect. To be subject to strict liability under the *Restatement (Third)*, the drug must be defective for departing from its intended design. Applying strict liability to these manufacturing defects would not always have a negative effect on public health and safety, since some pharmaceutical products (like cosmetic drugs) are not essential to health. Insofar as a blanket rule is required, the general rule of strict liability in the *Restatement (Third)* may be more desirable than a rule exempting all pharmaceutical products from strict liability. After all, limited exceptions to the general rule of strict liability in the *Restatement (Third)* can be adopted by the legislature, as illustrated by the blood shield statutes.

The approach adopted by the *Restatement (Third)* is not the only option, however. Rather than applying comment *k* to all pharmaceutical products and no other product, courts could conceptualize comment *k* in a more nuanced manner. The general rule would continue to be one of strict liability, with comment *k* providing an exception only when strict liability would pose a significant threat to public health and safety.

To evaluate this approach, consider the cases involving the transmission of electricity. Most courts have concluded that elec-

27. Restatement (Third) § 19 cmt. c.   **28.** Miller, *supra* note 20, at 484–85.

tricity is a product subject to the rule of strict products liability, but a "quite substantial minority of courts ... refuse to apply strict liability to electrical injuries, reasoning that the provision of electricity is a service rather than the sale of a product."[29] Like transactions involving blood, a number of courts have relied upon the product/service distinction to immunize the sellers of electricity from strict liability. The doctrinal distinction masks the real issue posed by these cases, however, for reasons that can be identified by an analysis based on comment k.

All courts presumably agree that electricity is socially valuable, and that a disruption in the supply of electricity would pose a threat to public health and safety. For purposes of comment k, the question then becomes one of the financial threat posed by strict liability. The cases of strict liability involve surges in electricity that have passed through the customer's meter—the surge departs from the intended specifications of the delivered product, rendering it defective. Do these cases occur with enough frequency or result in sufficiently severe consequences to threaten the financial viability of electric utilities? Different answers to this question help to explain the divergence in the case law. In the first case that imposed strict liability on electric utilities, the Wisconsin Supreme Court concluded that "the seller can more easily absorb or spread or insure against any financial losses which result" than the consumer.[30] Financial disruption of electric utilities was not a concern for this court and the others that have adopted the majority rule. By contrast, the courts that have adopted the minority rule and immunized electric utilities from strict liability often worry about the financial impact of strict liability upon electric utilities, reasoning that electric utilities are subject to rate regulation and not readily able to absorb liability losses.[31] The difference in the case law reflects a disagreement among the courts regarding the financial impact of strict liability upon the provision of electricity, a disagreement having nothing to do with the issue of whether electricity is a product or service.

Rather than rely upon the product/service distinction, the courts can instead rely upon comment k to determine whether electric utilities should be subject to strict liability. The comment k inquiry would avoid the unfortunate precedential effects that might be created by reliance on the product/service distinction. The courts that have deemed electricity to be a service may be forced to

29. 2 Madden & Owen on Products Liability § 20:7, at 469.

30. Ransome v. Wisconsin Elec. Power Co., 275 N.W.2d 641, 650 (Wis. 1979).

31. E.g., Bowen v. Niagara Mohawk Power Corp., 590 N.Y.S.2d 628, 632 (App. Div. 4th Dept. 1992).

conclude that computer software is also a service, even if the software in a product (like a traffic light or automobile) malfunctions and causes physical harm.[32] By foregoing the product/service distinction, courts could instead focus on the appropriate reasons for limiting strict liability under comment *k*.

Once a court determines that a product is "unavoidably unsafe," it must then decide upon the scope of liability. Comment *k* only applies if the product is accompanied by "proper direction and warning," and so the manufacturer is subject to liability for a defective warning. Whether comment *k* exempts the manufacturer from liability for defective design is a more difficult question to be discussed later.[33] The remaining issue is whether comment *k* immunizes the manufacturer from liability for all injuries caused by construction or manufacturing defects. In particular, can the plaintiff establish negligence liability by proving that the manufacturer adopted unreasonable quality-control measures that were the source of the construction or manufacturing defects?

The express language of comment *k* allows for these negligence claims. An "unavoidably unsafe" product must be "properly prepared" and is not "*unreasonably* dangerous." By alleging that the manufacturer failed to adopt reasonable quality-control measures, the plaintiff is claiming that the product was not "properly prepared," making it "unreasonably dangerous." The plaintiff typically will have a hard time proving negligence. Nevertheless, comment *k* prevents the plaintiff from establishing liability on the basis of defect alone—the result achieved by the rule of strict products liability. The plaintiff must prove that if the manufacturer had exercised reasonable care, the construction or manufacturing defect would have been avoided. This proof shows that the product was not "unavoidably unsafe" and is properly subject to liability in order to promote the adoption of reasonable manufacturing or quality-control measures.

32. In these circumstances, the program would be deemed defective under the malfunction doctrine. *See supra* section I. As a component supplier, the software designer would be subject to products liability if the software were deemed to be a product rather than a service. In a jurisdiction that has adopted the rule making electricity a service, the software designer could persuasively argue that it, too, provided a service not subject to strict products liability. A computer program, after all, is merely a series of instructions encoded in electronic impulses. Both electricity and software can be stored in a tangible medium (batteries; compact discs) or can be transferred to the consumer over an intangible medium (electric transmission lines; the Internet). Electricity and software potentially differ only with respect to the social consequences that would be produced by the application of products liability to these transactions. That difference has nothing to do with the product/service distinction, but instead directly implicates the policy considerations embodied in comment *k*.

33. *See* Chapter 6, section V.

III. Food Products

It can be surprisingly difficult to determine whether a food product is defective. A food product is often made from a recipe—the "design" of the product—but recipes routinely rely upon basic components of food that are generically defined. The recipe for a chicken enchilada requires chicken. Is the enchilada defective for containing a chicken bone that was swallowed by a customer in a restaurant, causing injury? The question cannot be simply answered by reference to a recipe that only requires chicken in the enchilada. What determines whether the chicken enchilada is defective for containing the bone?

The answer given by the *Restatement (Third)* ultimately reveals a great deal about the definition of defect:

> Faced with this indeterminacy, some courts have attempted to rely on a distinction between "foreign" and "natural" characteristics of food products to determine liability. Under that distinction, liability attaches only if the alleged adulteration is foreign rather than natural to the product. Most courts have found this approach inadequate, however. Although a one-inch chicken bone may in some sense be "natural" to a chicken enchilada, depending on the context in which consumption takes place, the bone may still be unexpected by the reasonable consumer, who will not be able to avoid injury, thus rendering the product not reasonably safe. The majority view is that, in this circumstance of uncertainty, the issue of whether a food product containing a dangerous but arguably natural component is [a construction defect] is to be determined by reference to reasonable consumer expectations within the relevant context of consumption.[34]

In effect, reasonable consumer expectations define the specifications for a food product, making a food product defective for departing from the design as defined in these terms.

In this respect, food cases do not comprise a special product category; the issue frequently arises in other product cases. Any product design is likely to be incomplete in important respects, much like a food recipe ordinarily does not fully specify every characteristic or component of the ingredients (like the size of chicken bones). A tire manufacturer can describe the components and proper assembly of the tire, but not specify how long the tire is intended to function. What if the tire fails after 2,000 miles? As one federal district court found, "[c]ommon experience indicates that

---

34. Restatement (Third) § 7 cmt. b.

no owner of a tire expects it to fail with less than 2,000 miles on its treads."[35] The tire had a manufacturing defect, not because the manufacturer's design stated that the tire would perform for more than 2,000 miles, but because the ordinary consumer reasonably expected the tire to perform at least that long. The problem of incomplete product design is not limited to food products; it potentially applies to any product.

Incomplete product designs create a gap filled by reasonable consumer expectations. To serve this function, reasonable consumer expectations must be the *default* or background definition of defect. The default definition is not required whenever there is a more concrete or particularized definition available, such as a departure from express design requirements or a violation of the risk-utility test. These varied definitions of defect flesh out the requirements of the default definition in particular sets of circumstances; they do not provide independent bases of liability substantively different than consumer expectations. For this reason, the *Restatement (Third)* can consistently define defective food products in terms of consumer expectations while also maintaining that consumer expectations do not provide an "independent standard for judging the defectiveness of product designs."[36] As the default definition of defect, consumer expectations appropriately fill the gap of incomplete product designs in food and other cases—a foundational role that does not make consumer expectations independent of the more particularized definitions of defect, such as the risk-utility test, applicable to other cases. The substantive equivalence of these varied definitions of defect has an important implication: *The definition of defect always depends upon reasonable consumer expectations, even if defect is not expressly defined in those terms.* This principle will help to clarify important issues regarding design and warning defects.[37]

---

35. McCann v. Atlas Supply Co., 325 F.Supp. 701, 704 (W.D. Pa. 1971).

36. Restatement (Third) § 2 cmt. g.

37. *But see* Henderson & Twerski, *supra* note 8, at 890 (arguing that the liability standard in food cases does "not apply to products generally [and therefore does not] support the thesis that the general design standard is based on consumer expectations").

Chapter 6

DESIGN DEFECTS

Many of the most important and vexing issues in products liability involve defective product design. In product cases involving damage claims over $100,000, the principal liability claim is one of strict liability for defective design.[1] These claims implicate the entire product line. A finding that the product is defectively designed means that all products with the design are defective. The potential extent of liability vastly exceeds the manufacturer's liability for defects in construction or manufacturing, which usually are aberrational departures from the rest of the product line. The large stakes at issue in design cases create a practical need for well-defined liability rules, which in turn has created a pronounced problem. "From the early days of products liability to the present, courts have said that the definition of design defect is elusive and difficult to discern."[2] The courts have had a hard time deciding whether design defects should be defined in terms of consumer expectations, the risk-utility test, or some combination thereof.

As we found earlier, this disarray in the case law is a predictable result of the ambiguous conception of consumer expectations in the *Restatement (Second)*.[3] To identify more precisely the problems created by this ambiguity, we will analyze how case-by-case litigation can influence a court's conception of consumer expectations. This evolutionary analysis confirms our earlier finding that consumer expectations and the risk-utility test are complementary.[4]

The courts have also struggled over other issues involving product design. By analyzing these issues, we can gain further understanding of how the important concepts of products liability aid doctrinal analysis.

1. *See* Alliance of American Insurers and the American Insurance Association, A Study of Large Product Liability Claims Closed in 1985 (1986) (finding that for claims in excess of $100,000 that were closed in 1985, the principal liability theory was based on strict liability, with 75 percent of those cases relying on defective design as the principal claim).

2. James A. Henderson, Jr. & Aaron D. Twerski, *Achieving Consensus on Defective Product Design*, 83 Cornell L. Rev. 867, 868 n.1 (1998).

3. *See* Chapter 1, section IV, and Chapter 4.

4. *See* Chapter 2.

I. A Stylized History of Design–Defect Jurisprudence: Emerging Consensus or Widespread Disagreement?

To understand the jurisprudence of defective product design, we need to see how it has evolved from the rule of strict products liability in the *Restatement (Second)*, the widely acknowledged textual source of modern products liability law. The evolution of design-defect jurisprudence can be depicted by the doctrinal developments that occur in two hypothetical jurisdictions facing a different series of design cases. Each jurisdiction begins with the text of the *Restatement (Second)*, first applying it to a case that substantially differs from the case first decided by the other jurisdiction. The different starting points yield different conceptions of the appropriate liability rule, creating the appearance of disarray and fundamental disagreement. Over time, as each jurisdiction faces the full range of cases, each adopts a liability rule requiring that defect be proved by reference to the risk-utility test in most cases. The disarray and disagreement in the case law evolves into a shared understanding of the appropriate liability rule.

This evolutionary analysis helps to explain the position reached by the *Restatement (Third)* and subsequently elaborated upon by its Reporters: "although a widely shared belief persists that the general standard for defective product design is unsettled ... thousands upon thousands of design defect decisions ... demonstrate[] that ... [c]onsensus has been achieved."[5]

Consensus has not yet been achieved, however, with respect to the way in which courts apply the risk-utility test, a potentially divisive source of disagreement that has not been adequately recognized. Should the safety of consumers be traded off against monetary cost as per the cost-benefit version of the risk-utility test? Or should safety considerations be given greater weight as a matter of fairness? Like the controversy regarding the relation between consumer expectations and the risk-utility test, the differing interpretations of the risk-utility test can be traced to the different evolutionary paths that have been taken by courts. Whether consensus will ever truly be achieved may depend on whether the courts recognize their common starting point.

A. A Warranty–Based Evolutionary Path

Consider a hypothetical jurisdiction, loosely based on the actual experience in California, that is the first jurisdiction to adopt the

---

5. Henderson & Twerski, *supra* note 2, at 868–69 (sentence structure omitted). The structure of the following discussion was inspired by this article. *Cf. id.* at 894.

Restatement (Second) rule of strict products liability. According to this rule, a seller is strictly liable for physical injuries caused by defective products that are unreasonably dangerous. To satisfy these requirements, the product "must be dangerous to an extent beyond that which would be contemplated by the ordinary consumer who purchases it, with the ordinary knowledge common to the community as to its characteristics."[6] This conception of defect works well for construction or manufacturing defects, which make products malfunction and perform more dangerously than "contemplated by the ordinary consumer." But how well does this conception work for design defects? The answer can depend upon the type of case first posing this issue to the courts.

Case 1. While using a coffeemaker in its normal and intended manner, the plaintiff was injured when the coffeemaker exploded. The explosion was caused by the design.

In this case, the court will have no trouble applying the *Restatement (Second)* rule of strict products liability. The design of the coffeemaker makes it incapable of performing its manifestly intended function, thereby breaching the implied warranty of quality.[7] Just as manufacturing defects frustrate consumer expectations, so does this type of product design.[8] The court can readily conclude that the product design is defective, subjecting the seller to strict liability for the plaintiff's injuries.

Today, this type of case is governed by the malfunction doctrine, which is now recognized as a distinctive liability rule governing a particular form of defect. The malfunction doctrine does not differentiate between manufacturing and design defects, because the defect is defined by the malfunction itself.[9] This attribute of the defect would probably not be noticed by the court, however, since the case is one of first impression. In the seminal case adopting strict products liability, the California Supreme Court held that the liability rule applies to "a defect in design and manufacture of which plaintiff was not aware that made [the product] unsafe for its intended use."[10] At the time, the court "simply was not thinking"

---

6. Restatement (Second) § 402A cmt. i.

7. McCabe v. L.K. Liggett Drug Co., 112 N.E.2d 254 (Mass. 1953) (finding that the implied warranty was breached by a coffeemaker that exploded during ordinary use because of its design).

8. *Cf.* Henderson & Twerski, *supra* note 2, at 890 ("When designs malfunction, violating built-in standards, courts often explain judgments for plaintiffs in terms of the designs having 'disappointed consumer expectations.' ").

9. *See* Chapter 5, section I (discussing malfunction doctrine).

10. Greenman v. Yuba Products, Inc., 377 P.2d 897, 901 (Cal. 1963).

of the potential differences between manufacturing and design defects.[11]

Having decided that strict products liability applies to design defects, the court in our hypothetical case would be troubled by the language in the *Restatement (Second)* limiting strict liability to defective products that are "unreasonably dangerous."[12] This limitation was intended by the drafters of the *Restatement (Second)* to preclude the possibility that the concept of defect would be drained of all meaning, resulting in the manufacturer being strictly liable for all injuries proximately caused by the product.[13] The limitation would be problematic for the court, however. The defect in this case is established by the basic malfunctioning of the coffeemaker, which frustrates consumer expectations and triggers liability. The "unreasonably dangerous" requirement is unnecessary and improperly adds a negligence element into an action of strict products liability, potentially prejudicing the plaintiff. For these reasons, the court could defensibly reject the requirement. Again, the experience in California is illustrative.[14]

At this point, design defects pose no special problems. The design defect for a malfunctioning product like the exploding coffeemaker can be inferred from the manufacturer's intentions (implied by the product's intended function), much like construction or manufacturing defects can be inferred from the manufacturer's intentions (implied by the product's blueprint or design). These defects frustrate the ordinary consumer's reasonable expectation that the product will perform as intended by the manufacturer.

Case 2. The plaintiff was injured by the exposed moving parts of a machine. She then filed suit against the manufacturer, claiming that the machine was defectively designed for not having an inexpensive guard that would protect users from the significant risk created by the moving parts of the machine. In defense, the manufacturer argues that the intended use of the machine does not involve the user coming into contact with its moving parts.[15] The

11. Robert L. Rabin, *Restating the Law: The Dilemmas of Products Liability*, 30 U. Mich. J.L. Reform 197, 203 (1997).

12. Restatement (Second) § 402A.

13. *See* William L. Prosser, *Strict Liability to the Consumer in California*, 18 Hastings L.J. 9, 23 (1966).

14. *See* Cronin v. J.B.E. Olson Corp., 501 P.2d 1153, 1163 (Cal. 1972) (rejecting the "unreasonably dangerous" requirement of § 402A in a case alleging

manufacturing defects and holding that "a distinction between manufacturing and design defects is not tenable").

15. *Cf.* Evans v. General Motors Corp., 359 F.2d 822, 825 (7th Cir. 1966) (applying Indiana law) (concluding that a manufacturer has a duty only to design a car reasonably fit for its intended purpose, and that "[t]he intended purpose of an automobile does not include its participation in collisions with other objects, despite the manufacturer's abili-

manufacturer also argues that the lack of the guard does not cause the product to fail in performing its manifestly intended function, nor can the lack of this safety feature frustrate consumer expectations: the absence of the guard was obvious and therefore expected by the ordinary consumer.

If the court were to conclude that liability depends only upon the manufacturer's intentions of product use and the obviousness of the risk, it would have to conclude that the machine is not defectively designed.[16] The court would be troubled by this outcome, though, for it seems clear that the manufacturer's arguments do not provide good reasons for limiting liability.

Products liability is supposed to give manufacturers an incentive to provide adequately safe products. The appropriate amount of product safety depends on product risk, which in turn depends on how consumers actually use products. Someone using a machine can accidentally come into contact with its moving parts, an unintended but foreseeable outcome. The design of the machine clearly should account for this possibility, just like the design of an automobile should account for unintended but foreseeable car crashes. The court could defensibly conclude that the concept of defect must be defined in terms of foreseeable product use rather than the manufacturer's intentions.

The court must then confront a hard question raised by the manufacturer's defense. The absence of a guard on the machine was obvious, so how can consumer expectations be frustrated by the lack of a guard? The difficulty posed by the problem could lead the court to reject the consumer expectations test, the path taken by many other courts.[17] A court committed to consumer expectations, however, could figure out a solution to the problem.

The court could first consider this issue from a negligence perspective. If a manufacturer can be liable in negligence to a consumer for the physical injuries proximately caused by an open and obvious risk, then such risks should not absolve the manufacturer of strict liability. As a matter of logic, a negligence inquiry can show that strict liability applies to patent dangers.

ty to foresee the possibility that such collisions may occur"), *cert. denied*, 385 U.S. 836 (1966).

16. *E.g.*, Campo v. Scofield, 95 N.E.2d 802, 804 (N.Y. 1950) ("If a manufacturer does everything necessary to make the machine function properly for the purpose for which it is designed, if the machine is without any latent defect, and if its functioning creates no danger or peril that is not known to the user, then the manufacturer has satisfied the law's demands."). For reasons to be discussed shortly, this case was overruled by Micallef v. Miehle Co., 348 N.E.2d 571 (N.Y. 1976).

17. 1 Madden & Owen on Products Liability § 10:1, at 602.

This approach to the problem, once again, can be illustrated with California case law. First, the California Supreme Court held that product sellers can incur negligence liability for open and obvious risks:

> [E]ven if the obviousness of the peril is conceded, the modern approach does not preclude liability solely because a danger is obvious.... "[T]he bottom does not logically drop out of a negligence case against the maker when it is shown that the purchaser knew of the dangerous condition. Thus if the product is a carrot-topping machine with exposed moving parts, or an electric clothes wringer dangerous to the limbs of the operator, and if it would be feasible for the maker of the product to install a guard or a safety release, it should be a question for the jury whether reasonable care demanded such a precaution, though its absence is obvious. Surely reasonable men might find here a *great danger*, even to one who knew the condition; and since it was so *readily avoidable* they might find the maker negligent."[18]

Having found that product sellers can be negligent for designing products with open and obvious, "readily avoidable" risks carrying "great danger," it logically follows that strict products liability can also apply to these risks, a result reached in another California case:

> It would indeed be anomalous to allow a plaintiff to prove that a manufacturer was negligent in marketing an obviously defective product, but to preclude him from establishing the manufacturer's strict liability for the same thing. The result would be to immunize from strict liability manufacturers who callously ignore patent dangers in their products while subjecting to such liability those who innocently market products with latent defects.[19]

The court could find added support in the doctrine of assumption of risk. For this doctrine to limit a manufacturer's liability, the plaintiff "must become aware of the defect and danger and still proceed unreasonably to make use of the product."[20] The plaintiff's awareness of an obvious risk does not mean she has made an informed choice to use a defective product, further showing why the manufacturer can incur liability for patent dangers.[21]

---

18. Pike v. Frank G. Hough Co., 467 P.2d 229, 235 (Cal. 1970) (quoting Fowler V. Harper & Fleming James, Jr., 2 The Law of Torts, § 28.5 at 1542–43 (1956)) (emphasis added).

19. Luque v. McLean, 501 P.2d 1163, 1169 (Cal. 1972) (citation omitted).

20. *Id.* at 1170.

21. *See* Chapter 10, section II (discussing assumption of risk); *see also* Chapter 2, section II.B (explaining why

The court has now resolved all of the difficult problems posed by the case. In effect, the plaintiff claims the machine is defectively designed for not containing an inexpensive guard that can "readily avoid" the "great danger" posed by the machine's exposed moving parts. Assuming the plaintiff's allegations are true, the court can find the product to be defective without a searching inquiry into the precise requirements of consumer expectations regarding product design. The court would have sufficient reasons for concluding that consumer expectations are frustrated by the open and obvious risk posed by the unguarded machine.

Case 3. The plaintiff was using a high-lift loader on uneven ground at a construction site. The loader rolled over and injured the plaintiff while he was using it to lift lumber. In his suit against the manufacturer, the plaintiff claims the loader was defectively designed in several respects: it was not equipped with seat belts or a roll bar, outriggers that might have given it greater lateral stability, an automatic locking device on its leveling mechanism, or a separate park gear.[22]

These allegations pose a problem for the consumer expectations test. Consumers can have expectations regarding seatbelts and a roll bar on loaders, but do they have meaningful expectations regarding complex technical matters like outriggers, automatic locking devices, and a separate park gear? When the ordinary consumer gives little or no consideration to a safety feature, how can consumer expectations determine whether the design is defective for not incorporating that feature?

The easy answer would be to deny liability: consumer expectations can't be frustrated when consumers have no expectations. This resolution of the issue would not be acceptable to courts in this jurisdiction, however. The lack of information makes consumers "powerless" to protect themselves by making safety choices, the reason why this jurisdiction has imposed a tort duty on product sellers.[23] The absence of information is ignorance. Consumers who have no idea of risk do not even contemplate safety measures. Such completely uninformed consumers are the ones most obviously in

the consumer's mere awareness of a risk does not necessarily enable her to make an informed safety decision).

22. Barker v. Lull Engineering Co., 573 P.2d 443 (Cal. 1978).

23. Greenman v. Yuba Products, Inc., 377 P.2d 897, 901 (Cal. 1963) ("The purpose of [strict products liability] is to insure that the costs of injuries resulting from defective products are borne by the manufacturers that put such products on the market rather than by the injured persons who are powerless to protect themselves."). See also Chapter 2, section II.B (explaining why the tort duty depends upon the ordinary consumer being uninformed about the product risk).

need of tort protection—the most "powerless" of all consumers. The absence of expectations does not justify the limitation of liability.

To evaluate all of the plaintiff's design claims, the court must figure out the content of consumer expectations for complex, technical matters. Not surprisingly, the court might look elsewhere to see how other jurisdictions have resolved the problem. "From the very earliest days of modern products liability law, courts and commentators have turned to the risk-utility test to avoid applying the consumer expectations test in cases involving vague expectations concerning complex designs."[24] The risk-utility test is the obvious complement to consumer expectations, providing a method for the court to resolve all of the different types of design defects alleged by the plaintiff:

> [A] trial judge may properly instruct the jury that a product is defective in design (1) if the plaintiff demonstrates that the product failed to perform as safely as an ordinary consumer would expect when used in an intended or reasonably foreseeable manner, or (2) if the plaintiff proves that . . . on balance the benefits of the challenged design outweigh the risk of danger inherent in such design.[25]

Case 4. The plaintiff was injured in an automobile crash and claims the car was defective for reasons involving complicated design considerations. Pursuant to *Case 3*, the trial judge instructed the jury in terms of consumer expectations and the risk-utility test. The jury returned a verdict for the plaintiff without specifying whether the defect involved the frustration of consumer expectations or failure of the risk-utility test. The defendant manufacturer appeals, arguing that the jury instruction regarding consumer expectations was inappropriate. According to the defendant, the alleged design defect was too complicated and beyond the contemplation of the ordinary consumer, so the jury should have been instructed only with respect to the risk-utility test.[26]

The court can decide this appeal by reasoning from prior precedents. As *Case 1* establishes, a jury instruction on consumer expectations is appropriate for product malfunctions like the exploding coffeemaker:

24. 1 Madden & Owen on Products Liability § 8:6, at 487 (citations omitted).

25. *Barker*, 573 P.2d at 457–58. The court also shifted the burden of proof to the defendant on the risk-utility issue,

an aspect of the case that is postponed for discussion until the end of this Chapter.

26. Soule v. General Motors Corp., 882 P.2d 298 (Cal. 1994).

For example, the ordinary consumers of modern automobiles may and do expect that such vehicles will be designed so as not to explode while idling at stoplights, experience sudden steering or brake failure as they leave the dealership, or roll over and catch fire in two-mile-per-hour collisions. If the plaintiff in a product liability action proved that a vehicle's design produced such a result, the jury could find forthwith that the car failed to perform as safely as its ordinary consumers would expect, and was therefore defective.[27]

As *Case 2* establishes, a jury instruction on consumer expectations is also appropriate for open and obvious risks like an unguarded machine posing a great danger that could be readily avoided by an inexpensive guard:

> In particular circumstances, a product's design may perform so unsafely that the defect is apparent to the common reason, experience, and understanding of its ordinary consumers. In such cases, a lay jury is competent to make that determination.[28]

Based on these cases, the court can conclude that the "the consumer expectations test is reserved for cases in which the *everyday experience* of the product's users permits a conclusion that the product's design violated *minimum* safety assumptions, and is thus defective *regardless of expert opinion about the merits of the design.*"[29] At minimum, the ordinary consumer expects that a product will not malfunction during normal use and is designed in a manner that eliminates great dangers at little cost.

> By the same token, the jury may not be left free to find a violation of ordinary consumer expectations whenever it chooses. Unless the facts actually permit an inference that the product's performance did not meet the minimum safety expectations of its ordinary users, the jury must engage in the balancing of risks and benefits [to determine whether the design is defective].[30]

Whether the jury should be instructed on consumer expectations or the risk-utility test accordingly depends upon the nature of the design defect. "[W]here the minimum safety of a product is within the common knowledge of jurors," the jury should be instructed only on consumer expectations. "The manufacturer may not defend a claim that a product's design failed to perform as safely as its ordinary consumers would expect by presenting expert

27. *Id*. at 308 n.3.

28. *Id*. at 310.

29. *Id*. at 308.

30. *Id*. at 309.

evidence of the design's relative risks and benefits." In all other cases, the jury must be instructed on the risk-utility test and can receive expert testimony to that effect.[31] Hence the jury in this case should have been instructed on the risk-utility test, since the allegation of defect involved complicated design considerations that were not within the common knowledge of jurors.

Case 5. The plaintiff was injured in a car crash. When the collision occurred, the car's airbag inflated, forcing the plaintiff's left arm into the windshield and its side pillar, causing the injury for which the plaintiff seeks compensation. The plaintiff based her case exclusively on consumer expectations. In defense, the manufacturer would like to prove that the design passes the risk-utility test.[32] The plaintiff objects, relying on the *Case 4* holding that the "manufacturer may not defend a claim that a product's design failed to perform as safely as its ordinary consumers would expect by presenting expert evidence of the design's relative risks and benefits." In response, the manufacturer relies on the *Case 4* holding that the product must "meet the *minimum* safety expectations of its ordinary consumers." According to the manufacturer, the minimum safety expectations of the ordinary consumer are necessarily satisfied by the more demanding risk-utility test. For this reason, the manufacturer concludes that the risk-utility evidence is highly relevant for evaluating consumer expectations: The risk-utility evidence rebuts the plaintiff's proof that the design frustrates consumer expectations.

The issue is a difficult one. The manufacturer is surely correct that evidence regarding the design's compliance with a more demanding safety standard is logically relevant for rebutting proof that the design fails a minimum safety standard. But if the manufacturer could present risk-utility evidence to the jury, the outcome of the case would depend entirely upon the risk-utility test, even though the plaintiff based her case on consumer expectations. Having received the risk-utility evidence, the jury could conclude that the design is defective only by rejecting the manufacturer's proof that the design passes the risk-utility test.[33]

---

31. *Id*. at 308–09.

32. This kind of issue was raised by Bresnahan v. Chrysler Corp., 38 Cal. Rptr.2d 446 (Ct. App. 2d Dist. 1995), although the content of the manufacturer's arguments in that case are different than those presented here.

33. Notice how this dynamic leads to the outcome in which the manufacturer effectively bears the burden of proof on the risk-utility test, an allocation of proof expressly adopted by the California Supreme Court. *See Barker*, 573 P.2d at 457–58; *see also Soule*, 882 P.2d at 311 n.8 (affirming the *Barker* burden-shifting rule).

Given its commitment to consumer expectations, the court would not be satisfied by a ruling that would effectively make all design cases turn on risk-utility evidence. To avoid this outcome, the court must reject the defendant's claim that consumer expectations establish minimum safety requirements that are less demanding than the risk-utility test.

The court can rule for the plaintiff on this issue by distinguishing between *actual* consumer expectations and *reasonable* consumer expectations. The tort duty is required when the ordinary consumer underestimates or otherwise fails to evaluate product risk, causing her to purchase products with insufficient amounts of safety.[34] The ordinary consumer does not actually expect enough product safety, and so a liability rule based on this form of expectation yields minimum safety requirements. A liability rule formulated in this manner is not problematic for malfunctioning products, since the defect is defined in terms of the malfunction itself and not consumer expectations. In the case now being addressed by the court, the product did not malfunction. Consequently, the defect cannot be defined in terms of actual consumer expectations. The element of duty depends upon the frustration of actual consumer expectations, making it analytically incoherent to define the separate element of defect in these same terms.[35] The two elements can be kept separate if duty is established by the frustration of actual consumer expectations and defect by the frustration of reasonable consumer expectations. Once the court defines defect in these terms, consumer expectations no longer establish safety requirements less demanding than the risk-utility test. The ordinary consumer reasonably expects the product design to pass the risk-utility test, contrary to the defendant's claim that the risk-utility test is a more demanding standard of liability.[36]

Having refined the consumer expectations test in this manner, the court can now rely on *Case 4*. If the design issues are within the common knowledge of the jury, then the case should be governed by reasonable consumer expectations. In such a case, the defendant manufacturer should not be able to introduce expert testimony regarding risk-utility factors as doing so "would invade the jury's function."[37] In all other cases, the jury should be instructed on the risk-utility test and can hear expert testimony regarding the risk-utility factors.

---

34. *See* Chapter 2, section II.B.

35. *See* Chapter 4.

36. *See* Chapter 2, section II.A.

37. *Soule*, 882 P.2d at 308.

Under this approach, consumer expectations and the risk-utility test may be truly complementary. In many design cases, the court can reach the right outcome by relying on the consumer expectations test. Prominent examples include products that fail to perform their manifestly intended function (*Case 1*); products that are obviously defectively designed by posing a "great danger" that can be "readily avoided" (*Case 2*); and products involving design issues that are otherwise within the common knowledge of the jury (*Case 4*). In all other cases, the court relies upon the risk-utility test to evaluate design defects. By taking this approach, the court has not abandoned consumer expectations but has instead "incorporate[d] risk-utility factors into the ordinary consumer expectation analysis."[38] The design-defect jurisprudence continues to be founded upon consumer expectations, even though a large number of cases rely on the risk-utility test to determine defective product design.

B.   A Negligence–Based Evolutionary Path

As the prior discussion suggests, the development of a jurisdiction's jurisprudence can importantly depend upon the order in which different types of issues are decided by the courts—the development of the common law can be *path dependent*.[39] To illustrate more fully this evolutionary aspect of the common law, we need to consider another hypothetical jurisdiction that has adopted the *Restatement (Second)* rule of strict products liability.

Case 1. Suppose the case is identical to *Case 3* in the other hypothetical jurisdiction involving a plaintiff who was injured by a loader that tipped over while being operated on a hill. The plaintiff alleges the design is defective for not having safety precautions ranging from the relatively simple (a seat belt) to the technically complex (lateral outriggers). Unlike *Case 3*, the plaintiff also claims that the loader is defective no matter how designed. According to this allegation, even the safest design cannot eliminate the substantial risk that the loader will tip over while being used on hills and other uneven surfaces, so the loader should not be marketed for this purpose.

Having just adopted the rule of strict products liability, the court would begin by analyzing the text of the *Restatement (Sec-*

---

38. Potter v. Chicago Pneumatic Tool Co., 694 A.2d 1319, 1333 (Conn. 1997).

39. For applications of this evolutionary concept to legal processes, see Oona A. Hathaway, *Path Dependence in the Law: The Course and Pattern of Legal Change in a Common Law System*, 86 Iowa L. Rev. 601 (2001); Mark J. Roe, *Chaos and Evolution in Law and Economics*, 109 Harv. L. Rev. 641 (1996).

ond). The court would not be troubled by the *Restatement (Second)* limitation of strict liability to defective products that are "unreasonably dangerous."[40] Unlike a construction defect, the court cannot evaluate the plaintiff's alleged design defects by reference to the manufacturer's intentions. The manufacturer intended to omit a seat belt, perhaps reasoning that a quick escape might be the safest precaution in the event the loader tips over. The court also cannot rely upon consumer expectations to evaluate all of the alleged design defects, given that consumers have, at best, vague expectations of the complex design issues. Within the text of the *Restatement (Second),* the court would find guidance from the "unreasonably dangerous" requirement. An "unreasonably dangerous" design renders the product defective, subjecting the seller to strict liability according to the express language of the *Restatement (Second).* Hence the court, like the majority of jurisdictions in the U.S., would conclude that the plaintiff must prove that the design is "unreasonably dangerous."[41]

The court must then determine the types of evidence that would be relevant for proving defective design. "Unreasonably dangerous" may connote many things. According to the influential torts scholar John Wade, the "unreasonably dangerous" requirement implicates the following factors:

(1) The usefulness and desirability of the product—its utility to the user and to the public as a whole.

(2) The safety aspects of the product—the likelihood that it will cause injury, and the probable seriousness of the injury.

(3) The availability of a substitute product which would meet the same need and not be as unsafe.

(4) The manufacturer's ability to eliminate the unsafe character of the product without impairing its usefulness or making it too expensive to maintain its utility.

(5) The user's ability to avoid danger by the exercise of care in the use of the product.

(6) The user's anticipated awareness of the dangers inherent in the product and their avoidability, because of general public knowledge of the obvious condition of the product, or of the existence of suitable warnings or instructions.

40. Restatement (Second) § 402A.

41. Shapo, 1 Law of Products Liability ¶ 8.04[1], at 4008 ("The great majority of courts that have defined defect for purposes of strict liability have required the claimant to show that the product was 'unreasonably dangerous.' ").

(7) The feasibility, on the part of the manufacturer, of spreading the loss by· setting the price of the product or carrying liability insurance.[42]

The court, like many others, would find this formulation to be appealing.[43] The Wade factors correspond to the *Restatement (Second)* factors for determining whether a risk is unreasonable for purposes of negligence liability and the *Restatement (Second)* factors for determining whether an activity is abnormally dangerous and subject to strict liability.[44] The Wade factors accordingly seem to be the appropriate for determining whether a design is unreasonably dangerous and subject to the *Restatement (Second)* rule of strict products liability. The Wade factors also address all of the design issues in the case. The plaintiff's defect allegations involve obvious risks (factors 3–6), technical matters (factors 3–5), and the issue of whether the product should ever have been marketed for use on uneven surfaces (factors 1–2). For understandable reasons, the court would conclude that the plaintiff's various allegations of design defect should be evaluated in terms of the Wade factors.

Unlike the other hypothetical jurisdiction, this jurisdiction immediately formulates its design-defect jurisprudence in terms of the risk-utility test. In this jurisdiction, design cases have no apparent dependence upon the concept of consumer expectations, unlike the other hypothetical jurisdiction.

C. Differing Approaches to the Same Destination?

Depending on the sequencing and mix of cases, a jurisdiction may adhere to consumer expectations as supplemented by risk-utility considerations, or reject consumer expectations altogether in favor of the risk-utility test for evaluating product design. Neither path has dominated. Half of the states apply the consumer expectations test in some manner.[45]

The different approaches have created the impression of a fundamental disagreement dividing the courts:

42. John W. Wade, *On the Nature of Strict Tort Liability for Products*, 44 Miss. L.J. 825, 837–38 (1973).

43. *See* 1 Madden & Owen on Products Liability § 8:4, at 459 ("Searching for some guidance in the murky sea of design defectiveness, appellate courts grasped quickly onto the Wade factors for use in ascertaining defects in design.").

44. Wade, *supra* note 42, at 837 n.41 (citing Restatement (Second) §§ 291–93 & 520).

45. John F. Vargo, *The Emperor's New Clothes: The American Law Institute Adorns a "New Cloth" for Section 402A Products Liability Design Defects— A Survey of the States Reveals a Different Weave*, 26 U. Mem. L. Rev. 493, 556 & 951 (1996).

Evolving separately from the law of warranty and the law of negligence, the consumer expectations and risk-utility tests for design defectiveness have developed largely as rival theories of design defect liability. Thus, for most of modern products liability law, most courts have determined design defectiveness exclusively by either one or the other standard and have refused to recognize the validity of the other.[46]

Over time, the apparent divide has considerably narrowed. Courts now agree on the need to evaluate product design by reference to a reasonable alternative design for those cases in which the defect cannot be readily determined by other means, like a product malfunction. Under this approach, the existing design is defective for not having a safety feature embodied in a reasonable alternative design. Courts also agree that a reasonable alternative design depends on risk-utility factors, supporting the conclusion that "consensus" has been achieved in this area of the law.[47]

While agreeing upon the relevance of the risk-utility test, the courts have not adopted a uniform approach for applying the risk-utility factors. On the basis of a national survey, Professor David Owen found widespread disagreement among the courts on this matter:

> First, there is no single clearly accepted view as to how the design defect balancing test should be described or formulated. A related finding is that there is considerable variation in how the balancing test is formulated among the states, among decisions within the same state, and often even within the same judicial opinion. Another finding is that courts today quite typically cobble together a variety of separate and often conflicting formulations of balancing tests borrowed, without analysis, from earlier opinions. Further, many courts acknowledge that a variety of factors should be balanced but neither discriminate between the various factors nor explain how they should be balanced or otherwise interrelate.[48]

The courts do not agree on whether the risk-utility factors should be balanced in a straightforward exercise of cost-benefit analysis, or whether the safety of consumers should be emphasized over cost concerns as a matter of fairness.[49] Widespread disagree-

46. 1 Madden & Owen on Products Liability § 8:6, at 475.

47. Henderson & Twerski, *supra* note 2, at 868–69.

48. David G. Owen, *Risk-Utility Balancing in Design Defect Cases*, 30 U. Mich. J.L. Reform 239, 242 (1997) (citations omitted).

49. For a good discussion of this "schism" in the risk-utility test, see Michael D. Green, *The Schizophrenia of*

ment about the roles of fairness and efficiency can create an impasse blocking the further development of design-defect jurisprudence. The case law need not evolve to a common point. For some courts, the lack of consensus is a reason for not altering an existing liability rule.[50]

The possibility of consensus may be further undermined by the *Restatement (Third)*, which conceptualizes the risk-utility test as "a reasonableness test traditionally used in determining whether an actor has been negligent."[51] The reasonableness test in negligence law is notoriously vague, lacking any well-defined balancing of the relevant factors.[52] Conceptualizing design defects in negligence terms is not a promising way to eliminate the vagueness of the risk-utility test.[53]

The prospects for consensus considerably brighten once we recognize that the design-defect jurisprudence in virtually every jurisdiction shares a common origin—the rule of strict products liability in the *Restatement (Second)*. If the courts acknowledge this common starting point, they should end up at the same destination.

The *Restatement (Second)* justifies strict products liability in terms of consumer expectations. As shown by the case law in our first hypothetical jurisdiction, courts adhering to consumer expectations will logically end up conceptualizing reasonable consumer expectations in terms of the risk-utility test. So understood, the relevance of risk-utility considerations is obvious: consumers reasonably expect a product design to balance risk (or safety) against utility factors (the various costs of precaution) in whatever manner best promotes consumer welfare. The best protection of consumer interests is provided by the cost-benefit version of the risk-utility test, ordinarily eliminating any conflict between the requirements

Risk–Benefit Analysis in Design Defect Litigation, 48 Vand. L. Rev. 609 (1995).

50. *E.g.*, Turner v. General Motors Corp., 584 S.W.2d 844, 849 (Tex. 1979) (rejecting risk-utility test in part because different commentators propose different sets of factors for evaluating design defects); Halliday v. Sturm, Ruger & Co., 792 A.2d 1145, 1159 (Md. 2002) ("Given the controversy that continues to surround the risk-utility standard in § 2 of the *Restatement (Third)*, we are reluctant at this point to cast aside our existing jurisprudence in favor of such an approach on any broad, general basis.").

51. Restatement (Third) § 1 cmt. a at 7.

52. *See, e.g.*, Kenneth S. Abraham, *The Trouble with Negligence*, 54 Vand. L. Rev. 1187 (2001).

53. *Cf.* Patrick J. Kelley & Laurel A. Wendt, *What Judges Tell Juries about Negligence: A Review of Pattern Jury Instructions*, 77 Chi.-Kent L. Rev. 587, 622 (2002) (finding that at most five jurisdictions rely on jury instructions consistent with the cost-benefit test for negligence, although the instructions are more plausibly interpreted in other terms).

of fairness and efficiency.[54] The concept of consumer expectations, therefore, provides the missing guidance on how to apply the risk-utility factors.

This interplay between consumer expectations and the risk-utility test is illustrated by the cases in which courts first express allegiance to consumer expectations as a reason for rejecting the *Restatement (Third)* approach to design defects, and then effectively adopt the *Restatement (Third)* substantive rules of liability.[55] According to the Reporters of the *Restatement (Third)*, these cases are best explained in terms of "rhetorical confusion [that] is largely unnecessary."[56] As we have found, these courts are defensibly emphasizing that the risk-utility test *depends* upon consumer expectations, contrary to the rationale for the risk-utility test adopted by the *Restatement (Third)*.[57] Having rejected this aspect of the *Restatement (Third)*, these courts can then defensibly adopt the *Restatement (Third)* risk-utility test as a matter of reasonable consumer expectations. The resultant liability rule may be no different than the *Restatement (Third)* rule, but the mode of justification does not involve "rhetorical confusion" that is "largely unnecessary." These courts improve upon the *Restatement (Third)* by supplying a consumerist rationale for the cost-benefit version of the risk-utility test.

By rejecting consumer expectations, the *Restatement (Third)* apparently has forced some courts to identify this relation between consumer expectations and the risk-utility test:

> [D]espite a rare appearance, the idea of mixing the two approaches to design defectiveness (or finding them equivalent) lay dormant during the 1980s as the consumer expectation test gradually lost ground to risk-utility in the battle for supremacy as an independent test of design defectiveness. Then, as if awakening like Rip Van Winkle from a lengthy slumber, courts in a small number of states in the 1990s resurrected the nearly defunct idea that the two independent design defect standards are equivalent, merely representing "two sides of the same coin."[58]

The *Restatement (Third)* may "awaken" courts in the other jurisdictions as well, making them aware of the substantive equiva-

---

54. *See* Chapter 2.

55. The most noteworthy being Potter v. Chicago Pneumatic Tool Co., 694 A.2d 1319 (Conn. 1997).

56. Henderson & Twerski, *supra* note 2, at 871.

57. *See* Chapter 4.

58. 1 Madden & Owen on Products Liability § 8:6, at 479–480 (citations omitted).

lence of the two tests for design defects. These jurisdictions should have no trouble incorporating consumer expectations into the risk-utility test, given that their design defect jurisprudence originates in the *Restatement (Second)*. Once the risk-utility test is widely conceptualized as the embodiment of reasonable consumer expectations, the risk-utility test will no longer suffer from the seemingly intractable problem of vagueness. The courts will have attained consensus.

II. Proof of Defect: Reasonable Alternative Design

"Simply as a linguistic matter, ... the term 'defect' has implicit within it the notion of comparison—something can be defective only if viewed against something else, which embodies a standard for evaluation."[59] In design cases, the evaluative standard is provided by a reasonable alternative design. By proving that there is a reasonable alternative design of the product, the plaintiff has shown that the actual design is unreasonably dangerous in violation of reasonable consumer expectations and negligence principles. Consequently, a claim of defective design requires proof of a reasonable alternative design, unless the plaintiff is claiming that the product is defective no matter how designed (an allegation of *categorical liability* discussed in the next section).

A. *Proving Defect Without the Risk–Utility Test*

Although a design passing the risk-utility test is a reasonable alternative to the actual design of the product, the plaintiff does not always have to rely on the risk-utility test to prove a design defect, nor does the defendant necessarily have to defend the design with risk-utility evidence. Other forms of proof can suffice in certain circumstances.

Product Performance. The plaintiff can establish defect by showing that the product malfunctioned during normal use.[60] By presenting evidence that satisfies the requirements of the malfunction doctrine, the plaintiff implicitly establishes the existence of a reasonable alternative design—one that does not cause the product to malfunction during normal use.[61] This proof does not depend on

59. Sheila L. Birnbaum, *Unmasking the Test for Design Defect: From Negligence [to Warranty] to Strict Liability to Negligence*, 33 Vand. L. Rev. 593, 603 (1980).

60. *See* Chapter 5, section I (discussing malfunction doctrine).

61. This conclusion assumes that the malfunction was caused by the design, the class of cases relevant for present purposes.

the risk-utility test, since the defect is established by the malfunction alone.

Safety Regulations. The plaintiff can show that a design is defective for violating a binding product safety statute or administrative regulation.[62] By establishing the violation of the regulatory requirement, the plaintiff has proven defect by reference to a reasonable alternative design—the one required by the safety regulation.

A related issue is whether the defendant can show that the design is not defective because it satisfies statutory or regulatory requirements. This issue is solely one of statutory interpretation. If the legislature intended the regulations to displace or preempt the requirements of state tort law, then the product's compliance with the statutory or regulatory requirement insulates the defendant from state tort liability with respect to this particular aspect of the product design.[63] Otherwise, the product's compliance with statutory or regulatory requirements is not an affirmative defense, but is only relevant evidence tending to show that the design is not defective. The court can still find the design to be defective.[64]

Market Comparisons. A product design can be evaluated in terms of other designs in the relevant market. The design can be compared to the design customarily supplied by the market or to the most technologically advanced design in the market. Each type of inquiry appears in the case law, although neither of these two market alternatives provides an appealing basis for definitively resolving the issue of defective design.[65]

As we found earlier, a customary market practice can involve sellers supplying unreasonably dangerous products to poorly in-

---

62. Restatement (Third) § 4(a). The plaintiff can also establish liability by relying on the doctrine of negligence per se. *See* David G. Owen, *Proving Negligence in Modern Products Liability Litigation*, 36 Ariz. St. L.J. 1003, 1004–13 (2004).

63. *See, e.g.*, Geier v. American Honda Motor Co., 529 U.S. 861 (2000) (finding that during period in which automobile manufacturers were required to phase-in the use of airbags in conjunction with other passive-restraint safety systems, federal regulations preempted state tort law claims concerning the defectiveness of automobiles designed without an airbag). For discussion of statutory interpretation, see William N.

Eskridge, Jr., Philip P. Frickey & Elizabeth Garrett, Legislation and Statutory Interpretation (2000).

64. Restatement (Third) § 4(b). For a wide-ranging, informative discussion of this issue, see *Symposium, Regulatory Compliance as a Defense to Products Liability*, 88 Geo. L.J. 2049 *passim* (2000).

65. For an overview of the different approaches taken by the various jurisdictions and a count of the number of jurisdictions following any given approach, see James Boyd & Daniel E. Ingberman, *Should "Relative Safety" Be a Test of Product Liability?*, 26 J. Legal Stud. 433 (1997).

formed consumers.[66] Due to market failures of this type, Judge Learned Hand famously concluded that "a whole calling may have unduly lagged in the adoption of new and available devices. It never may set its own tests. . . . Courts must in the end say what is required . . . ."[67] A customary design can be defective.

This same reasoning explains why the best available design in the market can also be defective. The courts frequently describe the issue as involving the "state of the art," although one should be careful about using this terminology.[68] "A few states take the position that conformance with the best available technology in actual use is an absolute defense to design liability."[69] The vast majority of states reject this affirmative defense, and for a good reason. Just as the customary design can be unreasonably dangerous, so can the best available design. Each design is produced by market forces having the potential to create safety problems requiring tort regulation. To repeat Judge Hand's admonition, "Courts in the end must say what is required."

Evidence regarding the existing technology in a product market can be relevant to the issue of defect, however. By showing that the precaution in question had not been incorporated into any other design and was not otherwise available in the market, the defendant properly supports its claim that the plaintiff's proposed reasonable alternative design was not technologically feasible. Nevertheless, "[i]f such a design could have been practically adopted at time of sale and if the omission of such a design rendered the product not reasonably safe, the plaintiff establishes defect."[70]

Rather than using industry practices to shield the defendant from liability, the availability of different designs in the market could give plaintiffs a sword to establish liability. This method of defining design defects is also problematic.

For example, automobile airbags had undergone extensive research and development by the early 1960s, and yet, two decades later, the price of airbags per vehicle was "extremely high."[71] If a design were deemed to be defective for not incorporating the best

---

66. *See* Chapter 2, section II.B.

67. The T.J. Hooper, 60 F.2d 737, 740 (2d Cir. 1932). *See also* Restatement (Third) § 2 cmt. d (rejecting custom as a defense in product cases).

68. *See* Restatement (Third) § 2 cmt. d Rptrs' Note ("The term 'state of the art' has been variously defined by a multitude of courts. For some it refers to industry custom or industry practice; for others it means the safest existing technology that has been adopted for use; for others it means cutting-edge technology.").

69. *Id*. at 81.

70. *Id*. § 2 cmt. d at 20.

71. Jerry L. Mashaw & David L. Harfst, The Struggle for Auto Safety 85, 208 (1990).

available technology, then automobile manufacturers would have been obligated to install airbags in every vehicle sold during this period, despite the extremely high cost. A liability rule requiring the best available technology can result in excessively costly product safety, thereby reducing consumer welfare.[72]

The plaintiff could also try to prove defect by showing that the design does not incorporate a customary safety feature. This form of proof has some appeal. Product markets require regulation by tort law when market forces produce an insufficient amount of product safety. In a market regulated by tort law, then, a customary practice is likely to involve the minimal amount of safety required by the tort duty. Consequently, a design lacking a customary safety feature probably is defective. To conclude that the design is defective for this reason, though, the court would have to confront a number of difficult issues. When a new safety technology is first incorporated into a specific product line, is custom defined by reference to that particular line (like high-end automobiles with airbags) or to the more general product class lacking the feature (high-end automobiles)? When defined by reference to the particular line incorporating the safety feature, the standard effectively defines defect by reference to the best available technology, a problematic evaluative standard that has been rejected by the courts. But once customary safety practices are defined by reference to more general product lines, the practices are more varied and custom is harder to identify. Rather than decide the difficult issue of what constitutes a customary safety feature, the courts have understandably concluded that the relevance of any such proof depends upon the particulars of the case. A product's failure to conform to an industry custom or standard ordinarily supports the allegation of defect but does not conclusively establish defect.[73]

Consumer Expectations. As we found earlier, in some cases the design can be evaluated directly in terms of consumer expectations. These cases involve design risks that are likely to be known by the ordinary product user and can be understood by the jury, particularly those posing a great danger that can be readily avoided at low cost. The jury evaluates the alleged defect by reference to a reasonable alternative design that must be affirmatively established by the plaintiff, but the design defect is so "apparent to the common reason, experience, and understanding of its ordinary consumers

---

72. For a formal demonstration of this point, see Boyd & Ingberman, *supra* note 65.

73. Shapo, 1 Law of Products Liability ¶ 11.02[7]. *See also* Owen, *supra* note 62, at 1017–25 (discussing role of custom in negligence actions).

... [that] a lay jury is competent to make that determination" without receiving expert testimony on the risk-utility factors.[74]

B. *The Risk–Utility Test*

According to the *Restatement (Third)*, except for cases "involving product malfunction, safety standard violation, or egregiously dangerous design," the "overwhelming majority of American jurisdictions" either "explicitly or implicitly" require "the plaintiff to establish the availability of a reasonable alternative design."[75] As a logical matter, in these cases the plaintiff must provide evidence of the risk-utility factors. A reasonable alternative design necessarily accounts for the risk posed by the actual design and the utility that would be lost by altering the design to incorporate the costly safety features proposed by the plaintiff.

The dominant definition of the risk-utility test is that a "design is defective if the product's risks exceed its utility."[76] This definition inappropriately suggests that defect depends on a comparison of total product risk with the total utility or benefit of the product, an interpretation adopted by some courts.[77] A comparison of total product risk with total product benefit would mean that most (all?) automobiles are not defectively designed for failing to incorporate important safety features. The total benefits of driving vastly exceed the risks posed by a car without an airbag, for example. In some circumstances, the total benefits of driving can exceed the risks posed by a car without good brakes. A risk-utility test formulated in these terms would absolve manufacturers from the tort obligation to incorporate numerous safety features into the product design. Instead of *macro-balancing* total product risks and utility, the risk-utility inquiry must *micro-balance* the cost of the proposed precaution with its safety benefit.[78] This formulation of the risk-utility test follows from the dominant definition of the risk-

---

74. *Soule*, 882 P.2d at 310 (sentence structure omitted). For more extensive discussion of these issues, see *supra* section I.A.

75. Restatement (Third) § 2 Rptrs' Note at 46. Critics of the *Restatement (Third)* argue that it departs from the case law by ordinarily requiring proof of a reasonable alternative design. *See, e.g.,* Frank J. Vandall, *The Restatement (Third) of Torts: Products Liability Section 2(b): The Reasonable Alternative Design Requirement*, 61 Tenn. L. Rev. 1407 (1994); Vargo, *supra* note 45. The *Restatement (Third)* clearly does not require proof of a reasonable alternative design in *all* cases, however, so this dispute seems to be another aspect of the more general debate concerning the relation between consumer expectations and strict liability, a form of liability that does not require proof of defect by reference to a reasonable alternative design.

76. David G. Owen, *Toward a Proper Test for Design Defectiveness: "Micro-Balancing" Costs and Benefits*, 75 Tex. L. Rev. 1661, 1672 (1997).

77. *Id.* at 1673.

78. These useful terms were formulated by Professor Owen. *See id.*

utility test once we account for the requirement that the design defect must be proven by reference to a reasonable alternative design: A "design is defective if the product's risks [that would be eliminated by the reasonable alternative design] exceeds its utility [that would be lost by adopting the reasonable alternative design]."

To illustrate, we can more fully consider the issue of whether an automobile design is defective for not having an airbag. The plaintiff's proposed reasonable alternative design adds the airbag to the existing design, and so the *risk* posed by the actual design (no airbag) refers to the risk reduction that would be produced by the airbag—the proposed reasonable alternative design. This safety benefit consists of the reduced probability P that occupants in cars would suffer injuries or losses having a monetary cost L. The total safety benefit or reduction in risk PL often involves both monetary and nonmonetary injuries like pain and suffering, but it can still be expressed in monetary terms as required by the risk-utility comparison.[79] The *utility* of the actual design (no airbag) refers to the disutility, cost or burden B that would be produced by the proposed design change. Most obviously, the cost of an airbag includes the added production costs of incorporating the airbag into the design. An airbag can have other costs. It may inconvenience drivers by accidentally inflating, for example. (The inconvenience many associate with seat belts provides a better example of such a cost.) An airbag, like other safety precautions, can also pose new risks. Airbags have killed children in low-speed collisions, thereby increasing expected accident costs in this respect. The sum of these various costs yields the total disutility, cost or burden B that would be produced by the airbag—the proposed reasonable alternative design:

$$B = increased\ production\ costs$$
$$+\ cost\ of\ inconvenience\ or\ reduced\ functionality$$
$$+\ expected\ accident\ costs\ created\ by\ airbag$$

These factors must be micro-balanced against the safety benefit PL of the airbag in order to determine whether that precaution is required by the risk-utility test, resulting in a finding of defect whenever the proof shows that the disutility of the proposed design change is less than the risk that would be reduced, a conclusion finding expression in the Hand formula for negligence: $B < PL$.[80]

79. *See* Chapter 9, section II.B (discussing computation of pain-and-suffering damage awards).

80. For further discussion of the relation between the risk-utility test and the Hand formula for negligence, see Chapter 2, section II.A.

C. Instructing the Jury

Whether a product is defectively designed ordinarily is a factual question to be decided by the jury. The way in which juries apply the risk-utility test can significantly depend upon the form of jury instructions. Consider the following pattern jury instructions for New York:

> A manufacturer who sells a product in a defective condition is liable for injury which results from use of the product when the product is used for its intended or reasonably foreseeable purpose.
>
> A product is defective if it is not reasonably safe—that is, if the product is so likely to be harmful to persons that a reasonable person who had actual knowledge of its potential for producing injury would conclude that it should not have been marketed in that condition. . . . It is sufficient that a reasonable person who did in fact know of the product's potential for causing injury and of the available alternative designs would have concluded that the product should not have been marketed in that condition, after balancing the risks involved in using the product against: 1. the product's usefulness and its costs, and against: 2. the risks, usefulness and costs of the alternative designs as compared to the product defendant did market.[81]

This instruction does not tell jurors how to balance the risk-utility factors. Insofar as jurors find it inappropriate to trade off lives and limbs for money, they will place significantly greater weight on the "risks involved in using the product," as compared to the way in which the alternative design decreases product "usefulness" and increases product "costs." The resultant imbalance can lead the jury to conclude that a design is defective, even though it passes the cost-benefit version of the risk-utility test.

Studies have found that lay individuals, jurors and judges emphasize safety considerations over monetary cost in a manner inconsistent with cost-benefit analysis. A survey of 100 judges found that most required precautions in excess of the cost-benefit amount when the risk threatened serious bodily injury.[82] Lay individuals and jurors also require more than the cost-benefit amount of safety for nonconsensual risks threatening serious bodily injury.[83]

---

81. N.Y. Pattern Jury Instructions—Civil 2:41 (2004) (tailored for defendant manufacturer in case involving a design defect that caused personal injury).

82. W. Kip Viscusi, *How Do Judges Think About Risk?*, 1 Am. L. & Econ. Rev. 26, 40–46 (1999).

83. W. Kip Viscusi, *Jurors, Judges, and the Mistreatment of Risk by the Courts*, 30 J. Legal Stud. 107 (2001).

Other studies have found that lay individuals, jurors and judges believe that the negligence standard is violated by corporate decisions based on a cost-benefit analysis of risks threatening serious bodily injury.[84]

The way in which jurors, judges and the public treat tradeoffs between cost and personal safety substantially affects the application of the risk-utility test in the courtroom. As Professor Michael Green observes:

> With this attitude widespread among the public who make up juries, how can trial lawyers defend a design case by pointing to a risk-benefit analysis performed by the manufacturer? The simple answer is that they can't and don't. Rather, lawyers will argue that the alternative design would compromise the product's function or create different risks in the product, but not that the costs of the alternative design outweigh the injury or death toll that might be avoided.[85]

Financial considerations are part of the risk-utility calculus, and yet defendants are unable to defend the design on this basis. This problem may explain why courts frequently emphasize that "the tort inheres in the product, not in the manufacturer's conduct."[86] The risk-utility test is supposed to evaluate the product rather than the manufacturer's decision to forego a safety investment out of cost concerns. By deflecting attention away from the manufacturer's conduct, the courts might be trying to help jurors understand that there is nothing inherently wrong about a product design that trades off safety considerations for financial ones.

Nevertheless, jury instructions that focus on the product are unlikely to make jurors more amenable to cost-benefit analysis. A product has no perspective for jurors to adopt. When evaluating the product design, jurors will naturally consider the reasons for the design, forcing the defendant to avoid any reference to the impact of the safety precaution on production costs and product price (both of which can be readily translated by the plaintiff into a greedy corporate concern for profits). Manufacturers will continue to have problems arguing that a safety improvement is not worth the increased costs.[87]

84. W. Kip Viscusi, *Corporate Risk Analysis: A Reckless Act?*, 52 Stan. L. Rev. 547 (2000).

85. Green, *supra* note 49, at 626–27 (citation omitted).

86. Shapo, 1 Law of Products Liability ¶ 8.03[2].

87. Consider pattern jury instructions in New Mexico:

The design of a product need not necessarily adopt features which represent the ultimate in safety. You should consider the ability to eliminate the risk without seriously impair-

The problem is not solved by the New York pattern jury instructions directing the jury's attention to the reasonable person rather than the manufacturer. The reasonable-person standard does not enable jurors to differentiate ordinary tort cases, like those involving drivers and pedestrians, from product cases. Like ordinary tort cases, one party (the driver or manufacturer) benefits or profits from the risky activity at the expense of the other (pedestrian or consumer). Given this similarity, jurors are unlikely to appreciate the important difference between the two types of cases. The fair tort rule emphasizes the protection of the pedestrian, potentially justifying more safety precautions on the part of drivers than is required by cost-benefit analysis. In product cases, the fair tort rule emphasizes the protection of the consumer. Unlike pedestrians, consumers internalize both the costs and benefits of tort liability, justifying the safety precautions required by the cost-benefit version of the risk-utility test. The two types of cases importantly differ in a manner that is obscured by jury instructions framed in terms of the reasonable person.[88]

The remaining possibility is to instruct the jury in a manner that defines the risk-utility test in terms of consumer expectations.[89] Even though the risk-utility test can be logically derived from the reasonable safety expectations of the ordinary consumer, the jury does not necessarily view the two tests as being substantively equivalent. According to numerous studies by cognitive psychologists, the way in which risky choices are described or framed to lay individuals can alter their decision making.[90] A framing effect

---

ing the usefulness of the product or making it unduly expensive.

Under products liability law, you are not to consider the reasonableness of acts or omissions of the supplier. You are to look at the product itself and consider only the risks of harm from its condition or from the manner of its use at the time of the injury.

N.M. Stat. Ann. Civ. UJI 13–1407 (Michie 2003).

The focus on the product requires that the instructions be framed in the passive voice ("the ability to eliminate the risk …"), creating the opening for lawyers to make the type of arguments discussed in the text. For an interesting interpretation of why liability rules emphasize products rather than conduct, see Anita Bernstein, *How Can a Product be Liable?*, 45 Duke L.J. 1 (1995).

88. *See* Chapter 2, section I (discussing differences between ordinary tort cases and product cases).

89. *Cf.* Stephen G. Gilles, *On Determining Negligence: Hand Formula Balancing, the Reasonable Person Standard, and the Jury*, 54 Vand. L. Rev. 813, 860–61 (2001) (advocating jury instructions that emphasize cost-benefit balancing only "as a gloss on how reasonable people make decisions about accident avoidance"). *But see* Birnbaum, *supra* note 59, at 615 ("Burdening a product defect analysis with the conceptual baggage of the hypothetical ordinary consumer adds essentially nothing of substance to a straightforward risk-utility balancing approach.").

90. The seminal study is Amos Tversky & Daniel Kahneman, *The Framing of Decisions and the Psychology of Choice*, 211 Sci. 453 (1981).

occurs when two "logically equivalent (but not transparently equivalent) statements of a problem lead decision makers to choose different options."[91] Jury instructions framed in terms of consumer expectations could make jurors more amenable to the option of trading off safety for financial considerations, yielding better decisions than jury instructions framed exclusively in risk-utility terms.

Research on risk perception indicates that lay people want risk decisions to be based on additional considerations besides expected damages, injuries and dollar costs. These considerations include voluntariness of exposure to the hazard; the degree to which the risks are dread, controllable or catastrophic; the degree of uncertainty surrounding the risk estimates; and the possible inequities in the distribution of benefits among persons who bear the risks.[92]

A great deal of this information can be conveyed by jury instructions that frame the risk-utility test in terms of consumer expectations. Consider how this change in perspective alters the New York pattern jury instructions:

A manufacturer who sells a product in a defective condition is liable for injury which results from use of the product when the product is used for its intended or reasonably foreseeable purpose.

A product is defective if it is not reasonably safe—that is, if the product is so likely to be harmful to persons and property that the ordinary consumer who had actual knowledge of its potential for producing injury would decide to forego that purchase in favor of the alternative product design proposed by the plaintiff. In making this decision, the ordinary consumer would compare the added risks involved in using the product as marketed by the defendant with any increased costs that would be created by the alternative product design proposed by the plaintiff. The costs of the alternative design include any increase in other risks, product price or operating costs, and any decrease in functionality or product performance. These higher costs are incurred by the ordinary consumer, who also benefits from any safety improvements in the alternative design. The ordinary consumer would reasonably decide to purchase the product defendant did market if the higher cost of the alternative design exceeds its safety benefit. For the product to be

91. Matthew Rabin, *Psychology and Economics*, 36 J. Econ. Lit. 11, 36 (1998).

92. Paul Slovic, The Perception of Risk 199–200 (2000) (citations omitted).

defective, the safety benefit of the alternative design must exceed any increased costs for the consumer.

These instructions could be improved upon, but they do show how the risk-utility test can be framed to emphasize that consumer choice determines the appropriate product design, and that consumers are the ones who both benefit from product safety and pay for it. Each of these factors importantly influences the decision making of lay individuals like jurors, but none of them are mentioned in the standard jury instructions on the risk-utility test.

This reasoning explains why many jurisdictions defensibly describe the risk-utility test in terms of consumer expectations, an approach sanctioned by the *Restatement (Third)*:

> [T]here are various ways in which courts make reference to consumer expectations without committing to consumer expectations as an independent test for design defectiveness.... Many states require proof of a reasonable alternative design as a prerequisite to reaching the jury, yet couch their jury instructions in more general language that often includes consumer expectations. The practice of these jurisdictions is fully compatible with the [liability rule for design defects in the *Restatement (Third)*.][93]

Even though the practice of these jurisdictions is fully compatible with the unadorned risk-utility test, it is likely to produce different outcomes. Two jury instructions can be substantively equivalent but framed in different manners that lead jurors to make fundamentally different decisions about the risk-utility factors. The actual requirements of the risk-utility test importantly depend upon whether it is framed in terms of consumer expectations.

III. Proof of Defect: Categorical Liability

In theory, a product can be defective no matter how it is designed—the entire product category can be defective. To establish *categorical liability*, the plaintiff must prove that the category consists of products having total risk greater than their total utility, making the entire category unreasonably dangerous. By implication, this proof shows that any product within the category is unreasonably dangerous and defective. The plaintiff does not have to prove that there is a reasonable alternative design for the product that was sold by the defendant, because no such design allegedly exists.

---

93. Restatement (Third) § 2 cmt. d
Rptrs' Note at 74.

Categorical liability may be viable in theory, but virtually no jurisdiction has recognized this form of liability.[94] The courts have not been willing to conclude that an entire product category is unreasonable. With respect to the issue of product design, the duty of a product seller is effectively limited to the provision of a reasonably designed product for the category in question.

This limitation of duty can be analyzed in terms of the actual safety expectations of the ordinary consumer, like any other limitation of duty. Recall that a tort duty is most defensible when the ordinary consumer would incur high information costs to evaluate the relevant risk-utility factors.[95] The information costs prevent the consumer from being well informed of the risk and can even cause her to forego the safety evaluation altogether. As information costs go down, the ordinary consumer is more willing to acquire the relevant risk-utility information and is more likely to consider the safety issue. For safety decisions involving low information costs, the ordinary consumer is presumptively able to make the appropriate safety choices and does not require tort protection. The tort duty therefore can exclude categorical liability if the ordinary consumer faces sufficiently low information costs in making risk-utility choices across product categories. In these circumstances, the ordinary consumer would not have frustrated safety expectations regarding her choice of category, and so the product seller could not incur tort liability merely by selling a product from one category rather than from another.

To assess the information costs faced by consumers who are choosing among product categories, we need to account for the other tort duties imposed on product sellers. The tort duty requires that the product must be free of manufacturing or construction flaws. The tort duty also requires that each product design within any category must be reasonably safe. These tort duties guarantee the reasonable safety of all products within any category, enabling the ordinary consumer to focus on the risk-utility comparisons across product categories.

In making choices across product categories, the ordinary consumer also benefits from the duty to warn, which guarantees that the product warning provides the ordinary consumer with the material information required for informed safety decisions.[96] Once the information already held by the ordinary consumer is supplemented by the information provided by the product warning, she presumably is able to make an informed categorical choice.

94. *Id.* § 2 cmt. e Rptrs' Note at 90.   **96.** *See* Chapter 7, section I.
95. *See* Chapter 2, section II.B.

Of course, consumers will make mistakes in choosing product categories. These consumer mistakes, though, must be compared to the alternative. Categorical liability would require courts to macro-balance the risk-utility factors for an entire product category. The micro-balancing of risk-utility factors for something like an automobile airbag can be quite difficult; a macro-balancing of risk-utility factors for a category like compact cars is vastly more difficult. The informational requirements are quite demanding, and a mistaken finding of categorical liability would drive beneficial product lines from the market, thereby harming consumers. Both consumers and courts are likely to make mistakes in evaluating product categories, but the courts could understandably conclude that the consumer is the more capable decision maker. The judicial resistance to categorical liability fosters consumer choice while avoiding the pitfalls of applying the risk-utility test to an entire product category.[97]

These reasons for resisting categorical liability can explain a range of cases, including many that do not directly raise the issue. To see why, first consider a case that clearly involves categorical liability. The plaintiff was a passenger in a Volkswagen microbus that crashed into a telephone pole, causing the plaintiff injury. The plaintiff claimed the microbus was defectively designed for placing the engine in the rear, thereby reducing the front-end "crash space" that would be afforded by an alternative design placing the engine in the front of the car, the design utilized by a "standard passenger car." On appeal, the court rejected this claim:

> The defendant's vehicle, described as "a van type multipurpose vehicle," was of a special type and particular design. This design was uniquely developed in order to provide the owner with the maximum amount of either cargo or passenger space in a vehicle inexpensively priced and of such dimensions as to make possible easy maneuverability. To achieve this, it advanced the driver's seat forward, bringing such seat in close proximity to the front of the vehicle, thereby adding to the cargo or passenger space. This, of course, reduced considerably the space between the exact front of the vehicle and the driver's compartment. All of this was readily discernible to any one using the vehicle; in fact, it was, as we have said, the unique feature of the vehicle. The usefulness of the design is vouchsafed by the popularity of the type. It was of special utility as a van for the transportation of light cargo, as a family camper, as a station wagon and for use by passenger groups too large for the average passenger car. It was a design that had

---

97. *See* Henderson & Twerski, *supra* note 2, at 885–887.

been adopted by other manufacturers, including American. It was a design duplicated in the construction of the large trucking tractors, where there was the same purpose of extending the cargo space without unduly lengthening the tractor-trailer coupling. There was no evidence in the record that there was any practical way of improving the "crashability" of the vehicle that would have been consistent with the peculiar purposes of its design. The only theory on which the plaintiffs posited their claim of negligent design was, to quote the language of their brief in this Court, that "The 1968 Volkswagen station wagon did not provide the protection for the front seat passengers as did the 'normal' or standard passenger car." ... Under this standard, any rear engine car would be "inherently dangerous ...." To avoid liability for negligent design, no manufacturer could introduce any innovative or unique design, even though reasonably calculated to provide some special advantage such as greater roominess. Such a strait-jacket on design is not imposed.... If a person purchases a convertible ... he cannot expect—and the Court may not impose on the manufacturer the duty to provide him with—the exact kind of protection in a roll-over accident as in the "standard American passenger car." The situation is similar when he purchases a microbus: The distance between the front and the passenger compartment is minified in order to provide additional cargo or passenger space just as the convertible is designed to provide openness. It is entirely impermissible to predicate a conclusion of negligent design simply because a vehicle, having a distinctive purpose, such as the microbus, does not conform to the design of another type of vehicle, such as a standard passenger car, having a different nature and utility.[98]

The allegation of design defect was one of categorical liability, since a microbus is in a different product category than a standard passenger car. But notice the various ways in which the case can be interpreted. It might seem as if the court is relying upon consumer expectations to absolve the manufacturer of liability for the open and obvious risks posed by a microbus. The case does not stand for this proposition, however, because the ordinary consumer was aware of both the risk and the safety alternatives. The ordinary consumer could have bought a standard passenger car instead of a microbus. By making a presumptively well-informed categorical choice, the ordinary consumer does not expect the microbus to have the same safety features as the standard passenger car. The case

---

98. Dreisonstok v. Volkswagenwerk, A.G., 489 F.2d 1066, 1073–75 (4th Cir. 1974) (applying Virginia law) (footnotes omitted).

therefore shows that the consumer's well-informed choice of a safety feature from among the set of relevant alternatives, rather than the obvious nature of the risk, is the reason for limiting categorical liability.

Other cases involve the same principle, although it is harder to determine whether the defect claim is one of categorical liability. Consider a case involving a police officer who was killed by gunshot wounds while wearing a bullet-proof, "contour style" vest. Plaintiff claimed the vest was defectively designed for not providing the more extensive bodily coverage available in other designs. Are contour bullet-proof vests a different product category than the other styles on the market? The appellate court never wrestled with the question in rejecting the claim of design defect:

> The contour style [worn by the decedent] was one of several different styles then on the market. It provided more protection to the sides of the body than the style featuring rectangular panels in front and back, but not as much protection as a wrap-around style.... This feature of the vest was obvious [at the time of purchase.] ... A person wearing the vest would no more expect to be shielded from a shot taken under the arm than he would expect the vest to deflect bullets aimed at his head or neck or lower abdomen or any other area not covered by the vest.... [T]he amount of coverage was the buyer's choice.... A manufacturer is not obliged to market only one version of a product, that being the very safest design possible.... Personal safety devices, in particular, require personal choices, and it is beyond the province of courts and juries to act as legislators and preordain those choices.[99]

Once again, the court appears to be limiting liability because the risk was obvious, but the case does not stand for the proposition that an open and obvious risk necessarily satisfies consumer expectations. The ordinary consumer had adequate knowledge of the relevant risks and was presented with a choice of safer alternatives. Having made a presumptively well-informed risk-utility choice to purchase the vest, the ordinary consumer does not expect the amount of safety offered by the other available designs she decided not to purchase. The availability of the relevant safety options, coupled with knowledge of the attendant risks, explains the limitation of liability.

Finally, consider a case that clearly does not implicate categorical liability. The presence or absence of most safety features does

99. Linegar v. Armour of America, 909 F.2d 1150, 1151–54 (8th Cir. 1990) (applying Missouri law) (paragraph structure omitted).

not change the product category. A car continues to be a convertible, whether or not it has an airbag. Suppose the manufacturer offers two versions of the product: one with the safety feature, and the other without. After reviewing cases of this type, the New York Court of Appeals concluded:

> We can ... distill some governing principles for cases where a plaintiff claims that a product without an optional safety feature is defectively designed because the equipment was not standard. The product is not defective where the evidence and reasonable inferences therefrom show that: (1) the buyer is thoroughly knowledgeable regarding the product and its use and is actually aware that the safety feature is available; (2) there exist normal circumstances of use in which the product is not unreasonably dangerous without the optional equipment; and (3) the buyer is in a position, given the range of uses of the product, to balance the benefits and the risks of not having the safety device in the specifically contemplated circumstances of the buyer's use of the product. In such a case, the buyer, not the manufacturer, is in the superior position to make the risk-utility assessment, and a well-considered decision by the buyer to dispense with the optional safety equipment will excuse the manufacturer from liability.[100]

The relevant principles governing these cases are the same as those governing cases of categorical liability. In all of the cases, the ordinary consumer is offered safety alternatives and faces low information costs, enabling her to make an adequately informed risk-utility choice. Having chosen a less safe alternative, the consumer does not expect the greater safety offered by a product configuration she decided not to purchase. The satisfaction of actual consumer expectations can explain why the seller's duty does not encompass such choices.

Although the courts have widely resisted categorical liability, the *Restatement (Third)* acknowledges the possibility of categorical liability for "manifestly unreasonable design" of products with "low social utility and a high degree of danger."[101] How could such an instance of categorical liability be squared with consumer expectations in light of the foregoing analysis? Perhaps the *Restatement (Third)* is wrong to acknowledge even a limited role for categorical liability, a conclusion finding support in the widespread criticism

100. Scarangella v. Thomas Built Buses, Inc., 717 N.E.2d 679, 683 (N.Y. 1999).

101. Restatement (Third) § 2 cmt. e.

leveled against the only case that has clearly adopted categorical liability.[102] But an alternative rationale for categorical liability remains to be considered, one that explains why the satisfaction of actual consumer expectations is not always a sufficient reason for limiting duty.

The analysis so far has been confined to the *consumer*, a concept including the buyer and users of the product. Excluded are third parties or bystanders. In situations of low information costs and a choice among safety options, consumers are able to make the safety choices that best promote their interests. In these circumstances, the rejection of categorical liability appropriately defers to consumer choice. Deference to consumer choice is not compelling, however, when third-party interests are at stake.

Consider a case in which the plaintiff was riding on a motorcycle that collided with a 1964 Buick Skylark:

> It is plaintiff's claim that this collision caused her left leg to be thrown into the opening of the rear wheel well containing ... protruding spinning blades of the hubcap. She received a severe lacerating injury to the outside of the lower leg just above the ankle. Her doctor described the injury as a "Mangling type injury with multiple lacerations of the foot." The bone was so severely severed that only some soft tissue held her leg together. Her father came to the scene of the collision and discovered the Buick's right rear hubcap with human flesh and blood on it. The highway patrolman verified the blood on the hubcap.
>
> The wheel cover was designed with the two ornamental blades protruding some three inches from the base of the cover itself. The flippers serve only the purpose of aesthetic design. These spinners or flippers were recessed two and one-eighth inches within the outer perimeter of the car's body shell. Within the five square feet of the car's rear wheel well there was no covering or protection from the blades. When the vehicle moved at a speed of 40 m.p.h. the blades revolved at 568 r.p.m. or nine and one-half revolutions per second. Plaintiff's expert witness, who held a Ph.D. in agricultural engineering and

---

102. O'Brien v. Muskin Corp., 463 A.2d 298, 306 (N.J. 1983) (finding an above-ground pool with vinyl bottom may be defective under risk-utility test despite lack of feasible alternative design). In response, the state legislature subsequently rejected categorical liability. N.J. Stat. Ann. § 2A:58C–3.b(3) (West 1990). For citations of the many critical scholarly critiques of *O'Brien*, see Restatement (Third) § 2 cmt. d Rptrs' Note at 89–90.

theoretical applied mechanics, testified that the protruding blades moving at high speeds in an unshielded area constituted an unsafe design to persons who might come within their vicinity.[103]

In finding that the plaintiff's defect claim was sufficient to support a finding of liability by the jury (which had not yet decided the matter), the court never considered categorical liability or the related doctrines involving consumer choice. The court undoubtedly would have found these doctrines to be entirely inapposite, as indeed they are. The consumer may have made a well-informed choice to purchase a wheel cover with propeller-like blades. The consumer's choice, though, does not provide a good reason for limiting the duty of the automobile manufacturer. The consumer's decision was made "only for the purpose of aesthetic design," a reason that pales in comparison to the risk that a bystander would be injured by the rapidly rotating blades. The consumer chose a wheel cover having a "manifestly unreasonable design" with "low social utility and a high degree of danger," the requirements for categorical liability in the *Restatement (Third)*.[104]

When the product risk largely threatens injury to bystanders, categorical liability can be defensible. Consumer choice ordinarily is desirable and properly promoted by the limitation of the seller's duty with respect to categorical liability. But in cases of bystander injury, the plaintiff is alleging that the consumer should not be given the choice in question. The purchaser of the Buick Skylark with rotating blades in the wheel well presumably made an informed choice and does not have frustrated safety expectations. Nevertheless, this product choice was unreasonable for the third-party bystander who suffered the injurious consequences. In these cases, duty does not have to be limited in order to foster consumer choice. The *Restatement (Third)* and many courts have defensibly concluded that categorical liability can be justified in the appropriate circumstances.

103. Passwaters v. General Motors Corp., 454 F.2d 1270, 1272 (8th Cir. 1972) (applying Iowa law).

104. Restatement (Third) § 2 cmt. e. In the one case that clearly adopted categorical liability, the plaintiff was a consumer and not a third-party victim. *O'Brien*, 463 A.2d 298. However, the only other case that has arguably adopted categorical liability did involve bystanders—the gun-shot victims of "Saturday Night Specials," an inexpen- sive handgun preferred by criminals. Kelley v. R.G. Indus., 497 A.2d 1143 (Md. 1985). This case was subsequently overruled by the state legislature. Md. Code Ann., Crim. Law art. 27 § 36–I (Supp. 1990). One view is that this "is probably a case based primarily on a theory of negligent entrustment" and not categorical liability. Restatement (Third) § 2 cmt. d Rptrs' Note.

IV. Considerations of Strict Liability: Shifting the Burden of Proof

To establish a defect of design, the plaintiff ordinarily must prove that the design is unreasonably dangerous for not incorporating the safety features of a reasonable alternative design—one passing the risk-utility test, for example. The liability rule requires proof that the product is unreasonably dangerous, making it a form of negligence liability that seems to fit poorly with the rule of strict products liability in the *Restatement (Second)*. Consequently, many courts have considered whether there is some role for strict liability in design cases.

Strict liability is particularly compelling when evidentiary problems prevent plaintiffs from adequately enforcing the duty of reasonable care. The evidentiary rationale for strict liability has been widely recognized by courts and persuasively justifies the rule of strict liability for construction or manufacturing defects.[105] The question naturally arises whether the risk-utility test involves evidentiary burdens that justify some role for strict liability in design cases. A role for strict liability can be created by shifting the burden of proof regarding defect. In a negligence case, the plaintiff bears the burden of proof. Shifting the burden to the defendant departs from the ordinary negligence rule while also reducing the plaintiff's evidentiary burden consistent with the rationale for strict liability.

A rule of this type was adopted by the California Supreme Court in the well-known case *Barker v. Lull Engineering Company*:

> Because most of the evidentiary matters which may be relevant to the determination of the adequacy of a product's design under the "risk-benefit" standard—e.g., the feasibility and cost of alternative designs—are similar to issues typically presented in a negligent design case and involve technical matters peculiarly within the knowledge of the manufacturer, we conclude that once the plaintiff makes a prima facie showing that the injury was proximately caused by the product's design, the burden should appropriately shift to the defendant to prove, in light of the relevant factors, that the product is not defective.[106]

This ruling has attracted a great deal of attention, although only a few other jurisdictions have adopted it.[107] In the vast majori-

---

105. *See* Chapter 4, notes 17–19 and accompanying text.

106. 573 P.2d 443, 455 (Cal. 1978); *see also* Soule v. General Motors Corp., 882 P.2d 298, 311 n.8 (Cal. 1994) (af-

firming the *Barker* burden-shifting rule).

107. Henderson & Twerski,, *supra* note 2, at 898–99 & nn. 131–32.

ty of states, the plaintiff bears the burden of proving that the product was defectively designed. By identifying the reasons why most jurisdictions could defensibly reject the *Barker* burden-shifting rule, we can better understand the evidentiary rationale for strict liability and its limitations.

The impact of the *Barker* burden-shifting rule has been well described by Professor Gary Schwartz:

> Prior to *Barker*, lawyers knew that proving a design defect was an expensive and uncertain endeavor. As a result, the victim with an injury "priced" at less than $25,000 [as of 1979] often encountered difficulties in finding a high-quality lawyer to take his case, even when the facts on the liability issue were reasonably good. It has been suggested that the implicit purpose of the *Barker* burden-of-proof rule is to enable competent lawyers to "small budget" such a case and thereby induce them to provide representation. Alternatively, the reduction in the burden of proof can be seen as an attempt to relieve the victim of the need to retain a lawyer who is already a products specialist.[108]

These observations explain how burden-shifting can better enable plaintiffs to enforce the duty of reasonable care, the animating ideal of the evidentiary rationale for strict liability.[109] A plaintiff's lawyer hired on a contingency-fee basis receives payment for her services only if the plaintiff receives compensation from the defendant, whether by settlement or judgment. The fee arrangement entitles the lawyer to a percentage of the plaintiff's compensation, typically ranging from 33 to 50 percent. The attorney's expected gross fee accordingly depends on the expected value of the lawsuit, or its "price" as Schwartz puts it, an amount equaling the compensable damages discounted by the probability the plaintiff will prevail.[110] The attorney's expected net proceeds or profit for taking the case equals the price of the case minus the attorney's cost of providing the representation. Insofar as the attorney's cost of representation is reduced by the *Barker* burden-shifting rule, a lawyer can earn a sufficient profit from cases with a lower price. By enabling attorneys to "small budget" design cases, the *Barker* rule will induce lawyers to take cases they otherwise would forego. The increased number of suits, in turn, provides more complete enforcement of the tort duty across the range of product cases, thereby

---

108. Gary T. Schwartz, *Foreword: Understanding Products Liability*, 67 Cal. L. Rev. 435, 464–65 (1979) (citations omitted).

109. *See* Chapter 1, section II (describing the evidentiary rationale for strict liability).

110. The concept of expected value is described in Chapter 2, footnote 14.

attaining the objective of the evidentiary rationale for strict liability.

Whether the *Barker* rule can be justified in this way depends on the circumstances in which burden-shifting is likely to reduce significantly the costs incurred by plaintiff attorneys, enabling them to "small budget" design cases. Realities of the litigation process strongly suggest that litigation costs will not be reduced in the appropriate set of cases.

Under the *Barker* rule, the mere fact of injury is not sufficient for the plaintiff to get to the jury. A party bearing the burden of proof can receive a directed verdict in its favor, so a manufacturer can satisfy its burden of proof and keep the case from the jury. In effect, the *Barker* burden-shifting rule operates as a rebuttable presumption.[111] The fact of injury creates a presumption of defective design that the manufacturer can rebut by presenting sufficient risk-utility evidence.

The presumption is unlikely to alter the plaintiff's trial strategy, again for reasons nicely articulated by Schwartz:

> [M]y discussions with plaintiffs' attorneys make clear that in a typical case, a plaintiff who has satisfactory facts will choose to ignore this aspect of *Barker*. *Barker* allows the plaintiff, having shown that the product's design caused his injury, to close his case and wait for the manufacturer to explain to the jury why that design is sensible after all; once the manufacturer has presented its pro-product evidence, the plaintiff can then bring forward his own evidence in an effort to counter the defense's presentation. Yet it would entail very poor trial strategy for a plaintiff to rely on this sequence, since it puts him on the defensive by allowing the manufacturer to get to the jury first with its explanation of the product's design, and why that design is a good one. If his facts are good, the plaintiff has a clear tactical interest in getting the jury to consider *his* version of the design issue first, before the manufacturer has a chance to tell its side of the story. Wishing to convey to the jury the strength of his case, the plaintiff will want to come out "with all guns blazing," presenting his strongest evidence as to the impropriety of the product's design.[112]

Since plaintiffs who have strong evidence are unlikely to rely on the *Barker* rule, burden-shifting in these cases will not signifi-

---

111. Schwartz, *supra* note 108, at 467 (concluding that "both the court's articulation of its rule and the court's reference to section 605 of the Evidence Code verify that the rule does amount to a presumption") (citations omitted).

112. *Id.* at 469.

cantly decrease litigation costs for attorneys or reduce the price at which the attorney is willing to take the case.[113] The *Barker* rule is unlikely to increase the number of claims based on strong evidence.

The evidentiary rationale for strict liability is only persuasive when the rule of strict liability enables plaintiffs with meritorious claims to overcome the evidentiary difficulties they would otherwise face in establishing negligence liability. An exploding soda bottle often is the result of negligent bottling procedures, but adequate proof of negligence is beyond the capabilities of virtually all plaintiffs, those with meritorious claims and those without. This explains why the evidentiary rationale for strict liability applies to construction or manufacturing defects, and also why its appeal diminishes considerably when those who benefit from strict liability are mostly plaintiffs with weak cases. These plaintiffs could not establish negligence liability even if they had good access to evidence, and so any evidentiary difficulties faced by this group does not persuasively justify the rule of strict liability.

Burden-shifting is likely to benefit only those plaintiffs with weak cases, and so the widespread rejection of the *Barker* burden-shifting rule is consistent the evidentiary rationale for strict liability. These cases further illustrate that *the rationale for reducing the plaintiff's evidentiary burden by adopting a rule of strict liability applies only when the evidence otherwise sufficiently shows that the product was defective.*[114]

V. Prescription Drugs and Medical Devices

In evaluating allegedly defective prescription drugs or medical devices, courts consider comment *k* of the *Restatement (Second)* rule of strict products liability, which exempts "unavoidably unsafe" products from strict liability as long as they are properly prepared and accompanied by an adequate warning.[115] Most courts have concluded that all pharmaceutical products are "unavoidably unsafe" and governed by comment *k*. Consequently, courts "have

113. *Cf.* Richard J. Heafey & Don M. Kennedy, *Product Liability: Winning Strategies and Techniques* § 4.04, at 4–9 (1994) (describing the manufacturer's failure to adopt a reasonable alternative design as "the heart of a plaintiff's case"). Note also that the *Barker* rule is unlikely to affect the defendant's trial strategy. "In fact, defense attorneys vigorously attempt to prove that a challenged design is not defective regardless of how the burdens of proof are allocated

by the court." Birnbaum, *supra* note 59, at 607.

114. *See* Chapter 5, section I (identifying this principle in the malfunction doctrine).

115. Restatement (Second) § 402A cmt. k. The complete text of comment *k* is provided in Chapter 5, section II, which discusses the application of this rule to construction or manufacturing defects.

traditionally refused to review the reasonableness of the designs of prescription drugs and medical devices."[116]

Initially, most courts "embraced the rule of comment *k* without detailed analysis of its language."[117] At the time, the concept of defect was not well understood, with most believing that it encompassed only those flaws that caused the product to malfunction.[118] For this simple conception of defect, comment *k* has evident appeal. As we found earlier, the rule of strict liability for construction or manufacturing defects has the potential to disrupt the supply of some products essential to public health or safety, like blood products, vaccines and other pharmaceutical products, so that the promotion of safety requires the limitation of strict liability provided by comment *k*.[119] With this conception of defect in mind, the courts understandably adopted comment *k* without detailed analysis.

After adopting comment *k* for all pharmaceutical products, the courts were then increasingly confronted by cases involving a different type of defect. Rather than alleging a defect based on product malfunction, the plaintiffs in these cases alleged defects involving the design of prescription drugs that caused injurious side-effects. These drugs performed according to their design specifications, were properly prepared, and were accompanied by an adequate warning as required by comment *k*. The plaintiffs, however, alleged that the defective design of the drugs meant that they were not "unavoidably unsafe," making comment *k* inapplicable by its express terms.

These allegations require a more careful analysis of comment *k*. To prove that the drug was defectively designed, a plaintiff ordinarily must show that there is a reasonable alternative design for the product that would have reduced risk. The proof of defect shows that risk was avoidable, establishing that the product was not "unavoidably unsafe." The exemption from liability afforded by comment *k* turns out to be no different than the exemption afforded by the requirement of defect—an "unavoidably unsafe" product must not be capable of being reasonably redesigned and is not subject to liability for that reason alone. In these cases, comment *k* does not expressly provide for an independent limitation of liability justifying the special treatment of pharmaceutical products.

---

116. Restatement (Third) § 6 cmt f Rptrs' Note.

117. Brown v. Superior Court, 751 P.2d 470, 476 (Cal. 1988).

118. *See* Chapter 4.

119. *See* Chapter 5, section II.

Despite the difficulties posed by the "unavoidably unsafe" language, a few courts decided to exempt pharmaceutical products from any liability for defective product design, reasoning that "the public interest in the development, availability, and reasonable price of drugs" makes it appropriate to limit liability to "the test stated in comment *k*."[120] This approach leaves the issue of design to the oversight of the Food and Drug Administration (FDA), the regulatory agency responsible for ensuring the safety and efficacy of drugs and medical devices.

Other courts opted for a different approach:

> The majority of jurisdictions that have adopted comment *k* apply it on a case-by-case basis, believing that societal interests in ensuring the marketing and development of prescription drugs will be adequately served without the need to resort to a rule of blanket immunity. A few courts have not specifically adopted comment *k* and have instead either fashioned their own rules or treated prescription drugs in the same manner as other products.[121]

The majority approach treats comment *k* as an affirmative defense, enabling the manufacturer to avoid liability by proving that the pharmaceutical product cannot be reasonably redesigned and is, therefore, "unavoidably unsafe." The plaintiff bears the initial burden of proving the design defect.

The *Restatement (Third)*, by contrast, has a special rule for drugs and medical devices requiring a prescription, one that "imposes a more rigorous test for defect" than does the liability rule governing the defective design of other products:

> A prescription drug or medical device is not reasonably safe due to defective design if the foreseeable risks of harm posed by the drug or medical device are sufficiently great in relation to its foreseeable therapeutic benefits that reasonable health-care providers, knowing of such foreseeable risks and therapeutic benefits, would not prescribe the drug or medical device for any class of patients.[122]

This liability rule has become a "lightening rod for criticism."[123] In a seminal case, the Nebraska Supreme Court rejected the rule for numerous reasons, the primary one being "that there is no support in the case law for application of a reasonable physician

---

120. *Brown*, 751 P.2d at 477.

121. Freeman v. Hoffman–La Roche, Inc., 618 N.W.2d 827, 836 (Neb. 2000) (citations omitted).

122. Restatement (Third) § 6(c).

123. James A. Henderson, Jr. & Aaron D. Twerski, *Drug Designs Are Different*, 111 Yale L.J. 151, 180 (2001).

standard in which strict liability for a design defect will apply only when a product is nòt useful for any class of persons."[124] The court decided to follow the majority approach and apply comment *k* on a case-by-case basis.

Even the Reporters of the *Restatement (Third)* have acknowledged that this rule does not restate the law:

> Most observers are in general agreement that the guidelines set forth a half-century ago in section 402A, comment *k* of the *Restatement (Second)* are unintelligible and that the cases seeking to interpret that section are confusing. In connection with [the liability rule of the *Restatement (Third)* governing defectively designed prescription drugs and medical devices], we plead guilty to the charge that we did not restate existing case law. One could hardly be expected to restate gibberish. Instead, we opted for a fresh look at the question of design liability for prescription products and utilized the case law to illuminate the underlying issues in this difficult area. Some cases did get it right, and we drew on them for support.[125]

The "fresh look" adopted by the *Restatement (Third)* explains why this liability rule has been a lightening rod for criticism, although it does not follow that the rule is wrong. That conclusion must be supported by analysis. Does the reasonable physician standard have "no support in the case law" as the Nebraska Supreme Court and other critics have claimed?

The *Restatement (Third)* liability rule applies only to drugs and medical devices that must be prescribed by a licensed health-care provider. The special role of the health-care provider explains the distinctive features of the liability rule.

A physician must select the drug or medical device that is in the best interests of the patient. A physician who prescribes treatment that is not in the patient's best interests is subject to malpractice liability for any injuries proximately caused by the treatment. Having decided upon the appropriate prescription drug or medical device, the physician must then tell the patient of the risks and therapeutic benefits so that the patient can give informed consent to the treatment. The failure to obtain the patient's informed consent is another source of malpractice liability for the physician.

Since the physician makes the initial risk-utility decision for prescription drugs and medical devices, and must then provide the

---

124. *Freeman*, 618 N.W.2d at 839.

125. Henderson & Twerski, *supra* note 123, at 180 (citations omitted).

reasons for that decision to the patient, these products are governed by the *learned intermediary rule*. This rule gives the manufacturer a duty to disclose the risks and therapeutic benefits of the product to the medical community, thereby enabling the physician "to make an individualized medical judgment, based on the patient's particular needs and susceptibilities, as to whether the patient should use the product."[126] An adequate warning to the medical community—the learned intermediary—fulfills the manufacturer's disclosure obligations, since the physician is responsible for conveying the information to the patient. If the manufacturer did not adequately instruct or warn the medical community, a patient who suffers injury as a result of the inadequate or defective warning can sue the manufacturer for breaching the duty to warn.[127]

Once these various rules are recognized, it becomes apparent why the *Restatement (Third)* liability rule asks whether the drug or medical device would be prescribed by "reasonable health-care providers" who were knowledgeable of the product's "foreseeable risks and therapeutic benefits." The learned intermediary rule ensures that the medical community has the requisite risk-utility knowledge, and if reasonable health-care providers having such knowledge would not prescribe the drug or medical device "to any class of patients," then the product is not in the best interests of anyone—the risks exceed the utility for any possible category of users, making the product defective in design.

Although the liability rule is defined in terms of the decision making of reasonable health-care providers, consumer expectations are still relevant. A useful analogy is provided by industrial equipment. Employers purchase and select these products for use by employees. Nevertheless, the employees who merely use these products still have safety expectations, making it possible to evaluate industrial products with consumer expectations. The same is true of prescription drugs and medical devices. Like the employer, the physician selects the product and makes the initial risk-utility decision, but the patient or user still has safety expectations as revealed by her informed consent to the treatment. By focusing on

126. Annot., 57 A.L.R.5th 1 (1998).

127. Sellers other than the manufacturer are liable only if they fail to exercise reasonable care in warning about the risks. Restatement (Third) § 6(e)(2). In this respect, the *Restatement (Third)* conforms to the limitation on strict liability provided by comment *k*. As will be discussed in Chapter 11, the rule of strict products liability is one of true strict liability for retailers and other nonmanufacturing distributors. Since comment *k* expressly provides only for an exemption from strict liability and not negligence liability, it permits the rule of negligence liability adopted by the *Restatement (Third)* for this class of product sellers.

the decision making of reasonable health-care providers, the *Restatement (Third)* liability rule does not depart from consumer expectations.[128]

According to the critics, the *Restatement (Third)* liability rule is too narrowly defined in terms of the product's ability to pass the risk-utility test for "any class of patients." A prescription drug can be beneficial for a small class of users and unreasonably dangerous for a large class of others. Under the *Restatement (Third)*, the drug would not be defectively designed. And since a drug or medical device will almost always be beneficial for at least some patients, the *Restatement (Third)* rule may have the practical effect of providing manufacturers with virtual immunity for design defects. As one court concluded, this rule "would change basic principles applicable to product liability suits. Such a fundamental shift should come from the legislature and not this court."[129]

This aspect of the *Restatement (Third)* rule is usefully illustrated by thalidomide, a drug that has caused a large number of serious birth defects and motivated the adoption of strict products liability in Europe.[130] The drug is not safe for use by pregnant women, but has significant health benefits for lepers. The drug, in other words, is unreasonably dangerous for a large class of users and beneficial for only a much smaller group. Since reasonable health-care providers would prescribe the drug to treat a complication of leprosy, the drug is not defectively designed. By limiting liability on this basis, the *Restatement (Third)* liability rule helps to make the drug available to the patients who would benefit from it, as a finding of defective design (defined by reference to women and lepers) would force the manufacturer to stop selling the drug to anyone, including lepers.[131] To protect against birth defects, the manufacturer must warn women about the risk.

128. *Cf. Brown*, 751 P.2d at 477 (stating that a "patient's expectations regarding the effects of a [prescription] drug are those related to him by his physician, to whom the manufacturer directs the warnings regarding the drug's properties"). *But see* Mele v. Howmedica, Inc., 808 N.E.2d 1026, 1037 (Ill. App. Ct. 2004) (rejecting the *Restatement (Third)* provision on defectively designed medical devices in part because it "completely eliminates appraisal of the consumer's expectations from determination of whether a medical device is unreasonably dangerous").

129. *Mele*, 808 N.E.2d at 1039.

130. This example comes from Michael D. Green, *Prescription Drugs, Alternative Designs, and the Restatement (Third): Preliminary Reflections*, 30 Seton Hall L. Rev. 207, 228 (1999). For a good discussion of the European adoption of strict products liability, see Jane Stapleton, Product Liability 37–65 (1994).

131. Once the drug design is found to be defective, a manufacturer that continues selling the known defective drug is subject to punitive damages. *See* Chapter 9, section III.

The *Restatement (Third)* liability rule therefore allows the manufacturer to limit the appropriate class of users with the product warning, something it cannot ordinarily do for other products. As we will find, the liability rule governing design defects does not assume that consumers will always following warnings, and so manufacturers may not be able to use warnings to limit their safety obligations regarding product design.[132] Unlike ordinary products, warnings for prescription drugs and medical devices depend upon the health-care provider, who has the duty to follow the warning and prescribe the product only to the appropriate class of patients. In designing these drugs or medical devices, the manufacturer can reasonably rely upon the duty running between the physician and patient. Insofar as this duty makes the physician responsible for ensuring that the warning will be followed, the liability rule for defective design can be defensibly limited in this respect.

For these reasons, the *Restatement (Third)* liability rule is more "rigorous" or demanding than the liability rule governing the defective design of other products. The distinctive features of the *Restatement (Third)* liability rule are based upon the tort duty running between health-care providers and patients and do not depart from basic tort principles.

Since the *Restatement (Third)* liability rule does not alter the relevant substantive principles, it does not provide blanket immunity for drug manufacturers. Consider the prescription drug Accutane, which critics claim is immune from design defect liability under the *Restatement (Third)*.[133] Accutane is used for the treatment of chronic acne. The warning states that Accutane can cause birth defects and should not be used by pregnant women. Most of the female users of the drug are of child-bearing age, however, and despite warnings to the contrary, pregnant women have taken Accutane. The manufacturer's epidemiological data "showed that from 1989 to 2000 there were 958 identified Accutane-exposed pregnancies. Of these, 834 were terminated.... There were 111 live births. Sixty of these children were examined or their records reviewed. Of these, 13 percent showed 'major malformations.'"[134] These injuries would seem to be irrelevant to the issue of defective design under the *Restatement (Third)*, since reasonable health-care providers would prescribe Accutane to male users and females who are not pregnant. If so, the *Restatement (Third)* apparently provides

---

132. *See* Chapter 7, section V.

133. George W. Conk, *The True Test: Alternative Safer Designs for Drugs and Medical Devices in a Patent–* *Constrained World*, 49 UCLA L. Rev. 737, 761–71 (2002).

134. *Id.* at 766–67 (citations omitted).

a practical immunity for design-defect liability as the critics have concluded. This conclusion, though, is quite contestable. The *Restatement (Third)* liability rule can support the imposition of liability for the injuries caused by Accutane-exposed pregnancies.

The *Restatement (Third)* liability rule assumes that there will be full compliance with warnings as mandated by the tort duty running between the physician and patient. In prescribing Accutane to a woman of child-bearing age, the physician must warn the patient not to become pregnant while using the drug. The physician usually cannot ensure that the patient will follow these instructions, nor must the physician take a paternalistic position on whether the patient will do so. A physician, therefore, can fulfill her tort obligations to an *individual* female patient by prescribing Accutane, but it is a separate question whether reasonable health-care providers would prescribe Accutane to the *class* of women who are of child-bearing age. With respect to this class of patients, reasonable health-care providers would consider the number of birth abnormalities caused by the drug. Having accounted for these injuries, reasonable health-care providers could conclude that Accutane should not be prescribed to women. The issue is one of fact, depending upon the other regulations governing the use of the drug.[135] Of course, reasonable health-care providers would still prescribe Accutane to men, and so the drug is not defectively designed for this simple reason. Nevertheless, the manufacturer could be liable for the injuries caused by Accutane-exposed pregnancies. If it is not reasonable to prescribe the drug to the class of women of child-bearing age, then the manufacturer should have warned that the drug is not designed for use by this group. Physicians would then be responsible for ensuring that the drug is never prescribed to this class of patients. The tort duty running between the physician and patient would eliminate the risk of Accutane causing birth abnormalities. The manufacturer did not provide such a warning, however, potentially exposing it to liability for the injuries caused by the inadequate warning.

The *Restatement (Third)* liability rule also does not necessarily foreclose a claim of defective design. In order to prove that Accutane is defectively designed, the plaintiff must show that there is a reasonable alternative design of the drug—one providing the same

---

135. The factual issue involves the number of Accutane-exposed pregnancies within the relevant group, a type of injury that the FDA has sought to reduce by regulation. Under the most recent regulations, "Female patients of childbearing age must take two pregnancy tests and use two forms of birth control to get the drug. And doctors and pharmacists must confirm that the requirements have been met." Gardiner Harris, *F.D.A. Imposes Tougher Rules for Acne Drug*, N.Y. Times, Aug. 13, 2005, at A1.

therapeutic benefits at lower risk. The manufacturer of Accutane has come up with a "micronized formulation" of the drug that makes it possible to achieve the same therapeutic benefits at much lower dosages. The reduced dosage makes it less likely that the drug will cause various side-effects. If presented with a choice between Accutane as marketed and the micronized formulation of the drug, reasonable health-care providers would choose the new, micronized formulation. No one would prescribe the existing formulation of Accutane to any class of patients, making it defective in design. This conclusion assumes that health-care providers had a choice between the two formulations of Accutane, when in fact physicians were only offered the single formulation that was available on the market. Design-defect liability, however, does not require that the reasonable alternative design was actually available to the ordinary consumer at the time of sale, nor does the *Restatement (Third)* liability rule expressly require as much. As long as the reasonable alternative design was feasibly available at the time of sale, it provides a basis for liability.[136]

The availability of drugs and medical devices depends upon the FDA regulatory process. The FDA must approve prescription drugs

---

136. The *Restatement (Third)* liability rule expressly states that it differs from the rule of design-defect liability governing other products, leading commentators to assume that defective drug design cannot be proven by reference to a reasonable alternative design. E.g., George W. Conk, *Is There a Design Defect in the* Restatement (Third) *of Torts: Products Liability*, 109 Yale L.J. 1087 (2000). As discussed in the text, the *Restatement (Third)* liability rule does importantly differ from the ordinary liability rule regarding defective design, although the reasons for these more demanding differences have nothing to do with the issue of whether defect can be proven by a reasonable alternative design. The *Restatement (Third)* never expressly rules out proof of defect with a reasonable alternative design. Moreover, there is no compelling reason for concluding that this ambiguity in the *Restatement (Third)* precludes such proof. Unless the defect is established either explicitly or implicitly by reference to a reasonable alternative design, the defect depends upon categorical liability. *See supra* section III. Because the courts have almost uniformly resisted categorical liability, the

Restatement (Third) does not include categorical liability "in the black letter." *Restatement (Third)* § 2 cmt e Rptrs' Note. Lacking any "black letter" support, there is no reason to assume that categorical liability governs prescription drugs and medical devices.

Whether the manufacturer of Accutane should be liable for not selling the micronized formulation is a separate question, one importantly depending upon the issue of whether the manufacturer's subsequent remedial improvements to a product can be relied upon by the plaintiff to prove defective design. Under the Federal Rules of Evidence, this proof of defect is not admissible. Fed. R. Evid. 407. *See generally* 2 Madden & Owen on Products Liability § 27:5 (discussing whether the manufacturer's subsequent change in design will be admissible proof). Any rationale for finding this proof to be inadmissible should account for the way in which patents alter the manufacturer's incentives regarding design changes, an issue not ordinarily relevant for other products. *Cf.* Conk, *supra* note 133, at 756–64 (discussing how the monopoly afforded by drug patents affects manufacturer design incentives).

and medical devices before they can be put on the market. In order to prove that the micronized formulation of Accutane could have feasibly been available at the time of sale, the plaintiff needs to show that it would have received FDA approval by this point in time. To do so, the plaintiff can prove that the micronized formulation of Accutane was technologically feasible at the time when the original Accutane formulation was first submitted to the FDA for approval. The original formulation received FDA approval, and the plaintiff's proof shows that the micronized formulation achieves the same therapeutic benefits at lower dosages. On the basis of these facts, a court could reasonably conclude that the micronized formulation would have received FDA approval within the same time frame as the original formulation, making it feasibly available at the time of sale.

As the issues surrounding Accutane illustrate, the manufacturers of prescription drugs or medical devices can incur liability for defective design in the precise set of circumstances in which liability is appropriate. The liability rule obligates manufacturers to submit the safest feasible design to the FDA for approval, something the FDA is not empowered to do.[137]

Like the majority rule that evaluates the alleged defectiveness of prescription drugs and medical devices on a case-by-case basis, the *Restatement (Third)* liability rule can promote the public interest in the development and availability of safe drugs and medical devices. The two rules do not provide these products with a blanket exemption from tort liability under comment *k*, giving manufacturers an incentive to provide reasonably safe drugs and medical devices in order to avoid liability for defective design.

Unlike the majority rule, the *Restatement (Third)* rule clearly identifies the relevant class of patients for purposes of evaluating the design. This aspect of the *Restatement (Third)* rule is defensibly based upon the tort duty running between the health-care provider and patient. In this respect, the majority rule is ambiguous, although it presumably should also account for the special nature of the doctor-patient relationship. The physician is responsible for ensuring that the drug or medical device is appropriately pre-

---

137. "[T]he FDA's regulatory authority for drugs is reactive, not proactive. The FDA responds to a New Drug Application submitted by a pharmaceutical manufacturer that has identified and tested a new drug to determine whether the drug is effective and safe. The FDA does not regulate the design of a drug and whether it might be formulated differently to improve the therapeutic benefit-to-risk ratio ...." Green, *supra* note 130, at 221 (citations omitted). The FDA review of medical devices is even less demanding. *See* Michael D. Green & William B. Schultz, *Tort Law Deference to FDA Regulation of Medical Devices*, 88 Geo. L.J. 2119, 2134–35 (2000).

scribed, making it reasonable for the manufacturer to design these products on this basis.

In the vast majority of cases, the drug or medical device will be appropriate for at least one class of patients, and so liability for defective design should be rare under both the majority rule and the *Restatement (Third)* rule. But to make the proper prescription, the physician must have received the requisite risk-utility information from the manufacturer. "With drugs, therefore, the liability game is with the warnings candle, not with design."[138]

138. Green, *supra* note 130, at 208–09.

Chapter 7

WARNING DEFECTS

As compared to claims for defective design, plaintiffs usually face an easier task in proving that the product defect involves an inadequate warning. "[I]t is easier for the jury to understand the need for better directions and warnings than to understand the deficiencies of some complex design, particularly when the testimony is by experts who know more about technical matters than explaining things to laymen."[1] The jury can readily understand that better warnings benefit consumers by informing them of product risks, a benefit made salient by the plaintiff's allegation that a better warning would have prevented her injury. The jury also does not have to wrestle with hard issues concerning the impact of warnings on production costs. A little more ink and paper is a negligible concern. Due to the apparent simplicity of the issues, plaintiffs in many jurisdictions do not have difficulty proving warning defects.

This may explain why critics of the tort system often use product warnings as exemplars of a malfunctioning tort system. A manufacturer of Halloween costumes has warned that its superhero costume does not enable the user to fly. Web sites provide descriptions of wacky product warnings. Something must be awry. Product sellers presumably devise warnings in the manner required by the relevant liability rules. Wacky warnings are symptomatic of some defect in the jurisprudence of product warnings.

A serious jurisprudential problem has been identified by Professors James Henderson, Jr., and Aaron Twerski:

> [N]egligence doctrine in the context of failure-to-warn litigation is little more than an empty shell. In most cases, the elements of the warnings cause of action require plaintiffs to do little more than mouth empty phrases. From the plaintiff's perspective, there is undoubtedly a certain attractiveness to a tort without a meaningful standard of care or any serious requirement of proving causation. From a broader social perspective, however, such a tort is too lawless to be fair or useful.[2]

1. Dix W. Noel, *Products Defective Because of Inadequate Directions or* Warnings, 23 Southwestern L.J. 133, 133–34 (1969).

2. James A. Henderson, Jr. & Aaron

Strong words indeed, ones that miss the mark according to others who find negligence doctrine to be inapposite for warning claims.[3] Liability for defective product warnings is predicated upon strict products liability, a distinct cause of action designed to free plaintiffs from the onerous evidentiary burdens of negligence liability. On this view, negligence doctrine should be an "empty shell" in warning cases.

The ongoing debate about the appropriate roles of negligence and strict liability, of the risk-utility test and consumer expectations, appears once again. In this respect, warning defects are no different than other defects. And like the other types of defects, the doctrinal issues in warning cases can be clarified by the underlying concepts.

I. The Duty to Warn

As we found earlier, a tort duty is most defensible when the ordinary consumer would incur high information costs in order to make the associated safety decision.[4] According to this conception of duty, the ordinary consumer strives to make product decisions that maximize her well-being or utility. A consumer maximizes utility by purchasing products that provide the greatest net benefit—the difference between the various benefits and costs of the product for the consumer. Due to information costs, the consumer must estimate these benefits and costs on the basis of limited information. When the ordinary consumer underestimates or fails to evaluate product risk and its associated cost, the resultant frustration of consumer expectations justifies a tort duty obligating product sellers to provide products that are properly manufactured and designed. The question, then, is whether the same informational problem that justifies the tort duties regarding construction and design defects also justifies the duty to warn.

Consider how a consumer's knowledge of risk affects her assessment of product benefits. Suppose that any benefit the consumer would get from a certain kind of use will be outweighed by the risk of injury created by such use. A consumer who is fully informed of the risk would not plan to use the product in this manner and would not attach any benefit to such product use. Consumers who do not appreciate the risk, however, may plan to

D. Twerski, *Doctrinal Collapse in Products Liability: The Empty Shell of Failure to Warn*, 65 NYU L. Rev. 265, 326 (1990).

3. *E.g.*, Mark McLaughlin Hager, *Don't Say I Didn't Warn You (Even Though I Didn't): Why the Pro–Defendant Consensus on Warning Law is Wrong*, 61 Tenn. L. Rev. 1125 (1994).

4. *See* Chapter 2, section II.B.

use the product in this way. These consumers expect to get a benefit from an undesirable product use, and this benefit might induce some consumers to purchase the product. Consequently, sellers have an incentive not to disclose information concerning undesirable product uses.

For example, an apartment dweller who enjoys barbecued foods may want to purchase an outdoor gas grill even though she cannot use the grill outdoors. There are substantial inconveniences created by barbecuing indoors (like smoke), but suppose that some individuals nevertheless would like to buy the grill. These individuals may not know that if the grill leaks gas in a confined area (an apartment), there are significant risks of explosion and poisoning. Apartment dwellers who know about these risks would not buy the grill, but those who are unaware of the risks may purchase the product. By voluntarily disclosing the risks, the seller would reduce sales and profits, giving it an incentive to keep quiet about the inappropriateness of grilling indoors.

The consumer's ability to estimate product costs also depends upon information about product risk. Consumers benefit from precautions that enable them to reduce the risk of product-caused injury in a cost-effective manner. Consumers who are not aware of a risk will not know of the need to take a precaution, however. These consumers would prefer to learn about the precaution, but if using the product in a safe manner is costly for the consumer, the product seller would not want to disclose this information. By making consumers aware of the desirable but costly precaution, the disclosure alerts some consumers to a product cost of which they would not otherwise be aware. The disclosure makes the product appear to be less desirable to these consumers, giving the seller an incentive to withhold the information.[5]

---

5. The concept is illustrated by a study involving a warning that informed users of a caustic drain opener about the need to wear rubber gloves in order to reduce by an average of .000061 the risk of hand burns severe enough to require medical treatment. The study found that 82 percent of the respondents would wear rubber gloves to reduce the risk of serious burn, even though the disutility, or cost, to users of wearing the gloves was $.17 per bottle. *See* W. Kip Viscusi, *Toward a Proper Role for Hazard Warnings in Products Liability Cases*, 13 J. Prod. Liab. 139, 153–56 (1991). The seller would not voluntarily disclose this information in a warning. Consider a consumer who is unaware of the risk of suffering hand burns severe enough to require medical treatment. For this consumer, disclosure of the risk would increase her estimate of the cost of the product by $.17 per bottle, and thereby reduce by $.17 her estimate of the product's net benefit. Disclosure of the risk would reduce consumer demand and likely decrease seller profits, giving the seller an incentive not to disclose. (If consumer demand were not reduced by this increase in cost, the seller would find it more profitable to raise the price of the product by $.17 per bottle and not disclose the risk.)

Product sellers may also have an incentive not to disclose information about unavoidable or residual product risks. Products that are designed, manufactured and used properly can still present a risk of injury to the consumer, like the side-effects caused by some drugs. These residual risks determine the accident costs the consumer can expect to incur by using the product.[6] Consumers who underestimate or do not evaluate the risk will underestimate the associated accident cost. By voluntarily disclosing information about residual product risks, the seller can alert these consumers to a cost of which they had not been aware. Once again, the seller does not want to diminish the appeal of its product for consumers, giving it an incentive to withhold the information.

To address these market failures, tort law gives product sellers a duty to provide adequate or nondefective warnings. The same informational problem that justifies the seller's duty to provide products free of defects in construction, manufacture and design also justifies the seller's duty to provide an adequate product warning.

II. The Characteristics of an Adequate Warning

An adequate warning depends upon the simple idea that information is good, which in turn has made warning cases deceptively simple. "[I]n failure-to-warn cases the common assumption is that warnings can be improved upon but can never be made worse; that is, the issue at stake is always whether the defendant ought to have supplied consumers with more, and by definition better, information about product risks."[7] More information is always better when the cost of warnings largely consists of ink and paper. This cost "is usually so minimal ... that the balance must always be struck in favor of the obligation to warn."[8] This approach makes it easy to identify the characteristics of an adequate warning: More is always better.

But if the liability rule assumes that more information is always better, then a product seller presumably should warn consumers that its Superman costume will not enable them to fly. Or consider aluminum extension ladders, which have had up to 44

---

6. *See* Chapter 3, section I (showing how residual risks affect the full price of the product and the consumer decision regarding insurance).

7. Henderson & Twerski, *supra* note 2, at 269–70.

8. Ross Lab. v. Thies, 725 P.2d 1076, 1079 (Alaska 1986); *see also, e.g.,* Anderson v. Hedstrom Corp., 76 F.Supp.2d 422, 440 (S.D.N.Y. 1999) (applying New York law) (holding that the "minimal" cost of product warnings "usually weighs in favor of an obligation to warn").

different warnings and directions.[9] These warnings all provide more information. If there is anything wacky about these warnings, the problem must reside in the idea that more information is always better.

Information costs explain why more information is not necessarily better. Every consumer incurs a cost by reading and remembering the various disclosures in a warning. Individuals will stop reading a warning if they find that the benefit of reading is not worth the effort. As the U.S. Supreme Court has recognized in a related context, a disclosure standard that requires an overabundance of information is not desirable, as it could lead sellers "simply to bury the [consumer] in an avalanche of trivial information—a result that is hardly conducive to informed decisionmaking."[10] Consider your own behavior. How often do you read warnings? When you don't read a warning, what is your reason for doing so?

As one federal appellate court explains:

> Extended warnings present several difficulties, first among them that, the more text must be squeezed onto the product, the smaller the type, and the less likely is the consumer to read or remember any of it. Only pithy and bold warnings can be effective. Long passages in capital letters are next to illegible, and long passages in lower case letters are treated as boilerplate.[11]

As implied by this passage, the characteristics of an adequate warning largely depend upon the information cost of processing and digesting information. All else being equal, more information is good. But to acquire new information, consumers must read and evaluate the warning. Too much information can be harmful by reducing the likelihood that consumers will read and comprehend the warning. According to two of the leading experts in risk assessment, "A major practical problem is ensuring that individuals read the warning label or acquire information in some other form, since there is no general assurance that individuals will do so."[12]

---

9. Steven Waldman, *Do Warning Labels Work?*, Newsweek, July 18, 1988, at 40.

10. TSC Indus., Inc. v. Northway, Inc., 426 U.S. 438, 448–49 (1976) (discussing the disclosure problem in the context of securities regulation).

11. Todd v. Societe BIC, S.A., 9 F.3d 1216, 1218–19 (7th Cir. 1993) (en banc) (applying Illinois law); *see also, e.g.,* Finn v. G.D. Searle & Co., 677 P.2d 1147, 1153 (Cal. 1984) (observing that if manufacturers were required to warn of "every ... possible risk," then the decision maker would be "inundate[d] ... indiscriminately with notice of any and every hint of danger, thereby inevitably diluting the force of any specific warning given").

12. Wesley A. Magat & W. Kip Viscusi, Informational Approaches to Regulation 8 (1992).

The characteristics of an adequate warning therefore can be determined by the following inquiry: What impact would the additional disclosure have upon the overall effectiveness of the product warning?

The effectiveness of a warning necessarily depends upon how well it performs on average. Consumers vary widely in terms of their knowledge, background, physical characteristics, and other traits that determine the kind of information an individual wants in a product warning. A warning cannot be tailored to satisfy each individual's needs, however, because the same warning is given to all product users. For example, even if a warning specified all information that could conceivably be relevant to some individual—"This Costume Will Not Enable You To Fly!"—the length of such a warning would render it unsatisfactory for most individuals. Due to the information cost that warnings create for each consumer, any given warning is unlikely to satisfy the needs of every product user. At best, a warning can perform better on average than alternative warnings, even though any given alternative might be beneficial for some individuals; that is, *an adequate warning satisfies the needs of the ordinary consumer.*

The ordinary consumer wants the warning to contain any disclosures that would significantly improve her risk-utility decisions. The ordinary consumer would not find it worthwhile to be warned about information she already has or can readily gain from product use. Such a warning does not improve the ordinary consumer's decision making but still creates an information cost for her—the time and effort to read the information in order to figure out that it is unhelpful.

Even if most consumers know a risk, the ordinary consumer may still prefer to be warned. Suppose that 60 percent of the consumers fully understand a risk and the remaining 40 percent do not adequately comprehend the risk. Before reading the product warning, any consumer does not know whether she is informed or uninformed about the risk in question. Each consumer finds that out only by reading the warning. The ordinary consumer therefore can be conceptualized as someone who knows there is a 60 percent chance that she fully understands the risk and a 40 percent chance that she does not. The ordinary consumer would want to be warned about the risk if the 40 percent chance of benefitting from the disclosure exceeds the cost of reading the disclosure. *An adequate warning can disclose risks that are known by the majority of consumers.*

The benefit an uninformed consumer expects to derive from a disclosure depends upon the likelihood of injury (the probability P) and the severity of harm (the loss L) that would be prevented by the warning. To use an extreme example, suppose the risk were virtually certain to kill the consumer, and that those who know of the risk can avoid it by proper product use, whereas those who are unaware of the risk will be killed by improper product use. Even if 99 percent of all consumers know of the risk, it would be disclosed in an adequate warning. The expected benefit of avoiding a 1 percent chance of dying clearly exceeds the information cost the ordinary consumer would incur by reading the disclosure, and so the ordinary consumer would prefer to be warned. In general, product risks are much smaller, such as a 1 in 10,000 risk of injury. As the frequency or severity of injury decreases, the expected benefit of disclosure (the reduction in risk PL) also goes down, making it less likely that the warning would be reasonably expected by the ordinary consumer.

As the expected benefit of disclosure decreases, there must be a larger proportion of uninformed consumers in order to justify the warning. To modify the prior example, suppose that 99 percent of all consumers know of a 1 in 10,000 risk of suffering moderate injury. The warning would now provide a vastly smaller benefit for the ordinary consumer, who faces a 1 percent chance of learning about how to avoid a 1 in 10,000 chance of injury. The expected benefit of disclosure, involving a discount factor of 1 in a million, is unlikely to make the warning worthwhile. *An adequate warning does not usually disclose ordinary product risks that are widely understood in the community.*

Indeed, a warning may not be required even if most consumers are unaware of the risk. For example, if only 40 percent of all consumers know about a risk that could cause trivial harm, the expected benefit of the warning is unlikely to exceed the cost of reading the warning. For the ordinary consumer, there is a 60 percent chance of deriving an insignificant benefit from the disclosure, an amount unlikely to justify the cost of warning. *An adequate warning does not disclose information about insignificant risks.*

The adequacy of a product warning also depends upon the method of disclosure, because the form of communication affects the likelihood that the ordinary consumer will benefit from the information. If, for example, the warning can be rewritten in a manner that will be more effective for more consumers without significantly increasing the ordinary consumer's cost of digesting the information, then the ordinary consumer would reasonably expect that the warning be rewritten. *The warning should be commonly understood without being overly long.* This does not mean that the warning must be written only in English. As long as someone who understands English is not significantly burdened by warnings written in another language, the warning may need to be provided in different languages. Such a warning would benefit a significant group of consumers who speak the foreign language without significantly burdening anyone else, and so the ordinary consumer would reasonably expect the warning to be written in this manner.

The design of the warning also affects the likelihood that it will improve the ability of the ordinary consumer to make safety decisions. Consider a poorly designed warning that has no apparent organization and tends to place the least significant risks at the beginning. The ordinary consumer cannot discern the organization of the information, so she will start reading the warning from the beginning. "Sequencing inevitably denotes relative importance and will have an impact on the weight a consumer attaches to the risk."[13] Since the first disclosures in this warning mostly describe the least significant risks, the ordinary consumer may decide that reading the entire warning is not worth the effort. "[A] hazard warning that is not in a prominent location on a product, or that ranks low in terms of the overall priority of the messages conveyed by the product label, is much less likely to be read than a warning that ranks high in this priority."[14] A poorly designed warning increases the likelihood that the ordinary consumer will not read the warning in its entirety, rendering the warning defective. *An adequate warning emphasizes risks in proportion to their significance.*

The conceptual characteristics of an adequate warning are broadly reflected in the liability rules. Proof of defect requires a showing that the warning inadequately disclosed a risk that was not obvious or otherwise widely known by consumers. The risk cannot be *remote*, but must instead be significant enough to affect materially the decision making of a sufficiently large group of uninformed consumers. What constitutes a sufficiently large group for this purpose depends upon the probability and severity of harm. All else being equal, an increase in either the probability or severity of harm reduces the size of the group that must benefit from the disclosure (compare the earlier example involving 1 percent of all consumers facing the certainty of death). A warning can be defec-

---

13. Henderson & Twerski, *supra* note 2, at 308 (citations omitted).

14. Magat & Viscusi, *supra* note 12, at 8.

tive for not disclosing any of these risks or because its format does not reasonably convey the requisite information.[15]

Although these requirements are widely accepted, their meaning is often unclear. For example, an adequate warning does not have to disclose obvious risks. "If anything is obvious about the obvious danger rule, it is that courts cannot agree on the definition of an 'obvious' risk."[16]

The meaning of an "obvious risk" can be clarified once it is conceptualized in terms of the consumer's informational problem. As Judge Guido Calabresi explains:

> [W]here the function of a warning is to assist the reader in making choices, the value of a warning can lie as much in making known the existence of alternatives as in communicating the fact that a particular choice is dangerous. It follows that the duty to warn is not necessarily obviated merely because a danger is clear. To be more concrete, a warning can convey at least two types of messages. One states that a particular place, object, or activity is dangerous. Another explains that people need not risk the danger posed by such a place, object, or activity in order to achieve the purpose for which they might have taken that risk. Thus, a highway sign that says "Danger—Steep Grade" says less than a sign that says "Steep Grade Ahead—Follow Suggested Detour to Avoid Dangerous Areas."[17]

As this passage shows, a risk is not obvious merely because the danger is apparent to the consumer. A risk is obvious only when the ordinary consumer adequately comprehends the probability of harm, severity of harm, and relevant precautionary alternatives. In these circumstances, the ordinary consumer can make a well-informed risk-utility decision, eliminating the need for the warning to supply the information. Without knowledge of all the risk-utility factors, a consumer who is only aware of the danger ("Steep Grade Ahead") may not be able to make the right safety decision ("Follow Suggested Detour to Avoid Dangerous Areas"), resulting in frustrated safety expectations requiring protection by tort law.

---

15. All of these requirements are expressed, explicitly and implicitly, in the Restatement (Third) § 2 cmts. i & k. *See also, e.g.,* Hildy Bowbeer et al., *Warning: Failure to Read this Article May Be Hazardous to Your Failure to Warn Defense,* 27 Wm. Mitchell L. Rev. 439 (2000).

16. Michael S. Jacobs, *Towards a Process–Based Approach to Failure-to-*

Warn Law, 71 N.C. L. Rev. 121, 134 (1992).

17. Liriano v. Hobart Corp., 170 F.3d 264, 270 (2d Cir. 1999) (Calabresi, J.) (paragraph structure omitted). The opinion contains a more extended, interesting discussion of obvious risks.

By evaluating warnings in this manner, the legal inquiry becomes more sensitive to the underlying issue common to all warning claims. The duty to warn is required because information costs prevent consumers from being well informed. A liability rule that does not acknowledges information costs predictably results in warnings with excessively high information costs, causing consumers to forego reading the warning. To avoid this self-defeating outcome, the legal inquiry must be sensitive to information costs.

III. Proof of Defect

Under the *Restatement (Third)*, the adequacy of a product warning is determined by the risk-utility test.[18] To establish defect, the plaintiff must prove that there is a reasonable alternative warning—one passing the risk-utility test. In evaluating the disutility or cost of the plaintiff's alternative warning, the finder of fact must consider information costs.[19] The disutility of disclosure must then be compared to the risk reduction or safety benefit that would be attained by the alternative warning.

The risk-utility test is the conceptually appropriate method for evaluating product warnings, but there is substantial concern that the courts cannot properly apply the test. According to the *Restatement (Third)*, the "defectiveness concept is more difficult to apply in the warnings context" than "for judging the safety of product designs."[20] Perhaps the jury or factfinder does not evaluate the evidence in the manner required by cost-benefit analysis, but that problem equally applies to the risk-utility test in design cases.[21] The distinctive feature of warning cases involves the intertwined or interrelated issues that can make application of the risk-utility test surprisingly complex.

Overly complex problems are difficult to adjudicate for reasons identified by Professor James Henderson, Jr.[22] "The characteristic of most legal problems that renders them adjudicable is the unique manner in which the various issues presented in a case are logically

---

18. Restatement (Third) § 2 cmt. n at 36 ("Regardless of the doctrinal label attached to a particular claim, design and warning claims rest on a risk-utility assessment.").

19. *Cf. id.* § 2 cmts. i-j (explaining requirements by reference to information costs).

20. *Id.* § 2 cmt. i at 29 (sentence structure omitted). For extended arguments that courts are unable to apply properly the risk-utility factors in warn-

ing cases, see Henderson & Twerski, *supra* note 2; Howard Latin, *Good Warnings, Bad Products, and Cognitive Limitations*, 41 UCLA L. Rev. 1193 (1994).

21. *See* Chapter 6, section II.C.

22. James A. Henderson, Jr., *Judicial Review of Manufacturers' Conscious Design Choices: The Limits of Adjudication*, 73 Colum. L. Rev. 1531, 1535 (1973).

related to each other." When "the parties are able to take up and consider each issue separately, in an orderly sequence," each litigant "will be able to isolate analytically any given issue in the case ... and to talk of a favorable decision in relation to that issue without simultaneously considering all of the others." Adjudication is poorly suited for resolving "polycentric" problems "in which each point for decision is related to all others," because as the litigant "moved from the first point of his argument to the second and then the third, he would find his arguments regarding the earlier points shifting beneath him."

The problem of polycentricity could plague warning claims due to the interrelationships among the disclosures in a warning. The information costs created by some disclosures can affect the consumer's willingness to read other disclosures. The prominence of some disclosures has the effect of deemphasizing others. The adequacy of a product warning depends on how all of its constituent parts work together, creating the potential for a polycentric problem in which "each point for decision is related to all others."

Consider the California model jury instruction for disclosures involving product use:

> A product is defective if the manufacturer of a product has a duty to warn of dangers, and fails to provide an adequate warning of that danger.

> A manufacturer has a duty to provide an adequate warning to the user on how to use the product if a reasonably foreseeable use of the product involves a substantial danger of which the manufacturer either is aware or should be aware, and that would not be readily recognized by the ordinary user.[23]

These instructions do little or nothing to address the problem of polycentricity. The instructions define the "adequacy" of the warning solely in terms of a particular risk involving a "substantial danger" that would not be "readily recognized" by the user. This risk is the one that injured the plaintiff; otherwise the absence of such a warning could not have caused the plaintiff's injury. By focusing the jury's attention on one salient risk, the instructions obscure or ignore the way in which that single risk disclosure affects the consumer's evaluation of other aspects of the warning. A particular disclosure, when considered in isolation, can seem beneficial. That same disclosure, when considered in terms of its impact on the effectiveness of the entire warning, can be pernicious. These important characteristics of the adequate product warning are not

---

23. The Civil Committee on California Jury Instructions, California Civil Jury Instructions (BAJI) 9.00.7 (July 2004).

highlighted by the jury instructions, making it hard for the jury to apply the risk-utility test in the appropriate manner. The *Restatement (Third)* understandably emphasizes the difficulty of applying the risk-utility test in warning cases.

In order for the jury to apply properly the risk-utility test, jury instructions must separate the interrelated issues posed by failure-to-warn claims, thereby enabling the jury to consider issues in the appropriate logical sequence. To see what this approach might entail, we need to consider the different types of warning claims—those involving the disclosure of unavoidable risks, the disclosure of instructions regarding product use, and the design or format of the warning.

Unavoidable Risks. A warning can be inadequate for not disclosing the residual or unavoidable risks that inhere in properly manufactured and designed products, such as the unavoidable side-effects caused by some drugs and vaccines. In these cases, the jury does not have to evaluate the claim with a full-blown risk-utility analysis. The inquiry can be broken down into a series of focused questions based upon a presumption that any disclosure already in the warning satisfies the risk-utility test. The presumption effectively makes product sellers responsible for each disclosure in the warning, while creating an important incentive for sellers not to overwarn.[24]

The plaintiff must first prove that the risk is not commonly known or otherwise obvious to the ordinary consumer. Assuming that this requirement is satisfied, the plaintiff must then prove that the risk would be material to the ordinary consumer. By presuming that each disclosure in the warning satisfies the risk-utility test, the materiality inquiry can first focus on the least significant risk in the warning. The presumption implies that the least significant risk is material, and so the plaintiff would establish materiality by proving that the requested disclosure involves a more significant risk. If the plaintiff is unable to provide such proof, then the requested disclosure must involve a risk less significant than any other risk in the warning. The plaintiff therefore must prove that the requested disclosure involves a material risk that would not undermine the effectiveness of the other, more important disclo-

---

24. In a market unregulated by tort law, sellers have an incentive to under-warn for the reasons discussed earlier in section I. Once tort law regulates the market transaction, the nature of the liability rule alters the seller's incentive to warn. If the liability rule is not sufficiently sensitive to information costs, the seller has an incentive to overwarn. Doing so protects it from tort liability for the failure to disclose while also reducing the overall effectiveness of the warning—and its impact on consumer evaluations of product cost—by making it less likely that consumers will seriously consider the warning.

sures already contained in the warning. Having done so, the plaintiff must finally prove that the ordinary consumer would read the disclosure. As the least significant risk, the disclosure is the one that would be read last by the ordinary consumer.

These requirements of the risk-utility test yield the following set of issues (framed as jury questions) that the factfinder must decide in order to evaluate the validity of the plaintiff's claim:

1. The plaintiff claims that the defendant should warn consumers about the risk of [___]. Is this risk so commonly understood or otherwise obvious to consumers that a warning about the risk is not likely to change significantly the ordinary consumer's understanding of the risk? If the answer to this question is yes, you must find for the defendant. If the answer is no, you must answer the next question.

2. The warning provided by the defendant already contains disclosures about other risks. Would the ordinary consumer attach greater significance to the risk disclosure requested by the plaintiff than to any other risk disclosure already contained in the warning? If the answer to this question is yes, you must find for the plaintiff. If the answer is no, you must answer the next question.

3. Would the ordinary consumer find the risk disclosure requested by the plaintiff to be significant or important in deciding whether to buy the product? If the answer to this question is yes, you must answer the next question. If the answer is no, you must find for the defendant.

4. If the risk disclosure requested by the plaintiff were put onto the warning, would it significantly diminish the effectiveness of the other disclosures already contained in the warning? If the answer to this question is yes, you must find for the defendant. If the answer is no, you must answer the next question.

5. Do you think the ordinary consumer would find it worthwhile to read the entire warning proposed by the plaintiff? If the answer to this question is yes, you must find for the plaintiff. Otherwise, you must find for the defendant.

As these instructions illustrate, a warning claim can have a number of interrelated issues that must be adequately separated in order for the jury to evaluate the warning with the risk-utility test. The evaluation requires the jury to compare the allegedly defective warning with the allegedly reasonable alternative warning proposed by the plaintiff. Such an express comparison is not routinely required by the courts, even though "the term 'defect' has implicit within it the notion of comparison—something can be defective only if viewed against something else, which embodies a standard for evaluation."[25] For the same reasons that courts require proof of design defect by reference to a reasonable alternative design, they should require proof of a warning defect by reference to a reasonable alternative warning.

Consider how these observations apply to the other types of warning claims.

Instructions Regarding Product Use. When the plaintiff alleges that the warning does not provide adequate instructions regarding product use, the risk-utility inquiry largely parallels the prior inquiry involving unavoidable risks. The primary difference is that the benefit of disclosure is defined differently. There are many ways to reduce risk (by not using the product, for example), but consumers would choose to take only those precautions costing less than the benefit of risk reduction. Hence disclosures regarding precautions can be material and beneficial to the ordinary consumer only if the precaution is cost-effective. Once this difference is taken into account, the prior analysis of unavoidable risks supplies a set of jury instructions:

1. The plaintiff claims that the defendant should warn consumers about the need to [___] when using the product. Is the need to take the precaution so commonly understood or otherwise obvious to the ordinary consumer that describing the precaution in the product warning is not likely to change significantly the ordinary consumer's understanding of the need to take the precaution? If the answer to this question is yes, you must find for the defendant. If the answer is no, you must answer the next question.

2. The warning provided by the defendant already contains disclosures about other precautions and risks. Would the ordinary consumer attach greater significance to the instruction requested by the plaintiff than to any other risk disclosure already contained in the warning? If the answer to this question is yes, you must find for the plaintiff. If the answer is no, you must answer the next question.

3. Would the ordinary consumer find it worthwhile to take the precaution described in the warning proposed by the plaintiff? If the answer to this question is yes, you must answer

25. Sheila L. Birnbaum, *Unmasking the Test for Design Defect: From Negligence [to Warranty] to Strict Liability to Negligence*, 33 Vand. L. Rev. 593, 603 (1980).

the next question. If the answer is no, you must find for the defendant.

4. If the instruction requested by the plaintiff were put onto the warning, would it significantly diminish the effectiveness of other disclosures or instructions already contained in the warning? If the answer to this question is yes, you must find for the defendant. If the answer is no, you must answer the next question.

5. Do you think the ordinary consumer would find it worthwhile to read the entire warning proposed by the plaintiff? If the answer to this question is yes, you must find for the plaintiff. Otherwise, you must find for the defendant.

The Method of Disclosure. A plaintiff can claim that the warning is inadequate because it does not emphasize adequately an unavoidable risk or instruction regarding product use. Two types of claims fall into this category.

First, the plaintiff may allege that the warning does not prioritize risks properly because it gives less significant risks greater emphasis than more significant risks. To establish that the warning is inadequate in this respect, the plaintiff must show that the risk which caused her injury is more significant than a different risk that is given greater emphasis in the warning. As a reasonable alternative to the existing warning, the plaintiff can propose a warning identical to the current warning with the exception that the two risk disclosures change places. If the change results in the greater emphasis of a more significant risk and a reduced emphasis of a less significant risk, the new format necessarily passes the risk-utility test. A potential problem with the plaintiff's claim is that there may be such a small difference between the significance of the risks in question that a minor restructuring of the warning is likely to offer little or no benefit. Consequently, the plaintiff must also show that the proposed alteration is likely to significantly improve consumer decision making.

These considerations suggest that in applying the risk-utility test to this type of claim, the jury needs to answer the following questions:

1. The warning provided by the defendant already contains a disclosure about the risk that caused the plaintiff's injury. The warning also contains a disclosure pertaining to the risk of [___]. Would the ordinary consumer attach greater significance to the disclosure of the risk that caused the plaintiff's injury than to the disclosure pertaining to the risk of [___]? If the answer to this question is yes, you must answer

the following question. If the answer is no, you must find for the defendant.

   2. Consider a warning identical to the warning supplied by the defendant except for one change in the format of the warning: the risk that caused the plaintiff's injury is described in the same place and manner as the disclosure pertaining to the risk of [___]. The disclosure pertaining to the risk of [___] is then described in the same place and manner as the disclosure pertaining to the risk that caused the plaintiff's injury. Now, if you consider this warning in its entirety, would this change in the format of the warning give the ordinary consumer a significantly better understanding of both risks? If the answer to this question is yes, you must find for the plaintiff. If the answer is no, you must find for the defendant.

The plaintiff could also allege that the warning does not adequately describe the risk that caused her injury. The plaintiff is not challenging the way in which the warning prioritizes risks, so the modification proposed by the plaintiff cannot give the risk in question greater emphasis than a more significant risk already described in the warning. The plaintiff may also be proposing an insignificant modification of the warning, making it important for the jury to consider whether the change significantly improves the warning:

   1. The plaintiff proposes that the warning be modified so that it describes the risk that caused her injury in the following way: [___]. Would the modification proposed by the plaintiff give the risk that caused her injury greater emphasis than any other disclosure involving a more significant risk? If the answer to this question is yes, you must find for the defendant. If the answer is no, you must answer the following question.

   2. Consider a warning that is identical to the warning supplied by the defendant except for the modification proposed by the plaintiff. Now, if you consider this warning in its entirety, would this change in the formatting of the warning give the ordinary consumer a significantly better understanding of the risks posed by the product? If the answer to this question is yes, you must find for the plaintiff. If the answer is no, you must find for the defendant.

These instructions, like the others, illustrate the surprising complexity of failure-to-warn claims, complexity that is largely ignored by the jury instructions commonly used today. Overly simple jury instructions obscure and deemphasize the role of information costs, giving manufacturers an incentive to overwarn. The

149

net result is that consumers often ignore product warnings, a self-defeating outcome for a liability rule that is supposed to improve upon consumer decision making. This outcome is not inevitable. The complexity may be manageable if jury instructions are formulated in the appropriate manner.[26]

IV. Considerations of Strict Liability: Unforeseeable Risks

An "overwhelming majority of jurisdictions" require the product seller to warn only of those risks that were reasonably foreseeable at the time of sale, although "[s]everal states take the position that a defendant manufacturer is charged with knowledge available at time of trial without regard to whether the defendant knew or reasonably could have known of the risk" at the time of sale.[27] A similar split has occurred among the members of the European Union.[28]

According to the courts, the divergence in the case law stems from an important substantive difference between the risk-utility test and consumer expectations.[29] By definition, the seller could not have reasonably known about an unforeseeable risk, implying that the seller could acquire knowledge of the risk only at an unreasonably high cost (otherwise the seller should have discovered the risk, making it foreseeable). The risk-utility test does not require a disclosure involving unreasonably high information costs, explaining why it requires the seller to warn only of risks that were foreseeable at the time of sale.[30] By this same reasoning, the ordinary consumer also does not know about an unforeseeable risk. When an unknown risk materializes into physical harm, the ordi-

26. *Cf.* Aaron D. Twerski et al., *The Use and Abuse of Warnings in Products Liability—Design Defect Litigation Comes of Age*, 61 Cornell L. Rev. 495, 525–28 (1976) (showing why a focus on the objectives of product-safety litigation make "clear that the problem of polycentricity is not of major significance" in design cases).

27. Restatement (Third) § 2 cmt. m Rptrs' Note.

28. The European Economic Community Directive on Liability for Defective Products allows the producer to avoid liability by showing "that the state of scientific or technical knowledge at the time he put the product into circulation was not such as to enable the existence of the defect to be discovered."

Council Directive 85/374/EEC of July 25 1985 on the Approximation of the Laws, Regulations and Administrative Provisions of the Member States Concerning Liability for Defective Products, art. 7(e), 1985 O.J. (L 210) 29. This article, commonly called the *development risk defense*, has been adopted by a great majority of the countries in the European Union, but not all. *See* Jane Stapleton, Product Liability 50–51 (1994) (summarizing adoption of defense by various countries).

29. *See, e.g.*, Green v. Smith & Nephew AHP, Inc., 629 N.W.2d 727, 745–46 (Wis. 2001).

30. *See* Restatement (Third) § 2(c) (limiting liability for warning defects to foreseeable risks).

nary consumer has frustrated safety expectations. If the frustration of these expectations justifies liability, the seller is liable for failing to warn about a risk that was unforeseeable at the time of sale. Under this formulation of consumer expectations, the seller's duty to warn is defined in terms of the knowledge available at the time of trial, even though the risk-utility test yields the contrary conclusion.

Perhaps sellers should be responsible for unforeseeable risks, but not for these reasons. An unforeseeable risk undoubtedly frustrates the actual safety expectations of the ordinary consumer. However, the frustration of actual consumer expectations only justifies the tort duty.[31] The substantive content of the duty—the liability rule defining warning defects—is a separate issue or element. When actual consumer expectations determine both elements, the facts that establish duty also establish the product defect. To keep the two elements separate, duty must depend upon the actual safety expectations of the ordinary consumer, with defect depending upon the reasonable safety expectations of the ordinary consumer.[32] The ordinary consumer reasonably expects a warning to include any disclosure having an information cost less than the associated safety benefit, an expectation that fully explains the other limitations of warning liability.[33] For this same reason, the ordinary consumer reasonably expects only those warnings required by the risk-utility test.

Rather than rely upon a substantive difference between consumer expectations and the risk-utility test, courts could instead make sellers strictly liable for not warning about unforeseeable risks pursuant to the evidentiary rationale for strict liability. For cases in which evidentiary problems substantially undermine the effectiveness of negligence liability, both consumer expectations and negligence principles can justify a rule of strict liability.[34] This type of evidentiary problem exists for the cases under consideration.

---

31. *See* Chapter 2, section II.B.

32. *See* Chapter 4.

33. Any liability rule that does not require a product seller to disclose remote risks or risks that are commonly known in the community relies upon information costs. If information costs were irrelevant, the provision of additional information would always provide some positive benefit for the ordinary consumer that would come at a negligible cost (ink and paper), requiring the

disclosure of the information. *See supra* section II.

34. *See* Chapter 1, section II (describing how negligence principles justify the evidentiary rationale for strict liability); *id.* section IV (explaining why the difficulty of proving that the seller used unreasonable quality-control measures can cause the ordinary consumer to reasonably expect the seller to guarantee that the product is not defective).

Consider the chemicals in commerce, including pesticides, cosmetic ingredients, drugs and food additives. A comprehensive 1984 study, which appears to have remained largely current as of the mid–1990s, "found that for approximately 80% of the estimated 48,523 unregulated chemicals in commerce, *no* toxicity information existed. For the remaining chemicals in commerce, . . . a full health assessment could not be completed for *any* of [them]."[35] Regulated chemicals, particularly drugs approved by the FDA, also frequently pose risks that are not known.[36] The most recent highly publicized example involves the pain-killer Vioxx, which had been marketed for years until studies showed that the drug poses an elevated risk of heart attack and stroke.[37]

For products having little or no toxicity information, the plaintiff could try to prove that the manufacturer should have known of the risk. "[A] seller bears responsibility to perform reasonable testing prior to marketing a product and to discover risks and risk-avoidance measures that such testing would reveal. A seller is charged with knowledge of what reasonable testing would reveal."[38] To prove that the seller negligently failed to discover the risk, the plaintiff must show what "reasonable testing would reveal." This proof is extraordinarily demanding. The plaintiff must establish the parameters of a reasonable research program covering all product hazards potentially posed by the manufacturer's full line of products, and then show that such a research program would have identified the particular product risk that caused the plaintiff's injury. Establishing an appropriate research budget and scope of research projects requires wide-ranging, costly proof. As a practical matter, plaintiffs ordinarily cannot prove that the manufacturer should have discovered a risk that was not otherwise known within the scientific community.[39]

---

35. Wendy E. Wagner, *Choosing Ignorance in the Manufacture of Toxic Products*, 82 Cornell L. Rev. 773, 782–83 (1997) (citing study by National Research Council of the National Academy of Sciences).

36. The FDA grants approval for a drug on the basis of short treatment studies in a limited number of patients. Consequently, a drug's adverse effects may not turn up until it has been used for a number of years by a large number of people with more diverse health characteristics, but drug companies ordinarily are not required by the FDA to test for such risks, including the risk that the drug causes cancer.

37. *See* Barry Meier et al., *Medicine Fueled by Marketing Intensified Trouble for Pain Pills*, N.Y. Times, Dec. 19, 2004, at A1.

38. Restatement (Third) § 2 cmt. m.

39. Ironically, the *Restatement (Third)* rationale for limiting liability to foreseeable risks implicitly recognizes the difficulty of proving negligence: "To hold a manufacturer liable for a risk that was not foreseeable when the product was marketed might foster increased manufacturer investment in safety. But such investment by definition would be a matter of guesswork." *Id.* § 2 cmt. a. Strict liability would only induce the manufacturer to make cost-effective re-

This evidentiary problem effectively immunizes the manufacturer from negligence liability for many reasonably knowable risks, thereby reducing the incentives of manufacturers to test for potential product hazards. The diminished incentive explains the paucity of toxicity data for chemicals, as does the history of the mass tort litigations. In most of these cases, the manufacturer "did not test its product adequately initially, failed to impart information when potential problems emerged, and did not undertake further research in response to adverse information."[40]

This evidentiary problem in a warning case is qualitatively similar to the evidentiary problem in a negligence case involving construction or manufacturing defects. One requires proof of a reasonable research program that would have discovered an unknown risk; the other requires proof of a reasonable quality-control program that would have discovered an unknown manufacturing flaw. The difficulty of proving negligence regarding quality control persuaded the courts to adopt strict liability, suggesting that the courts could also adopt a similar rule for warning cases.

As we found earlier, the evidentiary rationale for strict liability applies only to defective products.[41] In the warning cases under consideration, the risk is known at the time of trial but not at the time of sale. The same is true of construction or manufacturing defects. At the time of sale, the manufacturer did not know that the product had a construction defect or would otherwise malfunction, nor could it necessarily have found out by exercising reasonable care. The risk of defect only became apparent after the product had been sold and used. The evidentiary rationale for strict liability, therefore, applies to products that are known to be defective when evaluated in terms of information not available at the time of sale, a requirement satisfied by the warning cases involving unforeseeable risks.

Thus, the courts that have defined warning defects in terms of the knowledge available at the time of trial could defensibly rely upon the *Restatement (Second)* rule of strict products liability for construction and manufacturing defects. By eliminating the evidentiary burden that a plaintiff would face in trying to prove that the

search investments. If this amount is a matter of "guesswork," then how could the plaintiff prove that the manufacturer did not make reasonable research investments?

40. Margaret Berger, *Eliminating General Causation: Notes Towards a New Theory of Justice and Toxic Torts*, 97 Colum. L. Rev. 2117, 2135 (1997).

41. *See* Chapter 5, section I (identifying this principle in cases involving destroyed products); Chapter 6, section IV (identifying this principle in cases that reject a shift in the burden of proof regarding defective product design); *see also* Chapter 3 (discussing the requirement of defect).

seller could have prevented the defect by the exercise of reasonable care, the rule of strict liability gives sellers an incentive to reduce the incidence of defective products. In adopting the rule of strict liability for unforeseeable risks, courts have been strongly influenced by the idea that strict liability would give manufacturers an incentive to research potential product hazards.[42]

Reliance on the *Restatement (Second)*, however, limits the scope of strict products liability for many warning cases involving unforeseeable risks. Pursuant to comment *k*, a product seller should be immunized from strict liability when the imposition of such liability could threaten the disruption of a product market important for public health and safety.[43] Many courts have applied comment *k* to pharmaceutical products. Strict liability is ruled out, limiting warning liability for these products to those risks that were foreseeable at the time of sale.

What, then, explains the majority rule that limits warning liability to foreseeable risks for *all* products? The rationale for extending the *Restatement (Second)* rule of strict liability to warning cases depends upon the analogy between quality-control programs and research programs. Despite this important similarity, a construction or manufacturing defect importantly differs from a warning defect involving an unforeseeable risk. The two types of defects involve risks having different insurability properties, a difference that can justify the requirement of foreseeability in warning cases.

The insurability of a risk depends on the quality of data regarding the probability and the severity of loss. Insurers usually do not have difficulty collecting such data for construction or manufacturing defects. For example, the sales volume of a soda manufacturer can provide a solid statistical basis for determining the probability that a particular bottle will explode. The extent of liability for any given defect is also fairly predictable, being based upon the extent of injuries that could be suffered by the consumer

---

42. In the leading decision on the issue, the court concluded that "[b]y imposing on manufacturers the costs of failure to discover hazards, we create an incentive for them to invest more actively in safety research." Beshada v. Johns–Manville Products Corp., 447 A.2d 539, 548 (N.J. 1982). Economic analysis supports this conclusion, although it is a separate issue whether the rejection of the foreseeability require-

ment yields the optimal amount of research activity. Hindsight liability (knowledge at the time of trial rather than sale) increases the amount of research activity, but it could result in too much research. *See* Omri Ben–Shahar, *Should Products Liability Be Based on Hindsight?*, 14 J.L. Econ. & Org. 325 (1998).

43. *See* Chapter 5, section II.

and any bystanders. Construction or manufacturing defects typically have the actuarial characteristics required for insurability.[44]

Unforeseeable risks pose a hard actuarial problem, making the provision of insurance much more difficult, if not impossible. Good actuarial data depend upon a large sample size. To determine the likelihood that a warning is defective for not disclosing an unforeseeable risk, the relevant sample for statistical purposes cannot involve the number of products within a given product line, since each has the same warning. The statistical sample must instead involve a large number of different warnings, which must either come from different product lines or different manufacturers of similar products. Data involving different product lines or manufacturers may not be sufficiently similar in the relevant respects, complicating the actuarial analysis. The insurability problem is then exacerbated by the potential scope of liability. A warning defect involves the entire product line, whereas a construction or manufacturing defect involves a limited number of aberrations from the product line. The potential scope of liability for warning defects is vast, as starkly illustrated by the asbestos cases.[45] The magnitude of the liability exposure, coupled with the difficulty of estimating the likelihood of liability, makes it extremely difficult to insure against unforeseeable risks. An instructive example is provided by terrorism insurance.[46]

In deciding whether strict liability appropriately applies to a particular transaction, the courts have often based their decision upon the ability of the defendant to spread risk by purchasing insurance.[47] When liability insurance is not available or otherwise

44. A counterexample involves construction or manufacturing defects for many "unavoidably unsafe" products. *See* Chapter 5, section II.

45. "About 730,000 people have filed claims for asbestos-related injuries, costing a total of about $70 billion as of 2002, according to the RAND corporation...." Jonathan D. Glater, *Lawyers Challenged on Asbestos*, N.Y.Times, July 20, 2005, at C1.

46. Following the September 11th terrorist attacks on the World Trade Center, insurers became understandably concerned about the difficulty of estimating the probability of future terrorist attacks and the potential severity of those attacks.

Faced with a significant increase in uncertainty about the frequency and severity of future terrorist events, in-

ternational reinsurers responded to the event by excluding or significantly restricting terrorism coverage from most reinsurance policies. This in turn motivated primary insurers to exclude terrorism coverage from most commercial lines insurance policies. The Federal Terrrorism Risk Insurance Act ... nullified terrorism exclusions and provided a Federal reinsurance backstop for terrorism events.

J. David Cummins & Christopher M. Lewis, *Catastrophic Events, Parameter Uncertainty and the Breakdown of Implicit Long-Term Contracting: The Case of Terrorism Insurance*, 26 J. Risk & Uncer. 153, 153–54 (2003).

47. For example, in the first case that imposed strict liability on electric utilities, the Wisconsin Supreme Court based its decision on the finding that

155

exceedingly expensive, manufacturers might withdraw from the most vulnerable product markets or otherwise substantially increase the price of products. If these costs exceed any safety benefit that would be created by strict liability, the protection of consumer interests justifies the limitation of warning liability to the risks that were reasonably foreseeable at the time of sale.

Without data conclusively resolving the cost-benefit issue, we cannot determine which liability rule is in the best interests of consumers. This indeterminancy, however, explains why the courts can reach different conclusions about the appropriate liability rule while still relying upon substantively equivalent conceptions of products liability.

V. The Interplay Between Warnings and Product Design

Product warnings and design changes can be alternative methods of reducing product risk, making it necessary to determine the relation between these two types of safety precautions. Under what circumstances can a warning substitute for a design change? Rather than incorporating an airbag into the design of an automobile as required by the risk-utility test, could the manufacturer instead place a sticker on the dashboard proclaiming "WARNING: No airbags in car!"

Framed in this manner, the resolution of this issue seems straightforward. The fact that a danger is open and obvious to consumers does not preclude liability for defective product design in a "strong majority" of jurisdictions.[48] Given the demise of the patent-danger rule in design cases, it logically follows that a product warning—a method for making risks open and obvious to consumers—does not substitute for a design change otherwise required by the risk-utility test.[49]

Despite this seemingly straightforward resolution, the issue is made more difficult by comment *j* of the *Restatement (Second)* rule of strict products liability:

> Where warning is given, the seller may reasonably assume that it will be read and heeded; and a product bearing such a

"the seller can more easily absorb or spread or insure against any financial losses which result" than the consumer. *Ransome v. Wisconsin Elec. Power Co.*, 275 N.W.2d 641, 650 (Wis. 1979). Notice the tension between this case and the later Wisconsin case rejecting the fore-seeability requirement. *Green*, 629 N.W.2d at 745–46.

48. Restatement (Third) § 2 cmt. d Rptrs' Note at 84–85.

49. *See* Latin, *supra* note 20, at 1279–81.

warning, which is safe for use if followed, is not in a defective condition, nor is it unreasonably dangerous.[50]

In the airbag example, comment *j* does not create any problems. Comment *j* only applies when a product is "safe for use" if the warning is "followed," implying that the warning must enable consumers to reduce the relevant risk. A warning that the car has no airbag is unlikely to have any effect on driver behavior or risk reduction. Drivers who "follow" the warning cannot make the automobile "safe" with respect to the risks involved in a car crash, so comment *j* does not apply. The manufacturer can be subjected to design-defect liability.

For cases in which the consumer can safely use the product by following the warning, comment *j* creates a potential problem with respect to product design. Consider a machine with exposed moving parts posing a risk that could be eliminated by an inexpensive guard required by the risk-utility test. The risk could also be eliminated if consumers always followed the warning "Do Not Come Into Contact With Exposed Moving Parts." Comment *j* would seem to give the manufacturer the option of using the warning instead of redesigning the machine. The manufacturer can "reasonably assume" that the warning "will be read and heeded," and the machine would be "safe for use" if the warning is followed. The requirements of comment *j* apparently are satisfied, leading a number of courts to exempt manufacturers from liability for defective design in these cases.[51] This interpretation of comment *j*, though, lets manufacturers avoid design-defect liability by relying on the product warning to make a risk open and obvious. So understood, comment *j* implicitly revives the patent-danger rule, an outcome at odds with the case law rejecting that rule.

This interpretation goes awry by assuming that comment *j* applies to *any* product warning. The ordinary consumer would "read and heed" each and every warning only if it were always costless to do so. However, the consumer must incur costs in order to evaluate and comply with the warning, and these costs importantly limit the disclosures in an adequate warning.[52] Rather than inundating the consumer with unhelpful information—"Do Not Come Into Contact With Exposed Moving Parts!"—an adequate warning contains only those disclosures that would materially affect the decision making of the ordinary consumer. The product

---

50. Restatement (Second) § 402A cmt. j.

51. *See* Latin, *supra* note 20, at 1259–75.

52. *See supra* section II.

seller can only "reasonably assume" that an adequate warning "will be read and heeded." Comment j is logically limited to an *adequate* warning.[53]

This interpretation does not revive the patent-danger rule. The machine manufacturer, for example, cannot necessarily avoid liability merely by warning "Do Not Come Into Contact With Exposed Moving Parts." To comply with this warning, the consumer must be continually aware of the risk and act carefully to avoid the moving parts of the machine. The effort is quite costly for the consumer. If a guard on the machine could eliminate the risk at lower cost, the ordinary consumer would reasonably expect the guard to be included in the design of the machine. The ordinary consumer would not reasonably expect a warning when a reasonable alternative design could reduce that risk instead. An adequate warning, therefore, would not include disclosures of this type, and so the defect in design cannot be cured by reliance on comment j.

As illustrated by this example, the risk-utility test must account for the interplay between warnings and design, which is the approach taken by the *Restatement (Third)*:

> In general, when a safer design can reasonably be implemented and risks can reasonably be designed out of a product, adoption of the safer design is required over a warning that leaves a significant residuum of such risks. For example, instructions and warnings may be ineffective because users of the product may not be adequately reached, may be likely to be inattentive, or may be insufficiently motivated to follow the instructions or heed the warnings. However, when an alternative design to avoid risks cannot reasonably be implemented, adequate instructions and warnings will normally be sufficient to render the product reasonably safe.[54]

Under this approach, the first inquiry involves the amount of risk reduction likely to be achieved by a warning. Due to imperfect memory, lapses in attention, overconfidence, reflexive actions during emergencies or just plain disregard, consumers do not perfectly comply with product warnings.[55] These factors determine the

---

53. Moreover, the legislative history and contextual placement of comment j support the conclusion that it is limited to "unavoidably unsafe" products, which by their very nature cannot be reasonably redesigned. David G. Owen, *The Puzzle of Comment J*, 55 Hastings L.J. 1377 (2004). But if "a court feels impelled to interpret [comment j] more broadly, as applicable to all types of products, then [it] should be interpreted as saying nothing more than that a manufacturer may fulfill its informational obligations to consumers by providing adequate warnings and instructions." *Id.* at 1391.

54. Restatement (Third) § 2 cmt. l.

55. *See* Latin, *supra* note 20, at 1242–47.

amount of risk reduction that can be attained by a warning. Even if the warning does not leave a "significant residuum" of risk, it may be more costly for consumers to follow the warning than to eliminate the risk by redesigning the product. In these circumstances, the warning does not substitute for the design change. In the remaining class of cases, a warning would leave "a significant residuum" of risk, making it even more likely that a design change would be preferable. The warning involves the costs of compliance and the significant residual risk; the design change involves the costs of reconfiguration and perhaps some residual risk. The choice between warning and redesign depends upon a comparison of these costs; whichever one is less costly is required by the *Restatement (Third)*. In the prior example, the warning to avoid contact with the exposed moving parts of the machine creates compliance costs and a significant cost of injury for the residual risk, the sum total of which exceeds the costs of redesigning the machine and any residual risk. In these circumstances, the design change "can be reasonably implemented and the risks reasonably designed out of" the product, and so "adoption of the safer design is required over a warning."

Products passing this formulation of the risk-utility test have a nondefective design accompanied by an adequate warning containing disclosures that "will be read and heeded" by the ordinary consumer, making the product "safe for use." These products satisfy the risk-utility test in the *Restatement (Third)* and the requirements of comment *j* in the *Restatement (Second)*.

Chapter 8

CAUSATION

The element of causation links the violation of the plaintiff's tort right to the defendant's breach of duty. The plaintiff, like other consumers (or bystanders), has a tort right not to be physically injured by a defective product sold by the defendant manufacturer, distributor or retailer. By proving that the defendant sold the defective product that caused her physical harm, the plaintiff has proven that her tort right was violated by the breach of the corresponding duty held by the defendant, entitling her to receive compensation from the defendant wrongdoer.

Ordinarily, the element of causation is compatible with the safety objective of products liability. A manufacturer that incurs liability for the injuries caused by its defective products has a sufficient incentive to supply nondefective products. In some cases, however, plaintiffs face insurmountable evidentiary problems and cannot prove causation. In these cases, the element of causation bars recovery, effectively immunizing the seller of a defective product from tort liability. Due to evidentiary problems, the element of causation can undermine safety incentives and conflict with the safety objective of products liability.

This deterrence problem has one clear solution: the element of causation could be eliminated. A profit-maximizing seller cares only about the cost of liability and is otherwise unconcerned about the source of liability. If the seller incurred liability merely by placing a defective product on the market, it could have a sufficient incentive to supply nondefective products, depending upon the amount of liability. For this form of liability, all that matters is the fact that the defendant sold a defective product, making it unnecessary for the plaintiff to prove that the defect caused her injury.[1]

Eliminating the element of causation, or even reducing the plaintiff's burden of proof, is highly controversial. If liability does not depend upon proof that the defendant caused the plaintiff

---

1. Cf. Guido Calabresi, *Concerning Cause and the Law of Torts: An Essay for Harry Kalven, Jr.*, 43 U. Chi. L. Rev. 69, 85 (1975) ("One could do away with the *but for* test and employ other methods to [decide whether avoidance is worthwhile]. For example, one could simply guess at the size of injury costs that will be associated in the future with behavior causally linked to such injury costs."); William M. Landes & Richard A. Posner, The Economic Structure of Tort Law 229 (1987) (explaining why "the idea of causation can largely be dispensed with in an economic analysis of torts").

injury in violation of her right, then tort law no longer would be a system of *private law* that enforces individual rights and duties. Tort law would instead be a system of *public law* designed to further a public objective, in this instance one of product safety. A public-law rationale is profoundly problematic for those who claim that these liability rules are more properly called something like "product safety law" rather than tort law. As Professor Ernest Weinrib explains:

> Liability in tort law depends on the defendant's having inflicted harm on the plaintiff. We would not, I think, identify as tort law a system that ignored causation in compensating for disabilities. We might perhaps rejoice if eliminating the causation requirement allowed a more general treatment of injury, where compensation was triggered by the injury itself rather than by its tortious infliction. Again, however, such a more general treatment would be an alternative to tort law, not a version of it.[2]

By allowing the plaintiff to recover from the defendant without proof of causation, a tort rule would seem to run into the problems identified by Weinrib. This explains why some of the most controversial tort cases involve the issue of whether the plaintiff's burden of proof should be shifted or otherwise relaxed when the circumstances prevent the plaintiff from proving causation under the ordinary evidentiary rules. In a few recurring sets of circumstances, courts have adopted special causal rules that appear to ease the plaintiff's evidentiary burden. Do these rules unduly relax the plaintiff's burden of proof and tend to show that tort law is a form of public law designed to further an important social objective like product safety? Or do these rules instead adhere to the fundamental tort requirement of causation?

According to the *Restatement (Third)*, "Whether a product defect caused harm to persons or property is determined by the prevailing rules and principles governing causation in tort."[3] The tort principle of causation is supposed to govern all product cases, including those in which the plaintiff faces an impossible task of proving causation. Unlike our earlier inquiries that addressed how liability rules are shaped by the concern for product safety, we must now consider how the principle of causation tempers liability rules that might otherwise promote product safety.

---

2. Ernest J. Weinrib, *Understanding Tort Law*, 23 Val. U. L. Rev. 485, 494 (1989).

3. Restatement (Third) § 15.

I. Cause-in-Fact

The cause-in-fact element, often called *but for* causation, can be simply described: The defect in the product sold by the defendant must have been a factual cause of the injury for which the plaintiff seeks compensation. To establish this element, the plaintiff must prove, by a preponderance of the evidence, that but for the defect in the product sold by the defendant, the injury would not have happened.

This simple description of the cause-in-fact inquiry masks the various aspects or dimensions of causation. The defect must be capable of causing the general type of injury in question, an issue called *general causation*. The defect must also have caused the particular injury in question, an issue of *specific causation*. Finally, the injury-causing defect must have been in a product sold by the defendant, an issue of *individualized causation* addressing whether this particular defendant caused or was responsible for the plaintiff's injury.

In each of these dimensions, plaintiffs have run into trouble. Having proven the defect, in important categories of cases the plaintiff has difficulty proving either specific or individualized causation due to the nature of the accident, defect or even the product itself. In another category, the very nature of the defect undermines the plaintiff's ability to prove general causation. Given the plaintiff's proof of defect, liability in all of these cases would promote product safety, but can it be squared with the tort principle of causation? What does the right-duty nexus running between the plaintiff and defendant require of a causal inquiry plagued by factual uncertainty?

A. *Enhanced Injury*

In many product accidents, the defect enhanced the injuries that would otherwise have been suffered by the plaintiff. In many automobile accidents, for example, the plaintiff would have been physically injured even if the seat belt had not been defective. The defect in the belt aggravated or enhanced the plaintiff's injuries.

Ideally, "the manufacturer should be liable for that portion of the damage or injury caused by the [defect] over and above the damage or injury that probably would have occurred as a result of the impact or collision absent the [defect]."[4] The ideal outcome follows from the tort principle of causation—a defendant manufac-

---

4. Larsen v. General Motors Corp., 391 F.2d 495, 503 (8th Cir. 1968) (applying Minn. law).

turer should be liable only for those injuries caused by its breach of duty. The enhanced injuries are the only ones caused by the defect, and so the manufacturer's liability should be limited accordingly.

The ideal outcome is not always attainable. The nature of the car crash or other type of product accident can make it impossible for the plaintiff to identify the enhanced injuries caused by the defect. In a leading case involving this type of evidentiary problem, Benjamin Huddell suffered fatal brain injuries when his stalled car was rear-ended at high-speed by another car, throwing his head against a head restraint that contained "a relatively sharp, unyielding metal edge, covered by two inches of soft, foam-like material."[5] The plaintiff's expert testified that a nondefective head restraint would have enabled Huddell to survive the crash, but the plaintiff was unable to prove what injuries Huddell would have suffered had the restraint been properly designed. The limited evidence forced the court to confront a hard question. When the proof can only show that the defect caused some injury, is the burden on the plaintiff or defendant to prove the extent of enhanced injury? The party who must bear the burden of proof on this issue will lose, as there is no available evidence about the extent to which the defect enhanced the injuries.

The appellate court in *Huddell* overturned a jury verdict for the plaintiff on the ground that there was no proof of the extent of injuries caused by the defective head restraint.[6] "Without proof to establish what injuries would have resulted from a nondefective head restraint, the plaintiff could not and did not establish what injuries resulted from the alleged defect in the head restraint."

This ruling has been adopted by other jurisdictions, but a "strong majority of courts that have considered the question" and the *Restatement (Third)* do not require the plaintiff to prove the extent of enhanced injury caused by the defect for cases in which there is no proof capable of supporting such a determination.[7] To understand the rationale for the majority approach, suppose the car crash in *Huddell* was caused by the negligence of another driver. Now two tortfeasors are responsible for Benjamin Huddell's fatal head injury: the negligent driver and the manufacturer of the defective head restraint. If *Huddell* had involved these facts, the plaintiff would have recovered from the manufacturer. According to well-established tort principles, when the evidence does not permit

---

5. Huddell v. Levin, 395 F.Supp. 64, 68 (D.N.J. 1975).

6. Huddell v. Levin, 537 F.2d 726 (3d Cir. 1976) (applying NJ law).

7. Restatement (Third) § 16 cmt. d Rptrs' Note.

apportionment of an injury between two tortfeasors, the plaintiff can recover for the entire *indivisible injury* from either tortfeasor.[8] Reasoning that the defendant manufacturer in a case like *Huddell* would have been liable for the entire indivisible head injury if it had also been caused by another tortfeasor, most courts have concluded that the manufacturer's liability should not depend upon the fortuitous presence of another tortfeasor. Under the majority rule, the plaintiff must only prove that the defect caused an indivisible injury, with the defendant bearing the burden of proof regarding apportionment.

This rationale for the majority rule suffers from an obvious problem. Cases involving two tortfeasors are quite different than those involving a single tortfeasor. When the tortious conduct of two defendants combines to cause an indivisible injury, the only way to avoid injustice is to make the defendants bear the burden of proof on apportionment. Otherwise each defendant could escape liability merely because the other defendant also caused harm, the nature of which makes apportionment impossible. The plaintiff would receive no tort damages, even though she has proven that the entire injury was caused by the tortious conduct of the two defendants. To avoid this injustice, each defendant must be liable for the entire indivisible injury. The fair outcome can be achieved— the plaintiff is fully compensated and the damages are appropriately shared between the two defendants—only if the burden of apportionment is placed on the defendants.[9] This rationale clearly depends upon the fact that the *entire* injury was tortiously caused by the defendants. That fact, though, is absent from cases in which the defect only *enhanced* the injury otherwise suffered by the plaintiff in the product accident. Why does the rationale regarding indivisible injuries caused by multiple tortfeasors apply to the enhanced injuries caused by a single tortfeasor?

To address this issue, we need to distinguish between the two types of cause-in-fact inquiries involved in any tort case. The first causal inquiry is relevant to the liability phase of trial: Was the defendant's breach of duty a but for cause of an injury for which the plaintiff is entitled to compensation? Once the plaintiff has

---

8. Restatement (Second) § 433B(2) (providing that when the tortious conduct of two or more actors combines to bring about harm to the plaintiff, and one seeks to limit liability on the basis of apportionment, the burden of proof in doing so is placed upon that defendant).

9. This conclusion is valid even if the plaintiff sues only one defendant. After compensating the plaintiff for the entire injury, in principle the defendant has recourse against the other tortfeasor in an action for contribution or indemnity, resulting in an equitable apportionment of the tortiously caused indivisible injury between the two tortfeasors.

established liability, a different causal question arises in the damages phase: Did the defendant's breach cause the full extent of damages claimed by plaintiff? For each of these cause-in-fact inquiries, the plaintiff bears the burden of proof. The two types of causal issues, though, are not governed by the same evidentiary requirements. Causal issues regarding the extent of damages are subject to less exacting evidentiary requirements. These requirements explain why the plaintiff must only prove that the defect caused an indivisible injury, with the defendant bearing the burden of proof regarding apportionment.

As the U.S. Supreme Court has held, the plaintiff faces less demanding evidentiary requirements "[w]here the tort itself is of such a nature as to preclude the ascertainment of the amount of damages with certainty."[10] If ordinary evidentiary requirements were applied in these cases, "it would be a perversion of fundamental principles of justice to deny all relief to the injured person, and thereby relieve the wrongdoer from making any amend for his acts." To achieve justice, the evidence required of the plaintiff must fairly account for the factual uncertainty created by the defendant's tortious conduct.

Consider the tragic situation in which a promising third-year law student is permanently disabled by a product defect, leaving her unable to work. As part of the damages award, the student can collect the future earnings she will lose as a result of the product-caused injury. Various types of evidence show how much a law student is likely to earn in the future. But even the best evidence of projected future earnings cannot establish that this particular student, more likely than not, would in fact receive these earnings 30 or 40 years from now had she not been permanently disabled. Such certainty is not possible for damage calculations extending far into the future. The ordinary evidentiary standard—a preponderance of the evidence or the "more likely than not" standard—would bar many claims for lost future earnings. Barring the plaintiff from recovery would be unjust, though, because the factual uncertainty was created by the defendant's wrongdoing. Had the defendant's tortious conduct not permanently disabled the student, there would be no need to estimate the student's lost future earnings. Hence it would be "a perversion of fundamental principles of justice" if the uncertainty created by the defendant's tortious misconduct were to bar the plaintiff from recovering any damages for lost earnings. To avoid this injustice, tort law reduces the plaintiff's burden of proof

10. Story Parchment Co. v. Paterson Parchment Paper Co., 282 U.S. 555, 563 (1931).

regarding causal questions in the damages phase. The plaintiff is only required to establish the amount of damages with reasonable proof.[11] The plaintiff still bears the burden of proof, but the required amount of proof depends on what can fairly be demanded of the plaintiff in the circumstances created by the defendant's tortious misconduct.

The evidentiary rule applies to all enhanced injury cases, regardless of the number of tortfeasors. Consider again the *Huddell* case involving the defective head restraint. The plaintiff was only able to prove that a nondefective head restraint would have enabled the car's occupant, Benjamin Huddell, to survive the crash. Having shown that a nondefective head restraint would have been "survivable," plaintiff proved that the defect caused some injury (premature death). Any remaining causal issues involved the extent of damages caused by the defect. At the damages phase of the case, the plaintiff's burden of proof is satisfied by reasonable evidence. Due to the impossibility of apportioning damages, the evidentiary question is whether the plaintiff's proof that the defect caused some injury provides a reasonable factual foundation for making the defendant pay for the entire indivisible injury. It does. If the plaintiff were to bear the burden of proof and thereby necessarily lose the case (the rule adopted in *Huddell*), the defendant manufacturer would be exonerated from all liability because of the factual uncertainty created by its tortious conduct, a result contrary to the widely accepted evidentiary rule governing damages.

For good reasons, a strong majority of courts have rejected the rule in *Huddell*. In rejecting *Huddell*, the courts and the *Restatement (Third)* have relied on the rule governing indivisible injuries caused by multiple tortfeasors.[12] That rule, though, is a particular application of the more general principle that inherent factual uncertainty regarding the extent or scope of damages is a burden to be borne by a tortfeasor (or group of tortfeasors), rather than the plaintiff.[13] This principle persuasively explains why the *Restatement*

---

11. *See* Restatement (Second) of Torts § 912 cmt. a.

12. Restatement (Third) § 16 cmt. d Rptrs' Note at 244.

13. Consider a case involving two defendants who allegedly caused an indivisible injury. To make one of the defendants liable for any damages, the plaintiff must first prove that the defendant's tortious misconduct, more likely than not, caused at least some of the injury for which the plaintiff seeks compensation. Suppose the plaintiff can establish such liability against each of the two defendants. The next issue involves damages. By proving that the injury is indivisible, the plaintiff has proven that apportionment is impossible due to the factual uncertainty created by the defendants' tortious misconduct. The rule making each defendant liable for the entire indivisible injury therefore is a particular application of the more general principle that permits the plaintiff to prove the extent of damages with reasonable evidence.

(Third) can defensibly conclude that "when the plaintiff has proved defect-caused increased harm, the product seller is subject to liability for all harm suffered by the plaintiff if proof does not support a determination of what harm would have resulted if the product had not been defective."[14] Having proven that the defect caused her some injury that cannot be reasonably apportioned, the plaintiff satisfies her evidentiary burden with respect to the entire indivisible injury. Consequently, the *Restatement (Third)* liability rule "does not formally shift any burden of proof to the defendant."[15]

B. Market–Share Liability

Product cases have produced one of the most interesting causal issues in tort law. When generic, mass-produced products cause widespread injury due to identical defects in each unit, and a plaintiff is unable to identify which of the large number of manufacturers sold the product that caused her injury, can the plaintiff prove individualized causation by relying on a manufacturer's market shares as a proxy for the probability that it actually caused the plaintiff harm?

The issue originated in cases involving the synthetic drug diethylstilbestrol (DES), which manufacturers first marketed for use by pregnant women in 1947.[16] After millions of pregnant women had taken DES, the FDA in 1971 banned this use of the drug. Researchers had found that the drug can cause vaginal cancer and other reproductive-organ anomalies in the offspring of mothers who ingested DES during pregnancy. But throughout the entire period when manufacturers were marketing DES to pregnant women, these risks may have been foreseeable. For decades medical journals had provided evidence of the drug's hazards, and the manufacturers may also have been able to identify the risks by adequate testing. A warning that did not apprise consumers of any such foreseeable risk would render DES a defective product. Approximately 300 companies may have produced the drug over this period, although the exact number is uncertain. The market was quite fluid, with manufacturers frequently entering and exiting the market. The drug was truly generic and had no meaningful brand identification. Each manufacturer sold DES of identical composition, and pharmacists usually filled prescriptions with whatever brand was on the shelf. The lack of brand identity makes it difficult

---

14. Restatement (Third) § 16 cmt. d.

15. *Id.*

16. For an insightful and thorough discussion of the DES litigation, see Anita Bernstein, Hymowitz v. Eli Lilly and Co.: *Markets of Mothers* in Torts Stories (Robert L. Rabin & Stephen D. Sugarman eds., 2003).

for the plaintiff to identify the actual product seller under any circumstances, but the problem is even worse in the DES cases. After the plaintiff's mother purchased and ingested the DES, decades usually passed before the plaintiff offspring suffered injury. DES plaintiffs usually cannot identify which particular manufacturer sold the drug that caused his or her injury.

This problem is not solved by the evidentiary rationale for strict liability. The evidentiary difficulties faced by plaintiffs in proving negligence liability can justify strict liability, but that form of liability also requires proof of causation. The evidentiary rationale for strict liability does not address the issue posed by the DES cases: Can tort liability be justified for cases in which the plaintiff can prove that she was injured by a defective product, but the nature of both the product market and the defect make it extraordinarily difficult to identify which manufacturer caused the injury?

The answer is a resounding "NO" for many courts. Unless the plaintiff can prove individualized causation by identifying the DES manufacturer that caused her injury, she cannot recover in approximately one-half of the 20 or so jurisdictions that have considered the issue.[17]

As these cases illustrate, the causation requirement places an important limit on tort liability. So far, we have found that any form of products liability requires a deterrence rationale.[18] As the cases rejecting market-share liability show, products liability can promote product safety only within the limits established by the requirement of causation. The plaintiffs must prove individualized causation, even though this evidentiary burden effectively immunizes the mass manufacturers of generic products from tort liability. Lacking any credible threat of tort liability, these manufacturers are not sufficiently deterred from selling defective products. Nevertheless, courts have refused to relax the requirement of causation. To recover in tort law, the plaintiff must prove that the defendant caused the injury for which she seeks compensation, regardless of the consequences for product safety.

The DES cases have not been uniformly decided. About one-half of the jurisdictions that have addressed the issue have concluded that DES plaintiffs can recover on the basis of market-share liability, a leading version of which holds each manufacturer in the

---

17. *See* Restatement (Third) § 15 cmt c Rptrs' Note (collecting cases showing that no more than 20 jurisdictions have decided the issue, with 9 rejecting market-share liability).

18. Unless a liability rule is designed to reduce product risk, its justification requires that the seller be made an "insurer" of the product in violation of the requirement of defect. *See* Chapter 3, section III.

relevant product market severally liable in proportion to its market share.[19]

This split in the case law may stem from divergent opinions about the importance of causation. In rejecting market-share liability, courts typically reason that market-share liability "requires a profound change in the fundamental tort principle of causation. [W]e cannot pretend that any such theory is consistent with common law principles of tort liability."[20] The courts that have adopted market-share liability, however, do not reject the principle of causation, nor do they suggest that this form of liability represents a profound change in tort law. In the first case to adopt market-share liability, the California Supreme Court said that the liability rule is "grounded upon an extension of the *Summers* doctrine."[21] The Court was referring to the rule of alternative liability adopted in the famous case of *Summers v. Tice*.[22] Today "most courts appear to regard [*Summers*] as established law on its facts."[23] Insofar as market-share liability is a merely an extension of *Summers*, it does not depend upon divergent opinions about the principle of causation.

Indeed, the controversy surrounding market-share liability plausibly stems from a disagreement about whether the *Summers* doctrine properly extends to market-share liability. The California Supreme Court sought to justify market-share liability in these terms, but it never clearly explained the relevance of the *Summers* doctrine for market-share liability.[24] Nor has it adequately explained the *Summers* doctrine of alternative liability.[25] The courts that have rejected market-share liability are understandably wary of its connection with alternative liability. Our evaluation of market-share liability accordingly begins with the *Summers* doctrine.

19. Market-share liability was first adopted in Sindell v. Abbott Labs., 607 P.2d 924 (Cal. 1980). The California Supreme Court subsequently made clear that market-share liability involves several liability rather than joint and several liability. Brown v. Superior Court, 751 P.2d 470 (Cal. 1988). For other variations of market-share liability, see 2 Madden & Owen on Products Liability § 24.

20. Senn v. Merrell–Dow Pharmaceuticals, Inc., 751 P.2d 215, 223 (Or. 1988). *See also* Smith v. Eli Lilly Co., 560 N.E.2d 324, 334–40 (Ill. 1990) (providing a survey of cases rejecting market-share liability and stressing the common theme that the liability rule is a "radical" departure from tort principles).

21. *Sindell*, 607 P.2d at 928.

22. 199 P.2d 1 (Cal. 1948).

23. Dan B. Dobbs, The Law of Torts § 175, at 428 (2000).

24. *See* Zafft v. Eli Lilly & Co., 676 S.W.2d 241, 246 (Mo. 1984) (rejecting market-share liability in part because *Sindell* had not sufficiently articulated the relevant concepts).

25. *See, e.g., Senn*, 751 P.2d at 222 (rejecting both alternative liability and market-share liability in part because "none of the cases or commentaries presents a rigorous analysis of why [these doctrines are] 'fair' ").

In *Summers*, the plaintiff had been hunting quail with the two defendants, who negligently fired their shotguns in the direction of the plaintiff at about the same time. The plaintiff was struck in the eye by a single birdshot pellet, but it was not possible to identify which defendant caused the injury. In these circumstances, the California Supreme Court concluded that it was appropriate to shift the burden of proof to the defendants, requiring one or the other to prove that he was not the cause of the plaintiff's injury. If the defendants could not offer such proof, each would be jointly liable for the plaintiff's injury.[26]

This rule of alternative liability has been adopted by the *Restatement (Second)*:

> Where the conduct of two or more actors is tortious, and it is proved that harm has been caused to the plaintiff by only one of them, but there is uncertainty as to which one has caused it, the burden is upon each such actor to prove that he has not caused the harm.[27]

The rationale for alternative liability is based upon "the injustice of permitting proved wrongdoers, who among them have inflicted an injury upon the entirely innocent plaintiff, to escape liability merely because the nature of their conduct and the resulting harm has made it difficult or impossible to prove which of them has caused the harm."[28]

The rule of alternative liability applies to the DES cases. Each defendant manufacturer exposed the plaintiff to the same tortious risk by supplying the same defective product in the relevant market, just as each defendant in *Summers* exposed the plaintiff to the same tortious risk by negligently firing at him. Only one manufacturer was the cause of the plaintiff's harm, and only one shooter in

---

26. There is some dispute whether alternative liability involves joint liability or joint and several liability. As a logical matter, alternative liability must involve joint liability. The plaintiff must join all potential tortfeasors in order to establish alternative liability. A successful plaintiff therefore receives a judgment against each tortfeasor. In the event that the plaintiff cannot recover proceeds from a judgment-proof defendant, the plaintiff only has a worthless judgment and nothing more. The worthless judgment does not logically enable the plaintiff to recover those damages from the other defendants (the result achieved by joint and several liability), for otherwise there would be no reason for requiring the plaintiff to join all potential tortfeasors. Instead, the rule would only require the plaintiff to join all potential tortfeasors that are not judgment proof, or perhaps to join only one potential tortfeasor (who can then implead the other solvent torfeasors or seek contribution or indemnity in subsequent suits). The joinder requirement only makes sense for a rule of joint liability. Joint liability also produces the fair allocation of liability, unlike the rule of joint and several liability. *See infra* note 36 and accompanying text.

27. Restatement (Second) § 433 B(3) .

28. *Id.* cmt. f.

Summers injured the plaintiff. However, the nature of the tortious conduct engaged in by each manufacturer—the sale of a generic, defective product—and the resulting harm—cancer or other injury occurring long after exposure to the defect—has made it virtually impossible for the plaintiff to identify which particular manufacturer caused the harm, the same type of evidentiary problem confronted by the plaintiff in *Summers*. All of the requirements for alternative liability are satisfied in the DES cases.

To establish alternative liability, the plaintiff must join all potential tortfeasors in the lawsuit, as in *Summers*.[29] Due to the large number of DES manufacturers and the fluid nature of the market, this requirement has significantly limited the application of alternative liability in the DES cases. "[P]laintiffs' inability to join all tortfeasor participants has prompted the dismissal of the alternative liability count of several multi-party actions involving DES."[30] As a practical matter, alternative liability has not solved the evidentiary problem posed by the DES cases.

But why does the plaintiff have to join all of the potential tortfeasors? As an evidentiary matter, the alternative liability cases like *Summers* are indistinguishable from the DES cases in which the plaintiff is unable to sue all of the manufacturers. In both cases, the plaintiff was injured by the type of tortious conduct engaged in by all of the defendants, and the nature of that misconduct has made it impossible for the plaintiff to identify the actual tortfeasor. The only difference involves the inability of the DES plaintiffs to join all of the potential tortfeasors, but like the other evidentiary problems faced by the plaintiffs, this one was also created by the DES market. Why should this difference matter?

If alternative liability were to apply in a case not involving all potential tortfeasors, the plaintiff's burden of proof would not necessarily be reduced. Suppose the plaintiff sues a group of six DES manufacturers, each of which had 10 percent of the relevant market, and can prove, by a preponderance of the evidence, that each individual defendant sold a defective product (DES) that could have caused her injury. This evidence does not prove that any individual defendant, more likely than not, was the actual injurer. The evidence does show, however, that the *group* of DES manufacturers, more likely than not, caused the injury. When considered in relation to the group of defendants, the plaintiff has established

29. *See* Restatement (Third) of Torts: Liability for Physical Harm (Basic Principles) § 28 cmt. g (Proposed Final Draft No. 1, April 2005) ("Courts have insisted that all persons whose tortious acts exposed the plaintiff to a risk of harm be joined as defendants as a condition for alternative liability.").

30. 2 Madden & Owen on Products Liability § 24:4, at 652.

causation by a preponderance of the evidence, the amount of evidence ordinarily required by tort law.

To determine whether the plaintiff's burden of proof can be satisfied against the group, we need to consider an important class of cases involving multiple tortfeasors:

> The classic example is the case of two fires being swept by winds towards the plaintiff's property. Either fire is sufficient to burn the property. Before either fire reaches the property, they combine. The combined fire burns the plaintiff's property. If A negligently set one fire and B negligently set the other, each could claim that he is not a cause under the but-for rule, since, even if he had set no fire, the other fire would have burned the property. Since both A and B could make the same argument, a court that applied the unvarnished but-for test here would effectively bar the victim from any recovery from either of the two negligent defendants. The but-for test in such cases leads to a result that is almost always condemned as violating both an intuitive sense of causation and good legal policy.[31]

To avoid this problem, courts have rejected the "unvarnished but-for test" and allowed plaintiffs to recover by proving that a defendant's tortious conduct was a substantial factor in causing the harm. This alteration in the causal standard does not reduce the plaintiff's burden of proof. In the two-fire case, the plaintiff must prove, by a preponderance of the evidence, that each defendant negligently caused a fire. The plaintiff must also provide similar proof that the *group* of defendants—or the two fires—caused the injury for which she seeks compensation. The plaintiff's proof accordingly satisfies the ordinary evidentiary standard when applied to the group of defendants, even though the plaintiff is unable to prove causation with the "unvarnished but-for test."

If the two-fire cases are sufficiently analogous to the DES cases, then a DES plaintiff could prove causation by showing that the group of DES manufacturers, like the group of two defendants who negligently started fires, more likely than not caused the injury. One might draw a distinction based on the fact that each of the two negligently started fires was independently sufficient to burn the property. Even if one defendant had not negligently started one fire, the other defendant negligently started another fire that probably would have burned the property—that fire, after all, was a substantial factor in causing the damage. By contrast, it is unclear whether the conduct of each DES manufacturer was a

---

31. Dobbs, *supra* note 23, § 171 at 414–15 (paragraph structure omitted).

substantial factor in causing the plaintiff's harm, even though the breach of duty by each DES manufacturer may have been independently sufficient to cause injury to any individual DES plaintiff.[32] Tort liability, though, does not necessarily require that each defendant must have been a substantial factor in causing the harm, and so the cases can be analogous despite this difference.

Consider the *Summers* case. Only one of the two defendant shooters hit the plaintiff. If one defendant shooter had not acted negligently, then the harm would not necessarily have been caused by the other negligent defendant (who might have actually missed the plaintiff). In this respect, *Summers* differs from the two-fire cases. Otherwise *Summers* is analogous. As applied to each of the two defendant shooters, the "unvarnished but-for test" would absolve each of liability for the same reason it would absolve the two defendants of liability in the two-fire cases. Each defendant shooter could exculpate himself by relying upon the possibility that the other defendant caused the injury. Neither defendant disputes that the injury was caused by one of them, so the "unvarnished but-for test" would unfairly exculpate both from liability. This unfair result is avoided by the rule of alternative liability. The plaintiff in *Summers* proved, by a preponderance of the evidence, that each defendant acted unreasonably and could have caused the injury. The plaintiff also proved, by a preponderance of the evidence, that the *group* of shooters caused the injury. In a case of alternative liability, the plaintiff's proof satisfies the ordinary evidentiary standard when applied to the group of defendants, making liability appropriate even though the misconduct of each defendant was not a substantial factor in causing the injury.

According to a leading torts treatise, the relevant causal rule in all of these cases can be formulated in these terms:

> When the conduct of two or more actors is so related to an event that their combined conduct, viewed as a whole, is a but-for cause of the event, and application of the but-for rule to them individually would absolve all of them, the conduct of each is a cause in fact of the event.[33]

---

32. Due to the generic nature of DES, the plaintiff's mother would have purchased the pill from any available supplier. If every other defendant manufacturer had not acted negligently (and not sold DES), then the plaintiff's mother would have purchased DES from the sole remaining manufacturer in the market. So understood, the conduct of each defendant would have been inde- pendently sufficient to cause the plain- tiff's injury, just as in the two-fire cases. This conceptualization of the problem can explain why different jurisdictions have adopted different versions of mar- ket-share liability in the DES cases. *See infra* note 47.

33. Prosser and Keeton on Torts § 41, at 268. At least one court has expressly adopted this formulation in a

This causal rule shows why the plaintiff in our hypothetical DES case can prove causation against a group of manufacturers comprising 60 percent of the market. By a preponderance of the evidence, the plaintiff's proof shows that each individual defendant owed a duty to the plaintiff; each breached the duty in a manner that could have caused the injury; and the injury was caused by the group of defendants. In defense, each of the six defendant manufacturers does not contest this proof, but instead argues that there was only a 10 percent chance that it caused the plaintiff's harm. This defense does not provide any defendant with an exculpatory reason. Each defendant is relying upon the "unvarnished but-for test" in a manner that the courts have already found to be inappropriate. The but-for test would enable each defendant to avoid liability, even though each one admits that it might be the actual tortfeasor, and the plaintiff has proven that one of them is the actual tortfeasor. Like the two-fire cases and *Summers*, the "unvarnished but-for test" would unfairly exculpate all defendants from liability and is inappropriate. Unable to rely on that test, each defendant has no defense and is subject to liability. The two-fire cases and *Summers* show why the plaintiff can satisfy the ordinary burden of proving causation as applied to the group rather than to its individual members.

Liability in our hypothetical DES case therefore does not require any reduction in the plaintiff's burden of proof, leaving the problem of excessive liability as the reason for requiring the plaintiff to join all potential tortfeasors in the lawsuit. If our hypothetical DES plaintiff could establish alternative liability by joining 60 percent of the market, then the group of manufacturers would be jointly liable for the entirety of the plaintiff's injury. Joint liability would result in each of the six defendants incurring liability for one-sixth of the plaintiff's injury, whereas each had only 10 percent of the market. Each defendant would incur excessive liability, then, if its liability should be limited by the 10 percent likelihood that it was the actual cause of the plaintiff's injury.

In deciding upon the fair amount of liability, the court must compare the interest of the DES plaintiff who has established a right to receive compensation for the injury from the group of defendants, and the interest of each individual defendant as a member of the group.[34] The compensatory demands that the plain-

products case. Spaur v. Owens–Corning Fiberglas Corp., 510 N.W.2d 854, 858 (Iowa 1994). For reasons to be given in the text, this case conflicts with Mulcahy v. Eli Lilly & Co., 386 N.W.2d 67 (Iowa 1986) (declining to adopt market-share liability).

34. *Cf.* Brown, 751 P.2d at 487 (describing joint liability as frustrating *Sindell*'s goal of "achieving a balance be-

tiff can fairly place upon each member of the group depend upon that individual defendant's relation to the group. An individual who is responsible for the group's conduct can be held liable for the entire injury caused by the group, as in cases involving a concert of action among the defendants.[35] But in the DES cases, each individual manufacturer is not responsible for the group's conduct; the sale of DES by one manufacturer does not make it responsible for the sales made by other DES manufacturers. Since each individual defendant is not responsible for the group's conduct, and the group is the only known factual cause of the injury, each manufacturer should not be held responsible for the entire injury. Liability must be apportioned among the members of the group. Each individual defendant is a member of the group only by virtue of its responsibility for an independent tortious risk that could have injured the plaintiff. Each defendant's contribution to the total risk of injury therefore defines the extent of its responsibility for the group's conduct. In apportioning damages for the plaintiff's injury, the court can accordingly limit the liability of each defendant to the probability that its tortious conduct actually injured the plaintiff. Under this method of apportionment, the interest of the DES plaintiff who has established a right to receive compensation for the injury from the group of defendants exactly corresponds to the interest of each individual defendant as a member of the group.[36]

This reasoning explains why the courts insist that alternative liability requires joinder of all the defendants. Alternative liability gives the plaintiff 100 percent compensation for the injury from the jointly liable defendants. When the joinder requirement has been satisfied, the proportional liability of each defendant adds up to 100 percent. The imposition of joint liability on the group of all potential tortfeasors lets the plaintiff receive full compensation for the injury without requiring any individual defendant to incur liability in excess of the probability that it actually caused the injury.[37]

tween the interests of DES plaintiffs and manufacturers of the drug").

35. *See* Restatement (Second) § 876 (stating that a defendant may be jointly and severally liable if the defendant commits a tortious act in concert with another or pursuant to a common design, or a defendant gives substantial assistance to another knowing that the other's conduct constitutes a breach of duty). Similarly, an individual defendant can be responsible for the group's conduct under the theory of enterprise liability. *See* Hall v. E.I. Du Pont De Nemours & Co., 345 F.Supp. 353, 374–78

(E.D.N.Y. 1972) (holding all manufacturers in a specific industry liable when the plaintiff is unable to identify the specific manufacturer that caused the harm, and the industry jointly controlled the risk).

36. For this reason, alternative liability cannot involve joint and several liability. The imposition of several liability would make an individual defendant liable for more than its proportionate share of the injury.

37. The joinder requirement also explains why alternative liability is not a rule that compensates the plaintiff for

175

We can now see why the California Supreme Court could defensibly "extend" the *Summers* doctrine to market-share liability after modifying alternative liability to address the problem of excessive liability. The issue is complicated, and the court's reasoning is often confusing, but its opinions provide the necessary logic for the argument.

Since the plaintiff cannot join all potential tortfeasors as required by alternative liability, the court held that the plaintiff must instead join a "substantial share" of the market in order to establish market-share liability.[38] This requirement ensures that the group of DES defendants, more likely than not, caused the plaintiff's injury.[39] Once the plaintiff has satisfied this requirement and all of the other remaining requirements for alternative liability, she has established a right to compensation for the injury from the group of defendants. Alternative liability would make the defendants jointly liable for the entire injury, resulting in an unfairly excessive amount of liability for each individual defendant. Each of the DES defendants in our hypothetical case had only 10 percent of the market, and so each should be liable for 10 percent of the plaintiff's injury. To "protect ... defendants against excessive liability," the court in a later case concluded that the market-share liability involves several liability, with the liability of each DES defendant being limited by the probability that it actually caused the plaintiff's injury—an amount defined by its market share.[40]

Having altered the rule of alternative liability in these two respects, the court could defensibly conclude that market-share liability is "an adaptation of the rule in *Summers* which will substantially overcome [the] difficulties" faced by a plaintiff who

risk rather than injury. If the *Summers* doctrine involves compensation for risk rather than injury, then the plaintiff could sue only one shooter and show, by a preponderance of the evidence, that this individual defendant created a 50 percent chance of causing injury. The proof would sufficiently establish liability for the risk. This outcome is barred by the requirement that the plaintiff must join all potential tortfeasors, implying that alternative liability does not involve compensation for risk.

38. *Sindell*, 607 P.2d at 937.

39. *Sindell* says that the substantial-share requirement "significantly diminishe[s]" the "injustice of shifting the burden of proof to defendants to demonstrate that they could not have made the substance which injured plaintiff." *Id.* Insofar as the substantial-share requirement means that the plaintiff must satisfy the ordinary burden of proof regarding causation against the group of defendants, then the satisfaction of this requirement makes it fair to shift the burden of proof to the defendants. *Cf. id.* at 937 (indicating that the substantial-share requirement is less than 75–80 percent of the market); Murphy v. E.R. Squibb & Sons, 710 P.2d 247, 255 (Cal. 1985) (concluding that the substantial-share requirement is not satisfied by 10 percent of the market).

40. *Brown*, 751 P.2d at 486.

cannot join every potential tortfeasor in the lawsuit.[41] Market-share liability does not fully overcome this difficulty—the plaintiff receives compensation for only 60 percent of the injury in our hypothetical case. The plaintiff's recovery is limited by the rule of several liability, which makes the individual manufacturer responsible only for the defective products it actually sold, enabling the court to conclude that market-share liability avoids the unfairness that would arise if "one manufacturer would be held responsible for the products of another or for those of all other manufacturers if plaintiff ultimately prevails."[42] The plaintiff can prove causation by reference to the group of defendant manufacturers, but each defendant is only responsible for its contribution to the total risk of injury—the same outcome achieved by alternative liability.

Rather than rely upon the *Summers* doctrine, one could try to justify market-share liability in other ways.[43] A justification derived from the *Summers* doctrine has the advantage of depending upon the widely accepted rule of alternative liability.

This justification also sheds light on the differing judicial formulations of alternative liability and market-share liability. For example, some courts have suggested that alternative liability only applies to cases involving few potential tortfeasors, reasoning that fairness requires a high likelihood that any given defendant actually injured the plaintiff.[44] This limitation is problematic, though,

---

41. *Sindell*, 607 P.2d at 931.

42. *Id.* at 938.

43. For example, it might be possible to justify market-share liability if the destruction of a personal injury lawsuit were an actionable harm. In a case like *Summers*, Justice Rand of the Canadian Supreme Court justified alternative liability on the ground that the negligent defendants "violated not only the victim's substantive right to security, but ... also culpably impaired the latter's remedial right of establishing liability. By confusing his act with environmental conditions, he has, in effect, destroyed the victim's power of proof." Cook v. Lewis, [1951] S.C.R. 830, 832. This logic of evidential damages arguably justifies market-share liability. *See* Ariel Porat & Alex Stein, *Liability for Uncertainty: Making Evidential Damage Actionable*, 18 Cardozo L. Rev. 1891, 1938 n.128 (1997). This rationale for market-share liability does not persuasively justify the liability rule in California, however, because the California Supreme Court has expressly rejected the claim that the destruction of a personal injury lawsuit is an actionable harm. *See* Temple Comm. Hosp. v. Superior Court, 976 P.2d 223 (Cal.1999). For a different argument that market-share liability can satisfy the principle of causation, see Arthur Ripstein & Benjamin C. Zipursky, *Corrective Justice in an Age of Mass Torts* in Philosophy and the Law of Torts 214 (Gerald Postema ed., 2001) (arguing that market-share liability is unrelated to alternative liability but can be justified by the equitable powers of the court).

44. *E.g.*, Hymowitz v. Eli Lilly & Co., 539 N.E.2d 1069, 1074 (N.Y. 1989) (stating that alternative liability in part "rests on the notion that where there is a small number of possible wrongdoers, all of whom breached a duty to the plaintiff, the likelihood that any one of them injured the plaintiff is relatively high, so that forcing them to exonerate themselves, or be held liable, is not unfair").

because there is no evident reason why it is " 'fair' to impose joint liability without a preponderance of proof of causation in some cases (small number of defendants) but not in others (large number of defendants) when the character of defendant's conduct and plaintiff's difficulty of proof is the same in either instance."[45] Alternative liability does not need to be limited in this manner, however, as long as each jointly liable defendant is required to pay for a proportional share of the injury based upon the likelihood that it actually injured the plaintiff. If there is a small likelihood that an individual defendant actually injured the plaintiff, then the liability of that defendant is diminished accordingly, eliminating the problem of unfairly excessive liability.

Another important issue involves the type of evidence the defendant can provide to avoid market-share liability. The New York Court of Appeals has formulated a rule of market-share liability that does not let the manufacturer exculpate itself from liability by proving that it could not have sold the product that injured the plaintiff.[46] This proof, however, shows that the manufacturer was not in the group that injured the plaintiff, and so the evidence should exculpate the defendant from a rule of market-share liability that is derived from alternative liability.[47]

The most important issue involves the potential scope of market-share liability. Alternative liability is not necessarily limited to DES cases, nor is market-share liability. For example, market-share data may be appropriate for establishing liability in cases involving the gasoline additive methyl tertiary butyl ether (MTBE). The nature of the additive creates a risk of groundwater contamination that may be sufficiently fungible to rely upon market-share data for purposes of establishing several liability.[48]

45. *Senn*, 751 P.2d at 222.

46. *Hymowitz*, 539 N.E.2d 1069.

47. Perhaps one could argue that even if the defendant was not selling in the local market, it would have entered that market had no other DES manufacturer been available, which in turn would make it a member of the relevant group. This reasoning makes the market-share cases fully analogous to the two-fire cases and presumably justifies joint and several liability for each DES manufacturer. *See supra* note 32 (drawing this analogy). This reasoning explains the rule of market-share liability in Wisconsin, which is based upon the national product market because of its "fluid" nature and the fact that each DES manufacturer "contributed to the *risk* of injury to the public, and consequently, the risk of injury to individual plaintiffs." Collins v. Eli Lilly Co., 342 N.W.2d 37, 49–50 (Wis. 1984). Under this rule, the DES plaintiff can recover full damages for the entire injury from a single manufacturer in the national market. The liability rule, in other words, is one of joint and several liability that is entirely analogous to the two-fires case.

48. *E.g.*, In re Methyl Tertiary Butyl Ether ("MTBE") Products Liability Litigation, 175 F.Supp.2d 593 (S.D.N.Y. 2001).

The liability of each defendant, though, does not have to depend upon its share of the product market, nor must the product be fungible, as neither of these factors was present in *Summers*. As long as the plaintiff can prove the amount of tortious risk created by each defendant, then the amount of several liability for each defendant can be determined in the manner required by market-share liability.[49] The plaintiff must establish liability by a preponderance of the evidence, but the proof regarding the exact amount of each defendant's risk contribution involves the apportionment of liability—a damages question that is governed by the reasonableness evidentiary standard.[50]

Cases like this are exceptional, however. "Outside the DES context, market-share liability has been sparingly adopted. Its application has been largely rejected primarily on the ground that the product in question was not fungible."[51] Market-share liability should be rarely applied, but not because it requires fungible products or "a profound change in the fundamental tort principle of causation" as many courts have concluded. Market-share liability should be exceptional only because it depends upon a restrictive set of circumstances.

C. The Heeding Presumption in Warning Cases

A defective warning that was ignored by the plaintiff cannot have caused her injury, unless the defect involves the warning's failure to catch the consumer's attention by making the disclosure more prominent. To establish causation, the plaintiff must prove that she would have read and followed an adequate warning had one been given.[52]

The courts, with "widespread approval," have presumed that consumers would read and heed an adequate product warning.[53] The heeding presumption is tantamount to a presumption of causa-

---

49. A more descriptively apt name for the liability rule might be "proportional share liability." *See* Allen Rostron, *Beyond Market Share Liability: A Theory of Proportional Share Liability for Nonfungible Products*, 52 UCLA L. Rev. 151 (2004). Professor Rostron does not attempt to justify rigorously market-share liability, but instead thoroughly analyzes the types of proof required for liability purposes.

50. *See supra* section I.

51. In re Methyl Tertiary Butyl Ether ("MTBE") Products Liability Litigation, 175 F.Supp.2d at 621.

52. An exception occurs when the warning is directed to a third party, such as a doctor who prescribed a drug to the plaintiff. *See* Chapter 6, section V (discussing the learned intermediary rule).

53. 1 Madden & Owen on Products Liability § 9:11, at 590. The heeding presumption is contained in comment *j* of the *Restatement (Second)* rule of strict products liability, which we earlier found governs adequate warnings. *See* Chapter 7, section V.

tion, a seeming exception to the ordinary tort rule requiring the plaintiff to prove that the defendant's tortious conduct caused the injury for which she seeks compensation.

The heeding presumption is particularly puzzling when compared to the DES cases. If causation could be presumed rather than affirmatively proven, the courts would not have had to struggle with the issue of market-share liability. The DES cases affirm the importance of the requirement of causation, making it necessary for us to determine whether causation can be defensibly established by the heeding presumption in the two types of warning cases—those involving safety instructions, and those involving disclosures about residual risks.

Safety Instructions. The plaintiff can prove that a product is defective for not adequately instructing the consumer of the need to take a particular precaution while using the product. In a case of this type, the plaintiff also claims that if she had been warned of the need to take the safety precaution, she would have done so and avoided the injury for which she seeks compensation.

To establish the defect, the plaintiff must prove that a reasonable alternative warning would have provided the safety instruction. This proof should establish that (1) the ordinary consumer would find it worthwhile to follow the instruction; (2) the ordinary consumer was not otherwise sufficiently aware of the need to take the precaution; and (3) the ordinary consumer would find it worthwhile to read the warning in order to gain the information.[54]

This proof also satisfies the plaintiff's burden of proof on causation. The proof of defect establishes that the ordinary consumer would read and heed a warning that disclosed the safety instruction. The plaintiff, more likely than not, is like the ordinary consumer in these respects. By proving defect, the plaintiff has also shown by a preponderance of the evidence that she would have read and followed the safety instruction, thereby avoiding injury. The factual characteristics of an adequate warning make it logical for the court to presume causation in these cases.[55]

This proof only presumptively establishes causation. The defendant can rebut the presumption by showing that the plaintiff is not like the ordinary consumer. The plaintiff might have known of the risk, unlike the ordinary consumer. The plaintiff might also routinely or habitually disregard safety instructions in product warn-

---

54. *See* Chapter 7, section III.

55. *But see* Coffman v. Keene Corp., 628 A.2d 710, 717 (N.J. 1993) (concluding that the heeding presumption is not a logical or empirical assumption that can be derived from an empirically demonstrable probability).

ings, unlike the ordinary consumer. Such proof, if sufficiently persuasive, would show that the defective warning did not cause the plaintiff's injury.[56]

The heeding presumption is easily justified for this class of cases, as is the other method the courts have adopted for determining causation. Almost all of the courts that have not adopted the heeding presumption use a subjective standard for establishing causation.[57] Under this standard, the plaintiff can prove causation by testifying that she would have followed the safety instruction had one been given. Predictably, the plaintiff almost always testifies that she would have obeyed the warning.[58] Otherwise, why bring the case? As a practical matter, the defendant bears the burden of disproving causation under the subjective standard, the same result achieved by the heeding presumption.

Residual or Unavoidable Risks. The plaintiff can prove that a product is defective for not adequately apprising the consumer of a residual or unavoidable risk posed by a product that is manufactured, designed and used properly. In a case of this type, the plaintiff also claims that the residual risk caused the injury for which she seeks compensation.

To establish the defect, the plaintiff must prove that a reasonable alternative warning would have disclosed the residual risk. This proof should establish that (1) the ordinary consumer would find the risk to be material in deciding whether to buy or use the product; (2) the ordinary consumer was not otherwise sufficiently aware of the risk; and (3) the ordinary consumer would find it worthwhile to read the warning in order to gain the information.[59]

Once again, by proving defect the plaintiff has also proven that she would read and heed an adequate warning. The proof of defect establishes that the ordinary consumer would read a warning that adequately disclosed the residual risk and then consider that risk in making a decision about product use. The plaintiff, more likely than not, is like the ordinary consumer in these respects. By proving defect, the plaintiff has also shown by a preponderance of the evidence that she would have read and heeded or considered the adequate warning.

56. For an extensive discussion of these issues, see Sharpe v. Bestop, Inc., 713 A.2d 1079, 1088–93 (N.J. App. Div. 1998), *aff'd*, 730 A.2d 285 (N.J. 1999).

57. *See* Michael S. Jacobs, *Toward A Process–Based Approach to Failure-to-Warn Law*, 71 N.C. L. Rev. 121, 162–63 (1992).

58. "Rare indeed are cases involving the admitted failure by plaintiff to read an allegedly inadequate warning.... Plaintiffs invariably say that they would have read the missing or inadequate warning and that they would have heeded it as well." *Id.* (citations omitted).

59. *See* Chapter 7, section III.

In these cases, however, the heeding presumption does not necessarily link the defective warning to the plaintiff's injury. All users of the product are exposed to the residual risk, so the plaintiff could have avoided injury only if she would not have purchased or used the product upon being warned of the risk. For most residual risks, the ordinary consumer would still use the product had she known of the risk. Despite the risk of side-effects posed by many drugs, the vast majority of consumers still find the drugs to be worthwhile. The ordinary consumer would still take the drug, even if she had been adequately warned about such a side-effect. The plaintiff, presumably, would have read and considered an adequate warning and still suffered the injurious side-effect. In what way does the heeding presumption prove causation?

This problem is not satisfactorily solved by the subjective standard, which would enable the plaintiff to prove causation by testifying that she would not have used the product had she known of the residual risk. Suppose the warning is defective for not disclosing a residual risk that would increase the ordinary consumer's estimate of the product cost by 10 percent. The plaintiff cannot show that the ordinary consumer would not use the product following the disclosure. After all, how many products are there for which a 10 percent increase in cost or price would cause the ordinary consumer to forego the purchase or use of the product? Rather than trying to establish causation by reference to the way in which the ordinary consumer would respond to the disclosure, the plaintiff could try to prove that she is a *marginal* consumer—someone who would decide not to buy or use the product following the cost increase. Such consumers undoubtedly exist. When the price of the product increases by 10 percent, total demand for the product ordinarily will decline. Within the market as a whole, some consumers will choose not to use the product after learning of the risk. By proving that she is in this group, the plaintiff would establish causation under the subjective standard. This type of proof, though, is quite problematic. "Unless we provide our consumer with a questionnaire or otherwise directly inquire as to her preferences, the only signs we will see of her preferences are the choices she makes."[60] The choices that the plaintiff has made previously with respect to the product will typically be of little help in resolving a counterfactual inquiry into whether she would still prefer to use the product after its cost had been increased by 10 percent. The only available proof is the plaintiff's testimony concerning her own, unobservable preferences for the product. How can the jury decide whether the plaintiff is lying or telling the truth?

60. David M. Kreps, A Course in Microeconomic Theory 26 (1990).

Unlike the subjective standard, the heeding presumption does not require speculative proof or self-serving testimony by the plaintiff, while giving the manufacturer an incentive to provide adequate warnings. These two "public policy" reasons justify the heeding presumption according to courts.[61] This justification, though, does not satisfactorily explain why the heeding presumption establishes causation in these cases. As the DES cases show, the principle of causation must be satisfied, regardless of the consequences for safety incentives.

A justification for the heeding presumption can instead be supplied by the *Restatement (Second)* rule of strict products liability. This rule makes the activity of selling a defective product subject to strict liability. Like the rule of negligence, strict liability requires proof of causation. The form of the causal inquiry differs for the two liability rules, however, and that difference explains why the heeding presumption is a defensible form of proof regarding causation.

For purposes of negligence liability, the plaintiff must prove that the defendant's unreasonable behavior caused the injury, proof involving a counterfactual inquiry into whether the injury would have occurred if the defendant had exercised reasonable care. As applied to the cases at hand, this causal inquiry requires the plaintiff to prove that if the defendant had satisfied its duty and provided a nondefective warning, the injury would have been prevented. This causal inquiry routinely immunizes manufacturers from liability. For most residual risks, the ordinary consumer who reads the adequate warning and is informed of the residual risk would still use the product and suffer the injury. To recover, the plaintiff must show that she is not like the ordinary consumer in this respect, but rarely will plaintiffs be able to identify themselves as a marginal consumer. Evidentiary problems undermine the effectiveness of the negligence-based causal inquiry.

This evidentiary problem can justify a causal inquiry based upon strict liability, which does not require a counterfactual inquiry into what would have occurred if the defendant had satisfied its duty by providing an adequate warning. For purposes of strict liability, the defendant incurs a compensatory duty by virtue of engaging in the injury-causing activity subject to strict liability. One who engages in the abnormally dangerous activity of blasting, for example, has a duty to compensate others for the harms caused by the associated risk. As long as the blasting caused the injury in

---

61. The two rationales have been expressly called ones of "public policy" in a leading case adopting the heeding presumption. *Coffman*, 628 A.2d at 717–20.

question, the defendant has a duty to compensate. In these cases, the principle of causation is satisfied by proof showing that the risk subject to strict liability (like blasting) caused the injury in question. As applied to the cases at hand, this causal inquiry requires the plaintiff to prove that the risk subject to strict liability—the residual risk that was not disclosed in the warning, rendering it defective—caused the injury for which she seeks compensation. The plaintiff can satisfy this causal requirement without having to prove that she would not have used the product had she known of the risk.

As long as the plaintiff would read and heed an adequate product warning, a defective warning necessarily frustrates her reasonable expectations of product safety. The plaintiff did not reasonably expect to be injured by the residual risk, since the warning did not alert her to that possibility. In order for tort liability to protect this safety expectation, the defendant seller must compensate the plaintiff for the injuries caused by the risk, the result achieved by a causal inquiry based on strict liability.

This principle is usefully illustrated by an influential case in which a defendant car manufacturer expressly represented or warranted that the windshield of its automobile was made of glass that "will not fly or shatter under the hardest impact."[62] The driver of the car suffered eye injuries when a passing car kicked up a pebble that shattered the windshield. By misrepresenting that the windshield was shatterproof, the defendant manufacturer became liable for the driver's eye injuries. These damages protected the plaintiff's reasonable safety expectation by fully compensating him for the harm caused by the unexpected risk. The fact that the plaintiff would have faced the risk anyway—no other manufacturer supplied a stronger windshield at the time—was irrelevant.[63] The plaintiff had a reasonable safety expectation that he would not be injured by a shattered windshield, entitling him to compensation for that injury.

Like the express warranty, the rule of strict products liability protects reasonable safety expectations. The express warranty protects the reasonable safety expectations of a particular consumer as promisee, whereas strict products liability protects the reasonable safety expectations of the ordinary consumer. For the same reasons that the plaintiff could recover for the injuries caused by the

62. Baxter v. Ford Motor Co., 12 P.2d 409 (Wash. 1932).

63. The trial judge excluded expert testimony to the effect that no other manufacturer produced a better windshield at the time, and the appellate court affirmed. 35 P.2d 1090 (Wash. 1934).

shattered windshield, plaintiffs can recover for the residual risks that should have been disclosed in an adequate warning. The ordinary consumer who uses a product can reasonably assume that the warning contains all the information she needs to make an informed decision. When the warning does not adequately disclose a residual risk, the ordinary consumer uses the product on the mistaken expectation that the risk does not exist. The consumer's safety expectation is not affected by the fact that she would have used the product (and faced the risk) had she known the truth. Consequently, the consumer's reasonable expectation of safety is frustrated when the unexpected residual risk causes injury. The frustrated safety expectation triggers the rule of strict products liability, enabling the consumer to recover for the physical injuries caused by the unexpected residual risk.

This reasoning explains why most courts insist that warning claims involve strict liability, even though a warning defect is defined by negligence principles or the risk-utility test.[64] Warning cases would clearly depend upon strict liability if the issue of defect were determined by reference to the risks known at the time of trial rather than at the time of sale, but most courts reject this form of strict liability.[65] By adhering to negligence principles on the issue of defect while holding that warning cases are governed by strict products liability, these courts appear to be confused, particularly since they have been unable to identify the particular role of strict liability. This approach, however, makes sense when considered in causal terms. Due to the practical ineffectiveness of the negligence-based causal inquiry, the evidentiary rationale for strict liability justifies a causal rule of strict liability.

We can now understand why the heeding presumption does not force courts to depart from the principle of causation. The plaintiff's proof of defect satisfies her burden of proving that she would read and heed or consider an adequate warning. The defect involves the lack of warning about a residual risk. For the defect to frustrate the plaintiff's reasonable safety expectations, the unexpected risk must have injured the plaintiff. By providing this causal proof, the plaintiff has shown that the defect—the undisclosed residual risk—caused a compensable injury governed by the rule of strict liability.

---

64. *E.g.*, Carlin v. Superior Court, 920 P.2d 1347, 1351 (Cal. 1996) (holding that strict products liability was not equivalent to negligence liability merely because the liability rule had "incorpo-rated certain negligence concepts into the standard of strict liability for failure to warn").

65. *See* Chapter 7, section IV.

So understood, the heeding presumption satisfies the tort requirement of causation.[66]

The heeding presumption is rebuttable. The presumption is derived from the fact that the inadequacy of the warning was material to the ordinary consumer, enabling the defendant to disprove causation by showing that the plaintiff is not like the ordinary consumer in this respect. The defendant can show that the plaintiff already knew the risk or would not have read the warning, so that the defective warning did not actually frustrate the plaintiff's reasonable safety expectations.

Since the heeding presumption is based upon a form of strict liability, it can be limited by comment *k* of the *Restatement (Second)* rule of strict products liability. For cases involving "unavoidably unsafe" products, comment *k* requires negligence liability.[67] The court therefore could determine that a product, such as a medically necessary drug, is an "unavoidably unsafe" product for purposes of the heeding presumption. In that event, the plaintiff must prove causation without relying on the heeding presumption, the same burden faced by plaintiffs in medical malpractice actions based on informed consent.[68]

D. Scientific Uncertainty

Cases involving scientific uncertainty pose one of the most important questions now facing the tort system. In the paradigmatic case, the available scientific evidence indicates that the product contains a substance that *might* be carcinogenic, but the evidence does not establish that the substance *is* a carcinogen. When presented with such evidence, courts must decide whether the plaintiff has adequately proven that her cancer was caused by the allegedly defective product.

This causal issue potentially arises whenever we do not fully understand how a substance interacts with the body and produces

66. The heeding presumption could also sufficiently establish liability if the tort claim involves a right to informed decision making. "Considerable judicial authority identifies defendants' failure to provide for informed choice as a separate ground for a products liability action" involving a defective product warning. Restatement (Third) § 2 cmt. i Rptrs' Note at 95. By selling a product that inadequately disclosed residual or unavoidable risks, the defendant has violated the ordinary consumer's right to informed decision making. This rights violation presumptively applies to the plaintiff, and could justify a damages remedy for the physical injury. *See* Mark Geistfeld, *Scientific Uncertainty and Causation in Tort Law*, 54 Vand. L. Rev. 1011, 1021–23 (2001).

67. *See* Chapter 5, section II; Chapter 6, section V.

68. *E.g.*, Canterbury v. Spence, 464 F.2d 772 (D.C. Cir. 1972) (requiring the plaintiff to prove that he would not have undergone the medical procedure if he had known of the material side-effects that were not disclosed by the physician).

an adverse health outcome, like cancer. To assess whether such a substance may cause injuries, we observe health outcomes in populations of animals exposed to large amounts of the substance, study the biochemical effects of the substance on cells, organs and embryos, and compare the substance's chemical composition to other known health hazards. Though informative, these studies usually cannot determine whether the substance is hazardous. That determination typically requires a large-scale study comparing the incidence of adverse health outcomes in groups of exposed and nonexposed human beings, or comparing the incidence of exposure across injured and healthy groups. These *epidemiologic studies* are expensive, time-consuming, and require that a large number of people be exposed to the substance. Not surprisingly, the vast majority of potentially hazardous substances have not been subjected to epidemiologic study.[69] Substances are routinely introduced into the environment before there is conclusive scientific evidence regarding their health hazards. How should this scientific uncertainty affect the tort rights of an individual who has been exposed to such a substance and has the type of injury, such as cancer, that is reasonably attributable to the substance in light of the available scientific evidence?

After the U.S. Supreme Court's decision in *Daubert v. Merrell Dow Pharmaceuticals, Inc.*, an increasing number of courts have held that causation in these cases must be established by epidemiologic evidence showing that a population of individuals exposed to the substance faced at least twice the risk of suffering the injury in question.[70] Although these courts are still in the minority, they persuasively argue that epidemiologic studies are the only reliable evidence showing that the substance more likely than not caused the plaintiff's injury. Numerous commentators criticize this evidentiary requirement, arguing that it is inconsistent with fundamental tort principles, particularly when applied to substances that have not been subjected to epidemiologic study. According to these critics, the lack of conclusive scientific evidence, and the unfairness of placing the burden of factual uncertainty on plaintiffs, require the adoption of special rules, such as placing the burden on a

69. *See, e.g.*, Federal Judicial Ctr., Reference Manual on Scientific Evidence 193 (1994) ("It must be emphasized that less than 1% of the 60,000–75,000 chemicals in commerce have been subjected to a full safety assessment, and only 10–20% have any toxicological data at all."). Recall that the lack of scientific study on these issues is at least partially attributable to tort rules governing the manufacturer's knowledge of risk. *See* Chapter 7, section IV.

70. 509 U.S. 579 (1993). The trend in the case law is described by Lucinda M. Finley, *Guarding the Gate to the Courthouse: How Trial Judges Are Using Their Evidentiary Screening Role to Remake Tort Causation Rules*, 49 DePaul L. Rev. 335, 347–64 (1999).

defendant manufacturer to prove that its product is not hazard-ous.[71]

To evaluate this issue, we can consider a case in which a consumer has cancer and claims that a defect in the manufacturer's product caused the injury. The alleged defect involves the manufacturer's failure to warn about the residual risk of cancer. In support of this claim, the plaintiff relies on scientifically valid studies showing that the product contains a chemical known to be an animal carcinogen. The plaintiff also relies on other scientifically valid laboratory studies supporting the hypothesis that the chemical is a human carcinogen. Finally, the plaintiff has evidence, such as the expert opinion of medical doctors, showing that her cancer was probably not caused by exposure to other known carcinogens. The plaintiff, however, does not have epidemiologic evidence, because no such studies have been conducted. The question is whether the plaintiff should be able to recover for her cancer on the basis of the foregoing evidence.

The plaintiff's causal proof is problematic since the proof of carcinogenicity depends only upon animal studies and the other laboratory studies. The fact that large quantities of the chemical increase the risk of cancer for mice does not mean that the substantially lower quantity of the chemical in the product poses the same risk, or any risk, for humans. The proof is only indicative of carcinogenicity, just like the plaintiff's other proof involving laboratory studies of the chemical. All told, the proof does not establish that the chemical in the product, more likely than not, is a human carcinogen. Ordinarily, that proof can only be provided by an epidemiologic study, explaining why some courts require epidemiologic proof to establish that the product, more likely than not, is a human carcinogen.

Resolution of the matter is not so straightforward, however. The cases in which courts require epidemiologic evidence typically involve "a substantial body of epidemiologic evidence introduced by the defendant that tended to exonerate the agent as causal."[72] Once this factor is considered, it turns out that the courts do not require epidemiologic proof in all cases:

> Circumstances in individual cases ... are sufficiently varied
> that almost all courts employ a more flexible approach to proof

---

71. *See, e.g.,* Margaret Berger, *Eliminating General Causation: Notes Towards a New Theory of Justice and Toxic Torts,* 97 Colum. L. Rev. 2117, 2131–34 (1997); Finley, *supra* note 70, at 363–76.

72. Restatement (Third) of Torts: Liability for Physical Harm (Basic Principles) § 28 cmt. c(3) (Proposed Final Draft No. 1, April 2005).

of causation—except in those cases with a substantial body of exonerative epidemiologic evidence. Epidemiologic studies are expensive and can take considerable time to design, conduct, and publish. For disease processes with long latency periods, valid studies cannot be performed until the disease has manifested itself. As a consequence, some plaintiffs may be forced to litigate long before epidemiologic research is available. Indeed, sometimes epidemiologic evidence is impossible to obtain, which may explain why neither the plaintiff nor the defendant is able to proffer supportive epidemiology. Thus, most courts have appropriately declined to impose a threshold requirement that a plaintiff always must prove causation with epidemiologic evidence ....[73]

The majority approach is puzzling. The plaintiff ordinarily cannot prove causation merely by showing that the product defect increased the risk of harm.[74] In our hypothetical case, the plaintiff has not even shown that the product can ever cause cancer. Unless the plaintiff can prove that the product, more likely than not, actually causes cancer—proof that usually requires epidemiologic study—how can she show that the product increases the risk of cancer by an amount sufficient to satisfy the burden of proof? By permitting the plaintiff to prove causation in these cases, the "flexible approach" might reduce the plaintiff's evidentiary burden merely because she faces difficulty in acquiring epidemiologic proof. The courts, however, do not justify the flexible approach as a means of reducing the plaintiff's burden of proof. Moreover, plaintiffs in the DES cases also face a virtually impossible task of collecting the evidence required to prove causation, but that difficulty has not persuaded courts to relax the plaintiff's evidentiary burden. Evidentiary difficulties do not persuasively explain the flexible approach. The courts apparently believe that the approach adheres to the principle of causation, even though it does not require proof of cancer with epidemiologic study. But how is the principle of causation satisfied in these cases?

The case law has not provided a compelling answer. The courts, though, have addressed the issue as if it were purely one of causation, which is sensible insofar as the issue of causation is no different than the issue of defect. After all, if the product does not

---

73. *Id.*

74. "If nothing further were required [other than proof of tortious conduct and the concomitant increase in risk], plaintiff's burden of proof on causation would always be satisfied. Thus, only when the tortious conduct reason- ably could be found, after the fact, to have increased the risk of harm to a greater extent than the risk posed by all other potential causes would an inference from tortious conduct alone be permissible." *Id.* § 28 cmt. b.

cause cancer, then the warning cannot be defective for failing to state that the product is a carcinogen. In our hypothetical case, however, the warning can be defective even if there is no conclusive proof that the product is a carcinogen. That possibility explains why the plaintiff can recover without epidemiologic proof.

In the case under consideration, the plaintiff is claiming that the warning is defective for not alerting consumers to the possibility that the product might cause cancer. This allegation does not necessarily require proof that the product *is* a carcinogen. The warning can be defective for not letting consumers know of a reasonable scientific basis for concluding that the product *might* be a carcinogen. To recover for such a defect, the plaintiff can rely upon the types of evidence required by the flexible approach.

The proof of defect requires the plaintiff to show that the requested disclosure involves a risk that was foreseeable at the time of sale.[75] The risk is that the product might be carcinogenic. This risk is foreseeable, even though there is not conclusive scientific evidence of carcinogenicity. The plaintiff has proven that the product contains a chemical known to be an animal carcinogen, has other properties suggestive of human carcinogenicity, and has never been subjected to a scientific study finding that it is not carcinogenic. The plaintiff's proof provides a sufficient foundation for the administrative regulation of the product as a human carcinogen.[76] The proof does not show that the product, more likely than not, is a carcinogen. It does, however, provide a reasonable basis for concluding that the seller knew or should have known at the time of sale that the product might be carcinogenic, thereby satisfying the requirement of foreseeability.

The plaintiff must then show that a reasonable product warning would tell consumers that the product might be carcinogenic. As previously discussed, the warning must contain such a disclosure if it would be material to the ordinary consumer's decision of whether to purchase or use the product.[77]

To evaluate the materiality of the disclosure, consider the following bets. The first bet involves coin *A*, which you have been able to examine. Suppose you confidently believe the coin is fair because it comes up heads or tails with approximately equal frequency. The second bet involves coin *B*, which you have never seen and cannot examine prior to the bet. You do not know if coin *B* is two-headed, two-tailed, or otherwise fair. Without any further

---

75. *See* Chapter 7, section IV.

76. *See, e.g.,* Alon Rosenthal et al., *Legislating Acceptable Cancer Risk from* *Exposure to Toxic Chemicals*, 19 Ecology L.Q. 269, 270 (1992).

77. *See* Chapter 7, section III.

information about coin B, you might decide that each of these coin configurations is equally likely, so you estimate an equal likelihood of heads or tails (the equally likely two-headed and two-tailed coins cancel one another out, leaving the fair coin). You also estimate the same probabilities for coin A. Do you think the bets involving the two coins are identical, and does that make a difference?

If you're like most people, you will have much more confidence in your probability assessment of coin A than in your assessment of coin B. The difference is not relevant if you must bet now, for in that case you form a best estimate and bet accordingly. The best estimate for the two coins is the same, eliminating any relevant difference between them in this setting. The difference in your confidence of these estimates is relevant, though, if you have the option of obtaining more information prior to making the bet. When this option is available, you should be more willing to invest effort or money to obtain information about coin B than about coin A. If, for example, you can observe a toss of coin B and the outcome is heads, you can rule out the possibility that the coin is two-tailed. Observing the identical outcome from a toss of coin A, by contrast, is unlikely to change your opinion that the coin is fair. Consequently, "greater prior doubt (lesser degree of confidence) makes it more important to acquire additional evidence before making a terminal move" such as placing a bet.[78]

Now consider how this reasoning applies to the consumer's decision of whether to purchase a product that might be carcinogenic. Absent a warning, the consumer can reasonably assume that the product is not carcinogenic. By contrast, a consumer who is aware of the animal studies and other indicators of carcinogenicity would have much lower confidence in her assessment of the product risk. The difference in confidence may not matter if the consumer must use the product right now, but typically that is not the case. Consumers usually have the option of waiting to consume or use a product. Delayed consumption is costly for the consumer—she cannot derive any present benefit from the product—but the cost of delayed consumption can be less than the benefit of waiting to find out whether the product really is carcinogenic. Information about possible carcinogenicity, therefore, can influence the consumer's decision whether to purchase or use the product. Such a disclosure would reduce the consumer's confidence about the product's safety and may induce her to wait until further study has been done. In these cases, disclosure of the scientific uncertainty would be materi-

78. Jack Hirshleifer & John G. Riley, The Analytics of Uncertainty and Infor- mation 11 (1992).

al to the ordinary consumer's decision of whether to purchase or use the product. The absence of such a disclosure renders the warning defective.[79]

Hence, the plaintiff can establish a warning defect for cases lacking epidemiologic evidence. The question now is whether the plaintiff can also establish causation without epidemiologic proof pursuant to the flexible approach adopted by almost all courts.

In addition to the proof of defect, the plaintiff has also proven that her cancer was probably not caused by some other known carcinogen. By excluding these specific causes of the cancer in addition to proving that there is a reasonable basis for finding the product to be a carcinogen, the plaintiff has shown by a preponderance of the evidence that the product is the only reasonably identifiable cause of her cancer.

On the basis of this evidence, the court could decide that the defect injured the plaintiff in violation of the rule of strict products liability. As previously discussed, the plaintiff's proof of defect also presumptively proves that she would read and heed or consider an adequate warning.[80] Since the evidence also shows that the product is the only reasonably identifiable cause of the cancer, the plaintiff has established that the warning defect frustrated her reasonable expectations of safety. The warning created the mistaken expectation that the product does not cause cancer. The plaintiff now has cancer, and the product is the only reasonably identifiable cause. In these circumstances, the court could conclude that the warning defect frustrated the reasonable safety expectation of the plaintiff, the interest protected by the rule of strict products liability.[81]

Having established liability, the plaintiff must then prove damages. In proving the extent of damages caused by the defendant's breach of duty, the plaintiff must provide reasonable proof.[82] Reasonableness depends on what can fairly be demanded of the plain-

79. *Cf.* Restatement (Third) § 2 cmt. i ("Whether or not many persons would, when warned, nonetheless decide to use or consume the product, warnings are required to protect the interests of those reasonably foreseeable users or consumers who would, based on their own reasonable assessments of the risks and benefits, decline product use or consumption.").

80. *See supra* subsection C.

81. The sale of the defective product also establishes tort liability if the consumer has an independent right to informed decision making. *See supra* note 66. Regardless of the exact doctrinal basis, the liability is not one for mere risk exposure. The plaintiff has actually suffered injury (the cancer) and established a scientific basis that makes it reasonable to link the injury to the product defect. A reasonable linkage between the defect and injury can be sufficient to frustrate the consumer's reasonable expectation of safety, even if the consumer cannot have frustrated expectations when she has only been exposed to an unexpected risk.

82. *See supra* subsection A.

tiff in light of the defendant's breach of duty. The defendant failed to warn of the scientific uncertainty and therefore cannot rely on the uncertainty to disprove damages and exonerate itself from liability. The uncertainty is created by the lack of epidemiologic studies, and so the absence of such proof does not bar plaintiff's damages claim. The plaintiff only needs nonepidemiologic proof that provides a reasonable basis for concluding that the product caused her cancer. The plaintiff in our hypothetical case has submitted such evidence, enabling her to recover damages for the cancer as compensation for her frustrated safety expectations.

This form of liability provides an important safety incentive. As we found earlier, the vast majority of courts absolve a manufacturer of liability for unforeseeable risks, reducing its incentive to test for product hazards.[83] This safety problem is ameliorated if the manufacturer is responsible for the worst-case scenario that can be reasonably inferred from the current scientific understanding of the product. Rather than face liability for the worst-case scenario or otherwise disclose the problem to consumers and drive up their estimates of product cost, the manufacturer can engage in further research to clear up the uncertainty. The incentive to engage in research on product hazards is strengthened when manufacturers must account for scientific uncertainty.

This reasoning explains why "almost all courts have appropriately declined to impose a threshold requirement that a plaintiff always must prove causation with epidemiologic evidence."[84] Consumers have reasonable safety expectations regarding potential carcinogens and the like, depending upon the severity of the potential hazard, the reasonably available scientific evidence, and the consumer's willingness or ability to delay using the product. These factors are highly context-dependent, making it appropriate for the courts to adopt a flexible approach in determining the minimum evidence required of the plaintiff.

II. Legal or Proximate Cause (A Reprise of Duty)

A product defect can have injurious consequences extending far into the future. To limit the potential scope or extent of the seller's liability, tort law requires the plaintiff to prove that her injury was proximately caused by the defect.[85]

---

83. *See* Chapter 7, section IV.

84. Restatement (Third) of Torts: Liability for Physical Harm (Basic Principles) § 28 cmt. c(3) (Proposed Final Draft No. 1, April 2005).

85. *See generally* Joseph A. Page, Torts: Proximate Cause (2003).

The most widely adopted test for proximate cause is based on foreseeability, asking whether the plaintiff's injury was a reasonably foreseeable result of the defect. An alternative test holds the defendant liable for injuries directly caused by the defect, even if the harm was not foreseeable. "Importantly, some jurisdictions hold that a directness test is appropriate in strict products liability because foreseeability of harm is a negligence concept and not relevant in a strict liability case."[86]

This rationale for the directness test is based on consumer expectations, a concept that many courts and commentators equate with strict liability.[87] Consumer expectations do not justify liability rules that make the seller an "insurer" of the product, however—the liability rule must be formulated to reduce risk.[88] A foreseeable risk is one that is known or should be known by the manufacturer at the time of sale, enabling it to make safety decisions about the risk. So, too, an unforeseeable risk ordinarily does not factor into the manufacturer's safety decisions. Holding the manufacturer liable for unforeseen risks would not influence its safety decisions, eliminating any safety rationale for tort liability. Contrary to what some courts have concluded, the concept of consumer expectations justifies the limitation of liability to foreseeable risks.[89]

The foreseeability test for proximate cause requires reconsideration of the duty element. A product seller's duty is limited to foreseeable risks. Why, then, does the element of proximate cause also limit liability to foreseeable risks? What distinguishes the two elements?

Duty is a question of law to be determined by the judge. As a question of law, the judge must decide duty issues by reference to a category of cases and not merely the case at hand. For example, judges have determined that duty is limited to all foreseeable risks except those threatening certain types of injuries, such as pure economic loss or emotional harms unconnected to physical harm.[90] These duty rules are categorical in nature, excluding unforeseeable

86. 1 Madden & Owen on Products Liability § 13:2, at 786.

87. *See* Chapter 1, section III.

88. *See* Chapter 3, section III.

89. Liability for an unforeseeable risk can affect the manufacturer's decision to discover the risk by product testing, which in turn could have a beneficial safety effect if the discovered risks are large enough to influence safety decisions. *See* Chapter 7, section IV. Such a safety rationale is not applicable to the unforeseeable risks governed by the issue of proximate cause, which typically involve extraordinarily unlikely events that occur in highly individuated circumstances. A manufacturer that knew of these risks would not likely alter its safety decisions, nor would it engage in product testing to discover them.

90. The issues of economic loss and emotional harm are respectively discussed in Chapter 9, sections I and II.

risks, the risk of suffering pure economic loss, and the risk of suffering stand-alone emotional harms. A judicial decision that the defendant has no duty with respect to a general type of risk absolves the defendant and similarly situated product sellers of legal responsibility for risks of that type. Product sellers remain responsible for other risks. The judicial resolution of the duty question, therefore, determines the general risks to be evaluated by the standard of care, such as the risk-utility test.[91]

Once the element of duty has been established as a matter of law, the court must then address the separate issue of whether the particular risk that caused the plaintiff's injury is within the general category of foreseeable risks encompassed by the duty. This issue of proximate cause is a question of fact to be decided by the jury.

To see why, consider *Union Pump Co. v. Allbritton*.[92] The defendant pump manufacturer owed a duty to the plaintiff that included the foreseeable risk of the pump catching fire. On the basis of this duty, the plaintiff proved the pump was defective for catching on fire and igniting the surrounding area in a chemical factory. The plaintiff was a trainee employee who had just completed her shift before spending about two hours fighting the fire. After the fire had been extinguished, the plaintiff, while still wearing her firefighting gear, walked on a pipe rack—a shorter, but less safe route. She slipped on the wet metal, suffering injury. The pipe rack was wet because of the fire. This evidence established that the defendant owed a duty to the plaintiff; that the duty was breached by the sale of a defective product; and that the defect was a but for cause of the plaintiff's physical harm. The plaintiff's recovery depended only on whether her injury was proximately caused by the defect, an issue distinct from the element of duty.

In addressing the issue of proximate cause, the jury must decide whether the particular risk that caused the plaintiff's injury is within the general category of foreseeable risks encompassed by the duty. In making this determination, the jury effectively decides whether this particular risk is one that ought to influence the manufacturer's safety decisions.

Consider in this regard the concurring opinion in *Union Pump*, which concluded that the plaintiff's injury was not proximately caused by the defect:

91. *See* Mark Geistfeld, *The Analytics of Duty: Medical Monitoring and Related Forms of Economic Loss*, 88 Va. L. Rev. 1921, 1923–29 (2002) (showing why the standard of care is indeterminate unless first defined by the element of duty).

92. 898 S.W.2d 773 (Tex. 1995).

[Plaintiff's] injuries were the result of a needlessly dangerous shortcut taken after the crisis had subsided. Holding [defendant] liable for [plaintiff's] failure to use proper care is akin to holding it liable for an auto accident she suffered on the way home, even though the accident probably would not have occurred had she left after her normal shift. Foreseeability allows us to cut off [defendant's] liability at some point; I would do so at the point the crisis had abated or at the point [plaintiff chose to walk on the pipe rack].[93]

The force of the argument comes from the seeming absurdity of holding a pump manufacturer liable for an auto accident. The liability is absurd, though, only because the safety of a pump in a chemical factory should not depend upon a coincidental auto accident involving a firefighter. By analogizing the auto accident to the particular risk that caused the plaintiff's injury, the concurrence can persuasively argue that the risk was unforeseeable—it was something the manufacturer was not obligated to consider when making safety decisions.

Once proximate cause is conceptualized in this manner, it becomes apparent that the plaintiff had a much stronger case than the court recognized in ruling that no reasonable juror could have found the risk to be foreseeable. The plaintiff could first have argued that in considering the general risk of fire, the pump manufacturer should also consider the possibility that individuals will be injured as a result of fighting the fire. One source of injury stems from the physical and mental exhaustion inevitably caused by the firefighting effort. Tired individuals are more likely to make mistakes, resulting in injury. A good reason for pump manufacturers to reduce the risk of fire, therefore, is to reduce the risk that an exhausted firefighter will be less alert and vulnerable to hazards that she might otherwise be able to avoid. The plaintiff could then argue that she was injured by such a risk. Had the plaintiff deliberated about the matter, she probably would have realized that it was not a good idea to walk in fireman's hip boots on wet pipes. But the plaintiff did not deliberate. She had a "bad habit" of walking on the pipe racks, had just completed a full shift of work followed by two hours of firefighting, and was a trainee who was following her supervisor at the time of injury. By walking on the pipe racks, the plaintiff resorted to ordinary behavior despite the extraordinary circumstances posed by the fire. This behavior was predictable, given her mental and physical exhaustion foreseeably

93. *Id.* at 785.

caused by the firefighting, yielding the conclusion that the plaintiff's injury was proximately caused by the defect.

As this case shows, the seller's duty to control foreseeable risks requires elaboration by reference to the particular circumstances of each case. A duty to control the general risk of fire actually encompasses a wide range of individuated risks. Each case necessarily involves a particular instance of a general risk, requiring a case-by-case determination of whether the particular risk is part of the general risk encompassed by the duty. For this reason, the issue of proximate cause is a jury question.

Like any other factual issue, judges can determine proximate cause as a matter of law by concluding that no reasonable juror could find otherwise, the result in *Union Pump*. Since this finding of fact takes the form of a legal conclusion, it may seem to be equivalent to a finding of law that the defendant had no duty with respect to this particular unforeseeable risk. A legal conclusion concerning proximate cause, however, depends upon the reasonable-juror standard, whereas duty rules do not depend upon how a reasonable juror would decide the matter. The element of proximate cause is not interchangeable with the element of duty, even though they share the requirement of foreseeability and can be decided by the judge as a matter of law.[94]

94. *Cf.* Restatement (Third) of Torts: Liability for Physical Harm (Basic Principles) § 7 cmt. j (Proposed Final Draft No. 1, April 2005) (disapproving the judicial practice of basing a no-duty ruling on the lack of foreseeability in order "to protect the traditional function of the jury as factfinder").

Chapter 9

DAMAGES

Once the court has determined that the defendant is liable to the plaintiff, the jury must then determine the damages to which the plaintiff is entitled. Depending on the nature of the claim, the plaintiff may recover compensatory damages for personal injury, property damage, and economic loss. The plaintiff may also be able to recover punitive damages by proving that the defendant's tortious conduct merits such a sanction.

Many types of compensatory damages are easy to conceptualize, even if difficult to quantify in particular cases. Compensatory tort damages "are designed to place [the plaintiff] in a position substantially equivalent in a pecuniary way to that which he would have occupied had no tort been committed."[1] It is easy to understand how this compensatory principle can be satisfied for a plaintiff's financial losses, such as medical expenses, lost wages or earnings, and damage to tangible property having a recognized market value. A damages award equal to the amount of lost wages caused by the product defect, for example, returns the plaintiff to the pecuniary position for wage income that she would have been in if the product had not been defective.

Damages for nonmonetary injuries, commonly called pain and suffering, are much more puzzling. How do injuries like pain, fear, anxiety, disfigurement, and the loss of life's pleasures translate into a monetary damages award that returns the plaintiff "in a pecuniary way" to the position she would have been in if the product had not been defective? The difficulty of measurement has made these damages a target of tort reform, with many jurisdictions enacting legislation that limits or caps these damages.

Similarly, the quantification of punitive damages has been one of the most controversial issues in tort law. In a line of relatively recent cases, the U.S. Supreme Court has determined that the long-standing procedures used by courts to determine punitive damages can yield awards that violate the Due Process Clause of the U.S. Constitution. What are the criteria for determining whether any given award satisfies this constitutional requirement? What implications do they have for the role of punitive damages in product cases?

---

1. Restatement (Second) § 903 cmt. a.

The issues involving damages are not limited to questions of quantification or measurement. Defective products often cause injuries that are not compensable in tort law. For cases in which the defective product causes economic loss but no bodily injury or property damage, most jurisdictions deny the plaintiff recovery in tort altogether. Most jurisdictions also deny the plaintiff recovery when the defect causes pain and suffering not accompanied by physical harm. Why does the type of injury affect the plaintiff's ability to recover? As is true of the others, an analysis of these issues reveals a great deal about products liability.

I. Economic Loss

For cases in which the product defect causes *physical harm*—bodily injury or damage to tangible property—tort law provides the plaintiff with the greatest range of damage remedies. In these cases, the plaintiff can receive compensatory damages for the bodily injury, pain and suffering, property damage and the economic losses caused by the defect.

A different rule applies to cases in which the plaintiff suffers only economic or financial loss consisting of damage to the product itself and ensuing financial harms, such as repair costs, decreased product value, and reduced profits or earnings. For example, if a component in an industrial machine malfunctions because of a defect, causing an assembly line to shut down and the company to lose profits as a result, all the losses would be pure economic loss. In a "strong majority" of jurisdictions, a seller is not liable in tort for these damages pursuant to the *economic loss rule*.[2]

The economic loss rule has been controversial, generating a "particularly fierce battleground in products liability."[3] If the defective component in the preceding example caused physical damage to something other than the product itself—for example, if the defect caused the machine to catch fire and burn other property in the factory—the seller would be liable for the ensuing financial harms like lost profits.[4] Why should liability for economic loss turn on the

2. Restatement (Third) § 21 cmt. d Rptrs' Note.

3. Shapo, 2 Law of Products Liability ¶ 27.01 at 16,003.

4. Not surprisingly, disputes arise over what constitutes the "product itself" for purposes of the economic loss rule. When a defective component harms solely the entire manufactured product of which it is part, there is only damage to the "product itself." But what if the initial purchaser has added equipment to the entire manufactured product (like a boat), and the defective component causes injury to such equipment? According to the U.S. Supreme Court, in these circumstances the defect has injured "other property" and the economic loss rule does not apply. *See* Saratoga Fishing Co. v. J.M. Martinac & Co., 520 U.S. 875 (1997).

fortuity of whether the defect caused physical harm to something other than the product itself? Unable to find a satisfactory answer, a few jurisdictions have rejected the economic loss rule in all cases.[5] Other jurisdictions have adopted a variant of the economic loss rule, limiting it to cases in which the defect does not threaten physical harm.[6] Under this "intermediate rule," a plaintiff can recover damages for the reasonable financial expenditures required to reduce the risk of physical harm, even though the defect has not yet caused physical harm.

Despite these differing rules, the courts agree that a tort rule governing pure economic loss has important implications for contract law.[7] In the leading case that adopted the economic loss rule, the U.S. Supreme Court reasoned that the pure economic loss caused by a defective product "is essentially the failure of the purchaser to receive the benefit of its bargain—traditionally the core concern of contract law."[8] The owner of the malfunctioning industrial machine, for example, purchased the product on the expectation that it would produce profits. The defect frustrated the owner's economic expectations, the interest protected by the contract law of product warranties. If tort law governed all claims for pure financial loss, it would undermine the contract law of product warranties. To maintain the integrity of contract law, the Court ruled that recovery for any claim of pure economic loss must be based on contract law.

The economic loss rule returns us to the boundary between tort and contract law. In evaluating the respective roles of these two bodies of law, we have found that the appropriate rule depends upon whether consumers can adequately protect themselves with contracting. A tort duty is not required when the ordinary consumer can make good contracting decisions and does not have frustrated safety expectations.[9] As applied to the issue of pure economic loss, this principle means that the tort duty should not encompass the risk of pure economic loss if the ordinary consumer has good information about the risk and can adequately protect her interests by contracting with product sellers. Such a contracting rationale would justify the economic loss rule adopted by the strong majority

5. Restatement (Third) § 21 cmt. d Rptrs' Note at 305.

6. *See id.* at 304.

7. *See* Restatement (Third) of Torts: Liability for Physical Harm (Basic Principles) § 7 cmt. d (Proposed Final Draft No. 1, April 2005).

8. East River S.S. Corp. v. Transamerica Delaval, 476 U.S. 858, 870 (1986) (applying admiralty law). This case is the "leading decision espousing the position that the nature of the loss should be the determining factor" in deciding the scope of the tort duty. Restatement (Third) § 21 cmt. d.

9. *See* Chapter 2, section II.B.

of courts, which effectively limits the tort duty of product sellers by excluding the risk of pure economic loss.

To undertake this contracting analysis, we need to reconsider the nature of the safety decision that must be made by the consumer. So far, we have only considered a product risk that causes physical harm. In these cases, the seller incurs liability for the physical harm and any emotional or economic harm that was also caused by the defect. This liability is based upon the breach of a duty of care that can be defined in terms of the Hand formulation of the risk-utility test:

$$B < P \bullet (L_{Physical} + L_{Emotional} + L_{Economic})$$

This duty often is called the *general duty of care* because it expresses the general duty one has not to expose others to an unreasonable risk of physical harm. By definition, the general duty of care provides consumers with reasonable protection from the foreseeable risk of physical harm. The rationale for the duty is that the ordinary consumer does not have the information needed to make good contractual decisions, resulting in frustrated safety expectations requiring protection by the tort duty.

Now suppose that the product poses both a risk of physical harm to the consumer (denoted P_1) and a risk of pure economic loss (denoted P_2). If the tort duty were to encompass pure economic loss, the general duty of care would be expanded to include the additional risk that the defect might cause pure economic loss:

$$B < P_1 \bullet (L_{Physical} + L_{Emotional} + L_{Economic}) + P_2 \bullet (L_{Economic})$$

In general, the expanded duty of care requires more product safety than the general duty of care. (The added safety benefit for pure economic loss on the right-hand side of the equation can justify an increase in safety expenditures on the left-hand side.) The more expansive duty, though, cannot be justified on the ground that the increased product safety is required to protect consumers from an unreasonable risk of physical harm. That protection is already provided by the general duty of care.

Similarly, the informational problem that justifies the general duty of care does not justify the more expansive tort duty encompassing the risk of pure economic loss. Consumers who are poorly informed about the risk of physical harm have frustrated expectations requiring tort protection. By governing the manufacturer's safety decisions with respect to the risk of physical harm, the general duty of care can largely regulate the probability the product will cause any type of injury. In that event, any issues pertaining to pure economic loss largely depend upon the amount of loss and the cost-effectiveness of other methods for protecting against such losses. In this respect, the ordinary consumer has better information than the product seller. The consumer knows how the product will be used and has better information about the financial harms, like lost profits, that may be caused by a defect. This information enables the ordinary consumer to protect her interests by either contracting with the seller for warranty coverage, purchasing other types of insurance, or obtaining a supply of spare parts.[10] A tort duty encompassing pure economic harms, therefore, is not needed to protect the consumer interests at stake in these cases. The general duty of care protects the consumer's interest in physical security—the core concern of tort law—and the consumer can protect her pure economic interests by contracting.

Although a contracting rationale can justify the limitation of duty to exclude the risk of pure economic loss, the majority rule applies to all forms of economic loss, not merely the particular form we have just analyzed. A complete evaluation of the majority rule requires us to consider another class of cases involving pure economic loss.

Suppose an automatic braking system in a car is defective because the system operates during emergencies in a manner that "causes the average driver to perceive an actual brake failure and misapply the brakes."[11] To eliminate the risk, the braking system must be repaired. The repair, though expensive, costs less than the risk that the defective braking system will harm the consumer by causing her to misapply the brakes and crash:

$$B_{Repair} < P \bullet (L_{Physical} + L_{Emotional} + L_{Economic})$$

The consumer's repair decision implicates the same interests protected by the general duty of care. The defective automatic braking system works perfectly well in normal braking situations and does not disappoint the consumer's expectations in any respect other than the risk of physical harm—the defect is manifested only in emergency situations involving the risk of accidental crashes. For such a defect, the consumer must decide whether to incur repair costs in order to protect her interest in physical security. The nature of this decision is fundamentally equivalent to the safety

---

10. *See* William K. Jones, *Product Defects Causing Commercial Loss: The Ascendancy of Contract over Tort*, 44 U. Miami L. Rev. 731, 764–67 (1990). The informational advantage regarding loss is likely to be more pronounced for commercial buyers, explaining why some courts have granted recovery for pure economic loss in cases involving non-commercial buyers. *See, e.g.*, Lloyd F. Smith Co. v. Den–Tal–Ez, 491 N.W.2d 11, 17 (Minn. 1992).

11. Such a defect was alleged in Briehl v. General Motors Corp., 172 F.3d 623, 626 (8th Cir. 1999).

decision governed by the general duty of care (compare this equation with the first equation describing the general duty of care).

The repair decision importantly differs from the decision regarding pure economic losses that occur independently of the risk of physical harm (compare the prior two equations). For defects of this type (like the defective component of a machine in a factory assembly line), the consumer must decide whether to incur financial costs for the sole purpose of protecting a pure economic interest, such as future profits.[12] A defect of this type poses no future risk of physical harm (once the component failed, the assembly line shut down). The consumer's decision concerning such a defect does not implicate the interest in physical security. The decision only implicates the consumer's expectation regarding economic interests.

Despite the difference in the interests at stake, the majority rule on economic loss does not differentiate between these two types of economic loss. As long as the defect has caused injury only to the product itself, any ensuing economic losses are not recoverable in tort. It does not matter whether the defect implicates the same interests protected by the general duty of care.

This difference does affect the contracting rationale for the economic loss rule, however. To see why, consider the patent danger rule, which absolves the seller from any duty regarding open and obvious risks. Under this rule, an automobile manufacturer would have no duty regarding the defective braking system if the danger were obvious to consumers (a prominent warning of the risk presumably would suffice). The patent danger rule has been widely rejected. The ordinary consumer cannot necessarily make the correct contracting decisions merely because the danger is apparent, and that safety problem justifies the inclusion of these risks within the seller's tort duty.[13] By this same reasoning, the consumer faces contracting problems with respect to the defective braking system. In one case, the braking system involves an obvious risk (due to the warning). In the other case, the braking system involves a latent or hidden risk (the consumer only became aware of the problem after driving the car). If the ordinary consumer cannot make good contractual decisions regarding obvious risks, then she cannot make good contractual decisions regarding hidden risks. By rejecting the patent danger rule, the courts have relied upon a contracting problem that also applies to cases in which the consumer seeks

---

12. Recall that the concept of the consumer includes corporations and their employees. *See* Chapter 2, section I.

13. *See* Chapter 2, section II.B.

recovery for the economic costs of repairing the defective brakes. This contracting problem would seem to justify a tort duty regarding the cost of repair, but such recovery is denied by the majority rule on pure economic loss. The majority rule on economic loss is not persuasively justified by the ability of consumers to protect themselves by contracting.

Ultimately, the contracting rationale for majority rule depends only upon the form of damages rather than the substantive interests at stake: Pure economic losses are governed by the contract law of product warranties; to maintain the integrity of that body of contract law, product sellers cannot incur tort liability for pure economic loss. But since tort law is concerned with the protection of the consumer's interest in physical security, and that interest is implicated by certain forms of pure economic loss, the majority rule on economic loss disregards this substantive tort concern in order to protect the formal category of damages governed by contract law.

Like other liability rules that elevate form over substance, the majority rule on economic loss is most vulnerable when substantive concerns dominate the case at hand. This explains why the courts have effectively recognized two exceptions to the economic loss rule, each of which involves circumstances in which the safety concerns of tort law are paramount.

The first exception involves cases in which plaintiffs have sought to recover the financial expenses of medical monitoring. For example, in the cases involving the diet drug combination popularly known as Fen–Phen, the alleged defects involved the failure of the warnings to disclose the risk that the drugs might cause heart-valve damage.[14] Due to the nature of the risk, a plaintiff who does not yet have heart-valve damage may suffer that injury in the future. To protect herself, the plaintiff must undergo periodic medical testing. The tests are costly, and the plaintiff seeks tort recovery for these costs on the ground that the harm was caused by the product defect. As with the tort claims for repair costs, the monitoring claims would seem to be barred by the economic loss rule, as the cost of testing is financial and does not stem from an existing physical harm. Nevertheless, courts typically allow medical monitoring claims, reasoning that the claim involves the type of interest protected by tort law:

> [I]n light of the *Restatement (Second) of Torts'* definition of "injury," we are not obliged to accept [defendant's] implicit

14. *See* In re Penn. Diet Drugs Litigation, 1999 WL 962583 (Ct. C. P. Phil. Co. Pa., 1999).

claim that undergoing diagnostic examinations does not in itself constitute injury. The *Restatement* broadly defines injury as "the invasion of any legally protected interest of another." *It is difficult to dispute that an individual has an interest in avoiding expensive diagnostic examinations just as he or she has an interest in avoiding physical injury.* When a defendant negligently invades this interest, the injury to which is neither speculative nor resistant to proof, it is elementary that the defendant should make the plaintiff whole by paying for the examinations.[15]

The individual's interest in avoiding periodic medical testing is no different than her interest in avoiding physical injury—each implicates the individual interest in physical security, the core concern of tort law. In the medical monitoring cases, the security interest is the dominant consideration, leading most courts to the conclusion that "it is elementary that the defendant should make the plaintiff whole by paying for the examinations."

A similar exception to the economic loss rule involves asbestos abatement. In response to the health hazards posed by asbestos, the federal government and many states have enacted statutes requiring the removal or segregation of asbestos-containing materials from schools and public buildings. Private homeowners have also undertaken these abatement measures. The measures are quite expensive, leading property owners to seek tort compensation for the costs of abating the unreasonable risks posed by asbestos. In response, asbestos manufacturers and suppliers have invoked the economic loss rule, maintaining that abatement costs are entirely financial. The economic loss rule would seem to require dismissal of these claims. "In fact, most courts have done just the opposite, freely allowing property owners to sue in tort by adopting a 'liberal' definition of physical injury."[16] By holding that asbestos-containing material damages other property, "liberally" defined, these cases do not literally violate the economic loss rule. The holding is unpersuasive, however, because "asbestos-containing materials do not physically alter any part of the building or impair its structural integri-

15. Friends for All Children v. Lockheed Aircraft Corp., 746 F.2d 816, 826 (D.C. Cir. 1984) (citation omitted) (emphasis added). There has been a clear trend favoring recovery of medical monitoring costs. *See* James M. Garner et al., *Medical Monitoring: The Evolution of a Cause of Action*, 30 Envtl. L. Rep. (Envtl. L. Inst.) 10,024, 10,024 (2000). The appellate courts in seventeen states and the District of Columbia recognize such claims. *See, e.g.*, Badillo v. American Brands, 16 P.3d 435, 438–39 (Nev. 2001). The trend may have subsided, however. Recently some courts have rejected medical monitoring claims unless the plaintiff can establish a present physical injury. *E.g.*, *id.*

16. *See* Richard C. Ausness, *Tort Liability for Asbestos Removal Costs*, 73 Or. L. Rev. 505, 530 (1994).

ty."[17] The building materials containing asbestos also continue to perform the intended function of being fire resistant. The only reason to remove asbestos-containing materials is to reduce the risk of physical harm, not to restore the proper functioning of the building. Consequently, the asbestos abatement cases effectively involve an exception to the majority rule on economic loss, an outcome acknowledged by the *Restatement (Third)*:

> One category of claims stands apart. In the case of asbestos contamination in buildings, most courts have taken the position that the contamination constitutes harm to the building as other property. *The serious health threat caused by asbestos contamination has led the courts to this conclusion.* Thus, actions seeking recovery for the costs of asbestos removal have been held to be within the purview of products liability law rather than commercial law.[18]

The majority rule in the asbestos-abatement cases protects consumer expectations regarding product safety. The need to protect safety expectations also explains why most courts have been willing to provide a tort remedy for medical monitoring. As both issues illustrate, when the damages remedy would help to prevent a future physical harm, the security interest is at stake and the courts have had no trouble justifying tort liability.

For this same reason, many courts have rejected the majority rule on economic loss in favor of the intermediate rule, which is based upon the substantive interests at stake and not the form of damages. The intermediate rule distinguishes defects that merely disappoint the buyer from defects that are unreasonably dangerous to persons and property. Contract law governs cases in which the defect poses no threat of future physical harm, as with the broken-down assembly line. The defect frustrates the consumer's economic expectations regarding product performance and related financial matters, such as lost profits. This expectancy interest is the core concern of contract law, and so the intermediate rule protects the integrity of contract law by barring tort claims in these circumstances. But if the defect instead poses a threat of future physical harm, it frustrates reasonable consumer expectations of safety—the core concern of products liability. Now the tort duty can be justified without undermining the integrity of contract law, and so the intermediate rule does not apply the economic loss rule to defects of this type.[19]

---

17. *Id.* at 532.

18. Restatement (Third) § 21 cmt. e at 296 (emphasis added).

19. However, a number of these jurisdictions seem troubled by the distinction, leading them to add the require-

It should now be apparent why the economic loss rule has generated such a "fierce battle" in products liability. By focusing solely on the form of damages rather than the substantive interests at stake, the majority rule has been subject to the same pressures that are brought to bear on any rule that elevates form over substance.

II. Pain and Suffering

Pain-and-suffering damages provide compensation for physical pain and a variety of other harms such as fright, nervousness, grief, anxiety, indignity and the loss of life's pleasures. These harms all have the attribute of being a nonmonetary injury.

Since this tort award gives the plaintiff monetary damages for a nonmonetary injury, the practice involves a number of knotty problems. As the California Supreme Court explains:

> Thoughtful jurists and legal scholars have for some time raised serious questions as to the wisdom of awarding damages for pain and suffering in any negligence case, noting, inter alia, the inherent difficulties in placing a monetary value on such losses, the fact that money damages are at best only imperfect compensation for such intangible injuries and that such damages are generally passed on to, and borne by, innocent consumers.[20]

Due to the "inherent difficulties" of the practice, how can the jury determine the appropriate monetary award for a nonmonetary injury? And even if these damages can somehow be measured, they may be undesirable. "Innocent consumers" pay for tort damages in the form of higher prices. Does it make sense for consumers to pay money in order to receive a right to monetary compensation for an injury lacking financial impact?

Both of these problems largely explain why pain-and-suffering damages have been and continue to be the subject of tort reform. Since the 1980s, a large number of states have enacted legislative reforms to limit pain-and-suffering awards. A common reform involves a cap on these damages, such as $250,000.

For damages under the cap, the tort system must still face the problem of measuring or quantifying the damages. And the measurability problem only arises if there is some justification for giving

---

ment that the product must fail in a sudden and calamitous manner. *See id.* § 21 cmt. d at 304–05. This version of the rule is hard to understand, since the justification for tort liability depends only upon the nature of the interests at stake and not the nature of the product failure.

20. Fein v. Permanente Medical Group, 695 P.2d 665, 680–81 (Cal.), *appeal dismissed,* 474 U.S. 892 (1985).

the plaintiff *any* monetary compensation for a nonmonetary injury. A damages cap assumes that at least some damages can be justified. What, then, is the justification for pain-and-suffering damages, and what guidance does it provide for their measurement?

A. *The Desirability of Tort Damages for Pain and Suffering*

In the appropriate circumstances, tort damages can be analyzed as a form of insurance. Tort damages provide compensation in the event that the plaintiff suffers an injury covered by the liability rule. Insurance provides compensation in the event that the policyholder suffers an injury covered by the policy. The analogy between tort damages and insurance is complete in product cases involving injured consumers, since consumers pay for tort damages in the form of higher prices. The higher price represents the premium that consumers pay for the guarantee of tort compensation, making it defensible to analyze tort damages as a form of insurance.[21]

Many scholars have concluded that tort damages for pain and suffering are an inefficient form of insurance.[22] A nonmonetary injury does not reduce the consumer's wealth, nor does it necessarily increase her need for (or utility of) money. For injuries of this type, the consumer would prefer to save money on the premium by not purchasing the insurance. Why spend money on an insurance premium to insure against an injury that does not increase the need for money?

Even if pain-and-suffering damages are an inefficient form of insurance, these damages can still enhance consumer welfare. Any overinsurance for pain and suffering could be offset, perhaps completely, by underinsurance for other harms caused by the defective product. Such underinsurance undoubtedly exists. Insurance for any form of economic loss ordinarily is preferable for consumers, but there is no available insurance that would cover the consumer's legal expenses. As the courts have recognized, pain-and-suffering damages effectively compensate the plaintiff for her legal expenses.[23] This conclusion has empirical support. About one-half of

21. *See* Chapter 3 (analyzing the consumer's insurance decision regarding product-caused losses and describing the insurance function of tort damages).

22. For the seminal analysis underlying this conclusion, see Philip J. Cook & Daniel A. Graham, *The Demand for Insurance and Protection: The Case of Irreplaceable Commodities*, 91 Q.J. Econ. 143 (1977).

23. *E.g.*, Seffert v. Los Angeles Transit Lines, 364 P.2d 337, 345 (Cal. 1961) (Traynor, J., dissenting) (recognizing damages for pain and suffering is a proper means of enabling prevailing plaintiff to pay attorneys' fees not otherwise compensated by the litigation, but arguing majority erred in affirming excessive award).

total compensation received by plaintiffs involves damages for pain and suffering, whereas approximately one-third of the total compensation paid to plaintiffs is consumed by legal fees.[24] By serving as a form of insurance for legal fees, tort damages for pain and suffering become much more desirable for consumers.[25]

A pure insurance analysis of tort damages also omits any consideration of the safety benefit. Tort damages are only available for cases involving defective products, so they also provide a safety benefit by giving sellers an incentive to provide nondefective products. Once this safety benefit is added to the insurance benefit regarding legal fees, there no longer is a persuasive reason for concluding that pain-and-suffering damages are inefficient and should be eliminated.[26]

A separate question is whether the plaintiff should be able to recover for emotional harm, even though she has not suffered physical harm. A prominent example involves a plaintiff who does not have cancer and seeks damages only for "cancerphobia."

Cases involving pure emotional harm are analytically similar to the cases involving pure economic loss discussed in the previous section. If the tort duty were to encompass stand-alone emotional harms, the general duty of care would be expanded to include this independent risk:

$$B < P_1 \bullet (L_{Physical} + L_{Emotional} + L_{Economic}) + P_2 \bullet (L_{Emotional})$$

The more expansive duty cannot be justified on the ground that the increased product safety protects consumers from an unreasonable risk of physical harm. That protection is already provided by the general duty of care limited to cases involving physical harm:

---

24. *See* James S. Kakalik & Nicholas M. Pace, Costs and Compensation Paid in Tort Litigation 68–69 & tbl. 7.2 (1986) (describing study showing that for average tort lawsuit in 1985, approximately 30 percent of total compensation paid to plaintiffs was used to pay plaintiffs' legal fees and expenses); 2 American Law Institute, Reporters' Study, Enterprise Responsibility for Personal Injury: Approaches to Legal and Institutional Change 201 (1991) (providing data on pain-and-suffering awards).

25. Moreover, compensating plaintiffs for their legal fees through higher damages awards may be more efficient than compensating plaintiffs directly for these costs. *See* Louis Kaplow, *Shifting Plaintiffs' Fees Versus Increasing Damage Awards*, 24 Rand J. Econ. 625 (1993) (showing that use of higher damage awards is more efficient than shifting plaintiffs' fees, since substituting higher damage awards for fee shifting would not affect deterrence but would eliminate the suits of plaintiffs with the highest litigation costs).

26. *See* Mark Geistfeld, *Placing a Price on Pain and Suffering: A Method for Helping Juries Determine Tort Damages for Nonmonetary Injuries*, 83 Cal. L. Rev. 773, 796–803 (1995).

$$B < P_1 \bullet (L_{Physical} + L_{Emotional} + L_{Economic})$$

As long as the general duty of care effectively regulates the risk of physical harm, tort damages for pure emotional harms must largely find justification in an insurance rationale. The insurance properties of the pain-and-suffering damages award are now the dominant consideration, unlike cases involving physical harm. Insofar as insurance for nonmonetary injuries is inefficient, tort damages for these stand-alone emotional harms are also inefficient. The plaintiff's ability to recover for emotional harm therefore can defensibly depend upon whether the plaintiff has suffered physical harm.

For cases in which the defect has not caused the plaintiff an existing physical harm, the availability of pain-and-suffering damages largely depends on "two factors: (1) the need for a plaintiff to show a physical consequence (including both physical impact and physical manifestation) and (2) the need for a plaintiff to show that the emotional distress is reasonable, based on the chance that disease will manifest."[27] The first limitation is problematic, whereas the second can be justified if implemented appropriately.

The physical-consequence requirement governs tort cases like those involving drivers and pedestrians. The rationale for the requirement does not depend upon the pedestrian's insurance preferences, since the pedestrian does not pay for the driver's liability costs. All else being equal, pedestrians undoubtedly prefer to be compensated for their emotional harms, whether or not the harm is accompanied by a physical consequence. Any limitation on the pedestrian's right to compensation for pure emotional harms must be justified by the need to protect the interest in physical security, the core concern of tort law. When evaluated in this manner, the physical-consequence requirement can be justified.[28]

Product cases are different. Unlike pedestrians, consumers must pay for any tort right to compensation, making the desirability of compensation dependent upon consumer insurance preferences. Insofar as pain-and-suffering damages are an inefficient form of insurance, they must provide a significant safety benefit in order to benefit consumers. The physical consequence is not a compensa-

---

27. Andrew R. Klein, *Fear of Disease and the Puzzle of Futures Cases in Tort*, 35 U.C. Davis L. Rev. 965, 978 (2002).

28. *See* Mark Geistfeld, *The Analytics of Duty: Medical Monitoring and Related Forms of Economic Loss*, 88 Va. L. Rev. 1921, 1929–35 (2002) (explaining why recovery for stand-alone emotional harms must be circumscribed by seemingly arbitrary rules like the "zone of danger" test in order to limit the number of tort claimants and ensure that the tortfeasor typically has sufficient assets to pay damages for the physical harms caused by the wrongdoing).

ble physical harm, however, for otherwise the ordinary damages rule would apply, entitling the plaintiff to full damages for both the physical and emotional harms. A special damages rule is required only because the physical consequence is not encompassed by the general duty of care. But as long as the general duty of care gives product sellers a sufficient incentive to supply nondefective products, liability is not required in these cases to promote deterrence. The liability instead largely functions as a form of insurance for the pain and suffering that accompanies the physical consequence. But if the damages are justified as a desirable form of insurance—a difficult proposition in any event—then there no longer is any reason to limit recovery with the physical-consequence requirement. The plaintiff should be able to recover any time a defective product causes nonmonetary injury. An insurance rationale, therefore, does not persuasively explain the physical-consequence requirement, nor does a deterrence rationale. The requirement is hard to justify in product cases, even though it is defensible in ordinary tort cases like those involving drivers and pedestrians.

The plaintiff can also recover by proving that the emotional distress is reasonable, based on the chance that she will get the disease. This proof connects the emotional harm to the physical harm encompassed by the general duty of care. Properly formulated, this liability rule can serve as a means of enforcing the general duty of care. If the plaintiff can only sue the manufacturer once, then her recovery for pure emotional harm (like cancerphobia) would bar future recovery for the disease itself (cancer). In these circumstances, the emotional-harm liability substitutes for any physical-harm liability, thereby enforcing the general duty of care. But if the plaintiff can sue for the emotional harm and then file suit later to recover for the disease itself, then the first action for pure emotional distress no longer enforces the general duty of care and is hard to justify.[29]

Thus, the rules governing the availability of tort damages for pain and suffering largely conform to the principle that products liability should promote consumer welfare. When the plaintiff has

29. *See generally* Klein, *supra* note 27 (proposing a rule under which the plaintiff's recovery for pure emotional distress bars later suit for physical injury). The issue is complicated if the plaintiff receives damages for medical monitoring—a form of liability that enforces the general duty of care—in addition to emotional distress damages. Now the emotional distress damages serve as a form of compensation for the plaintiff's legal expenses, enhancing the insurance value of the award and making two potential causes of action easier to justify. *Cf.* Mauro v. Raymark Indus., Inc., 561 A.2d 257 (N.J. 1989) (permitting medical monitoring claim coupled with damages for emotional distress and relaxing single-controversy doctrine in order to give the plaintiff a chance for future recovery in the event he gets the disease).

suffered physical harm, the availability of a damages remedy for pain and suffering is likely to be efficient and increase consumer welfare. This justification becomes much more tenuous when the plaintiff only suffers from stand-alone emotional harms. In cases of this type, the pain-and-suffering damages are more likely to be inefficient and their availability is correspondingly limited. The courts have not always formulated these limitations in the manner that fully promotes consumer welfare, but the problem stems from their failure to recognize the important differences between ordinary tort cases and product cases.

B. Determining Damages for Pain and Suffering

Regardless of their theoretical appeal, tort damages for pain and suffering may be undesirable in practice if there is no defensible method for calculating the award. How should an intangible, nonmonetary injury be translated into monetary damages? The courts have been unable to come up with a good answer. Judges provide jurors with vague guidelines on how to determine these damages, as illustrated by the following pattern jury instructions from California:

> No definite standard [or method of calculation] is prescribed by law by which to fix reasonable compensation for pain and suffering. Nor is the opinion of any witness required as to the amount of such reasonable compensation. [Furthermore, the argument of counsel as to the amount of damages is not evidence of reasonable compensation.] In making an award for pain and suffering you should exercise your authority with calm and reasonable judgment and the damages you fix must be just and reasonable in the light of the evidence.[30]

Not surprisingly, jurors have reported that they "find the guidance that is given to them on how to compute damages to be minimal...."[31] In one products case, jurors said they used a process of "guesstimation" to determine pain-and-suffering damages.[32] Another study found that jurors "used different methods of calculating the awards."[33]

30. California Jury Instructions—Civil, BAJI 14.13 (2005).

31. Shari S. Diamond, *What Jurors Think: Expectations and Reactions of Citizens Who Serve as Jurors* in Verdict: Assessing the Civil Jury System 282, 297 (Robert E. Litan ed., 1993).

32. Edith Greene, *On Juries and Damage Awards: The Process of Deci-*

sionmaking, 52 Law & Contemp. Probs. 225, 230 (1989).

33. Neil Vidmar, *Empirical Evidence on the Deep Pockets Hypothesis: Jury Awards for Pain and Suffering in Medical Malpractice Cases*, 43 Duke L.J. 217, 254–55 (1993).

The vague jury instructions predictably result in highly variable damage awards. Plaintiffs who suffer more severe injuries tend to receive higher awards, indicating some degree of *vertical equity*, but those with similar pain-and-suffering injuries often are awarded significantly different amounts of damages, indicating a lack of *horizontal equity*.[34] Vague jury instructions produce highly variable damage awards by permitting jurors to rely upon a variety of methods for calculating pain-and-suffering damages. Different methods predictably yield different results. One method can produce a damages award twice as great as the amount produced by a different method.[35]

To address this problem, one commonly proposed reform involves a scheduling of damages based upon previous awards for nonmonetary injuries of the same type.[36] Another proposal involves more exacting judicial review that evaluates the present award in terms of its comparability with prior awards for similar injuries.[37] Both approaches would result in less variable awards across cases, but are subject to a fundamental problem. If the existing method for awarding these damages is so problematic, why rely on the results produced by this method to determine future awards? Garbage in. Garbage out.

Of course, at least some variability is inevitable. By definition, a nonmonetary injury has no objective monetary equivalent. But even if there is no objectively correct damages award, there can still be a right way to think about these damages.

Consider the fundamental requirement of defect, the most important limitation of liability in product cases. As we found, tort liability requires a product defect because consumers reasonably expect to receive tort compensation only as a means of giving sellers an incentive to supply nondefective products.[38] Tort compensation for pain and suffering is justified by a safety rationale, and

---

34. *See, e.g.*, Randall R. Bovbjerg et al., *Valuing Life and Limb in Tort: Scheduling "Pain and Suffering,"* 83 Nw. L. Rev. 908, 924 (1989).

35. *Cf.* Edward J. McCaffery et al., *Framing the Jury: Cognitive Perspectives on Pain and Suffering Awards*, 81 Va. L. Rev. 1341 (1995) (study finding that the way in which jury instructions are worded will have a substantial impact on the amount of "full compensation" that individuals would award for a given pain-and-suffering injury, with some instructions yielding a fully compensatory pain-and-suffering award twice as great as the amount yielded by other instructions).

36. *E.g.*, Bovbjerg et al., *supra* note 34.

37. *E.g.*, David Baldus et al., *Improving Judicial Oversight of Jury Damages Assessments: A Proposal for the Comparative Additur/Remittitur Review of Awards for Nonpecuniary Harms and Punitive Damages*, 80 Iowa L. Rev. 1109 (1995).

38. *See* Chapter 3, section III.

that justification provides guidance for calculating the damages award.

A product is defective under the risk-utility test if there is a safety investment costing less than the expected injury costs the consumer would face if the investment were not made: $B < P \bullet (L_{Physical} + L_{Emotional} + L_{Economic})$. This requirement can be implemented in a tort case only if the pain-and-suffering injury (the term $L_{Emotional}$) is somehow monetized; added to the associated terms involving the cost of the physical and economic harms ($L_{Physical}$ and $L_{Economic}$); and then compared to the cost of precaution B. Without a monetary amount for the pain and suffering, there is no way to determine the safety expenditures required by the risk-utility test.

The risk-utility test reflects the reasonable safety decision that would be made by the ordinary consumer having good information about the risk-utility factors.[39] Since the consumer incurs either the cost of a safety precaution or the associated cost of injury, she must decide how much she is willing to pay for a safety investment that would eliminate the risk of incurring the pain-and-suffering injury. The monetary measure that the consumer would reasonably adopt in making the safety decision provides an appropriate basis for calculating the damages award.

To see why, suppose there is a 1 in 10,000 risk of suffering the nonmonetary injury (the term P). To make the associated safety decision, the consumer must decide upon a monetary valuation of the nonmonetary injury (the term $L_{Emotional}$). That amount cannot be objectively determined, but instead depends upon the consumer's subjective preference for spending money to eliminate this particular risk of experiencing the pain and suffering. Suppose the consumer honestly says she is willing to pay no more than $10 to eliminate the risk. Since $10 is the most the consumer would pay to eliminate the risk, she must be indifferent between incurring the $10 cost or otherwise incurring the expected cost of the pain and suffering:

$$\$10 = P \bullet L_{Emotional}$$
$$\$10 = (1/10,000) \bullet L_{Emotional}$$
$$\$100,000 = L_{Emotional}$$

In making the safety decision defined by the risk-utility test, the consumer would prefer that this particular pain-and-suffering injury be monetized at $100,000. A different injury, or even a different probability of injury, would yield a different number. The monetization of the pain-and-suffering injury does not represent

---

39. *See* Chapter 2, section II.A.

the "value" of the injury or the amount of money the consumer would accept in exchange for suffering the injury with certainty. When framed in those terms, the amount could be infinite for the most severe nonmonetary injury—the loss of life's pleasures due to premature death. The value of the injury, however, is not relevant to the safety question involved in this particular case. The issue is one of determining the appropriate expenditure on product safety for eliminating a 1 in 10,000 risk of suffering the nonmonetary injury in question, and for this purpose, the consumer would prefer that the pain and suffering be monetized at $100,000.

This method for monetizing the pain-and-suffering injury is based upon established economic methodology commonly employed by regulatory agencies, such as the Environmental Protection Agency, in devising regulations for the protection of human health and safety.[40] The method is also consistent with tort requirements.

Monetary damages for pain and suffering are not supposed to "restore the injured person to his previous position," but should instead "give to the injured person some pecuniary return for what he has suffered or is likely to suffer."[41] The $100,000 damages award satisfies this requirement by providing redress for the violation of the plaintiff's tort right. To violate the plaintiff's right, the defendant must have breached the duty of care in a manner that caused injury to the plaintiff. The rights violation links the duty of care to the injury, making it appropriate to formulate the damages remedy in these terms. Like other consumers, the plaintiff has a tort right protecting her reasonable expectations of product safety. Consumers reasonably expect to receive tort damages solely because of the safety incentives created by tort liability. The $100,000 damages award in the foregoing example provides the correct safety incentive for the nonmonetary injury suffered by the plaintiff, making it the appropriate "pecuniary return" for the plaintiff's injury.

Moreover, this damages measure compensates the plaintiff for an existing injury in the manner that appropriately accounts for the underlying risk. The jury cannot base the damages award on the amount of money the victim would require to accept the certainty of suffering the injury—the damages must somehow depend upon risk rather than certainty.[42] In the foregoing example, a

---

40. *See, e.g.*, George Tolley et al., Valuing Health for Policy: An Economic Approach (1994).

41. Restatement (Second) of Torts § 903 cmt. a.

42. Courts do not let jurors determine the award by asking themselves how much money they or anyone else would want in exchange for experiencing the plaintiff's injury. *See generally* L.R. James, *Annotation, Instructions in a*

damages remedy of $100,000 links the injury and its underlying risk in the manner required by the duty of care.

To implement this approach, the jury could first be informed about the methodology and its rationale. The jury could then be provided with a specific probability, such as 1 in 10,000, that the defect would cause the particular pain-and-suffering injury in question. (The probability in each case can be based upon the reasonably available evidence, which is the evidentiary standard governing damage determinations.) The jury could also be told how to conceptualize a probability of this magnitude. For example, the jury might benefit from learning that there is an average risk of 1 in 10,000 that an individual will die in a commercial plane crash over the course of 100 flights.[43] The jury also receives evidence about the injury in question, making it relatively well-informed about the nature and severity of the pain and suffering. On the basis of all this information, the jury is likely to provide a reasonably defensible determination of the damages award for pain and suffering.[44] That award can then be added to the damages for the other injuries, like medical expenses, to yield the total damages award for the plaintiff.[45]

Rather than telling juries to award pain-and-suffering damages that are "just and reasonable," this approach would enable judges to provide more precise guidance. They can ask jurors to determine

Personal Injury Action Which, in Effect, Tell Jurors That in Assessing Damages They Should Put Themselves in Injured Person's Place, 96 A.L.R.2d 760 (1964); *see also* 4 Fowler V. Harper et al., The Law of Torts, § 25.10, at 563–64 (2d ed. 1986) ("All agree that [full compensation for pain and suffering] does not mean the sum that the plaintiff—or anyone else—would be willing to suffer the injury for."). The courts have rejected this method for determining damages because it invites sympathy or bias by the jurors. James, *supra*, at 761. The source of the sympathy or bias must involve neglect of the underlying risk of injury for reasons that can be illustrated by a severely disabling physical injury. An individual may not be willing to accept any amount of money to suffer this injury with certainty, whereas she would be willing to accept a finite amount of money to face a low risk of suffering the injury. A damages award based upon the certainty of injury therefore can vastly exceed an award based upon the actual risk of injury faced by the plaintiff, so

jury instructions framed in terms of the certainty of injury clearly bias the determination of damages for physical injury. The only way to eliminate the bias is to base the damages award on the underlying risk of injury.

43. *See* Stephen Breyer, Breaking the Vicious Circle: Toward Effective Risk Regulation 5 (1993).

44. *See* Geistfeld, *supra* note 26, at 832–40.

45. To keep the jury from double-counting damages, the jury instructions must explain that the pain-and-suffering damages depend upon the plaintiff's willingness to pay to eliminate only the risk of the pain and suffering. The risk must exclude the other injuries suffered by the plaintiff. Inclusion of these other injuries would increase the maximum amount of money that the plaintiff would be willing to pay, thereby increasing the damages award in a manner that includes compensation for both these injuries and the pain and suffering.

the maximum amount of money the plaintiff would have been willing to pay to eliminate the relevant risk (such as 1 in 10,000) of experiencing this particular pain-and-suffering injury. The jury must collectively make the decision that would have been made by the plaintiff as consumer, an appropriate task given the extensive consumer experience of virtually all jurors. Different juries presumably will reach different damage decisions, since there is no objectively correct damages award. The issue is solely one of consumer preference. But by framing the issue as one of consumer preference regarding safety, the approach provides a rationale for the damages award and may help jurors apply the risk-utility test in the appropriate manner.[46] The damages award would no longer be the mystical result of some process of "guesstimation," but instead would be formulated to provide redress for the rights violation suffered by the plaintiff-consumer.

III. Punitive Damages

Once the plaintiff has established the right to compensatory damages, she also can receive punitive damages by proving that the defendant acted with fraud, malice or in wanton disregard of the plaintiff's tort rights. These extracompensatory damages "are aimed at deterrence and retribution."[47]

Punitive damages are not typically awarded to a prevailing plaintiff. According to data collected by the U.S. Department of Justice, in 1992 punitive damages were awarded in 5.9 percent of the trial cases won by plaintiffs in the jurisdictions being studied. For products liability cases, the rate was 2.2 percent. In 1996, punitive damages were awarded in 4.5 percent of the trial cases won by plaintiffs. For product cases not involving asbestos or breast implants, the rate rose to 12.8 percent. In 2001, punitive damages were awarded in approximately 5 percent of the trial cases won by plaintiffs, with the same rate applying to product cases.[48]

---

46. *Compare* Chapter 6, section II.C (describing the resistance of juries to consider safety issues in the manner required by the risk-utility test).

47. State Farm Mut. Auto. Ins. Co. v. Campbell, 538 U.S. 408, 416 (2003).

48. Carol J. DeFrances et al., U.S. Dep't of Justice, Civil Justice Survey of State Courts, 1992: Civil Jury Cases and Verdicts in Large Counties, http://www.ojp.usdoj.gov/bjs/pub/pdf/ cjcavilc.pdf; Carol J. DeFrances & Marika F.X. Litras, U.S. Dep't of Justice, Civil Justice Survey of State Courts, 1996: Civil Trial Cases and Verdicts in Large Counties 9 tbl.8, 17 (1999), *available at* http://www.ojp.usdoj.gov/bjs/pub/- pdf/ctcvlc96.pdf; Thomas H. Cohen, U.S. Dep't of Justice, NCJ No. 206240, Tort Trials and Verdicts in Large Counties, 2001 (2004), *available at*

Though awarded infrequently, punitive damages have been a focal point in the debate over tort reform. Public scrutiny is invited by the enormous punitive awards in some product cases, like the $4.9 billion punitive damages award a California jury levied against General Motors.[49] Punitive damages are controversial because of the way in which an otherwise defensible principle of liability has been applied in the courtroom.

To identify the rationale for punitive damages, consider a product that is defective for not containing a safety precaution required by the risk-utility test: $B < PL$. By making the seller liable for the expected injury costs (PL), the tort rule gives the seller an incentive to adopt the less costly safety precaution (B) in order to avoid liability and reduce costs. For the incentive to operate in this manner, the seller must face expected liability costs equal to the expected injury costs. Suppose the seller knows that only one-third of the consumers with meritorious claims will actually sue and recover. To maximize profits, the seller would make the safety decision by comparing the cost of the precaution (B) with its expected liability costs $(1/3 \bullet PL)$. Now the cost of the safety precaution can exceed the seller's expected liability costs $(B > 1/3 \bullet PL)$, giving the seller an incentive to sell the defective product. To restore the seller's safety incentive, successful plaintiffs must have a right to extracompensatory or punitive damages. If each plaintiff who recovers compensatory damages were to receive treble damages, the seller's expected liability costs would equal the expected injury costs $(1/3 \bullet PL \bullet 3 = PL)$. When punitive damages are formulated in this manner, the seller once again has the incentive to comply with the risk-utility test, because it would make the safety decision by comparing the cost of safety precaution with the expected injury costs $(B < 1/3 \bullet PL \bullet 3 = PL)$.

Although the appropriate amount of punitive damages depends upon the seller's conduct towards the entire market, the award can be justified by the individual tort right held by the plaintiff. A manufacturer of a mass-marketed product does not give individualized treatment to each consumer. The manufacturer treats each consumer as nothing more than a member of a group—the market or those individuals whose aggregate demand determines the most profitable characteristics of the product. To protect the individual right held by each consumer, the court must consider how the manufacturer has behaved towards the group of consumers in the market. If the manufacturer decided to sell a defective product for

at   *at*   http://www.ojp.us-doj.gov/bjs/pub/pdf/ttvlc01.pdf.

49. Andrew Pollack, *$4.9 Billion Jury Verdict in GM Fuel Tank Case,* N.Y. Times, July 10, 1999, at A8.

the reason that not enough consumers would file tort claims, then it has acted with malice or conscious disregard of the individual right held by each consumer, including the plaintiff. To protect the plaintiff's tort right, the damages award must give the manufacturer an incentive to comply with the duty it owed to the plaintiff, an incentive that necessarily depends upon how the manufacturer is likely to behave towards the market as a whole.

This attribute of punitive damages has created significant practical problems. In the previous example, the computation of the appropriate damages award in each particular case assumed that the punitive damages in other cases would be determined in the same manner, with each plaintiff receiving treble damages. Punitive damages, though, are not coordinated across cases and jurisdictions. Moreover, the punitive awards do not have to be coordinated across cases to achieve deterrence. In the preceding example, only one or a few plaintiffs has to receive a particularly large amount of punitive damages ($4.9 billion?) to restore the seller's safety incentive. However, plaintiffs who subsequently sue could still seek punitive damages as retribution or punishment for the way in which the defendant's tortious conduct violated their individual tort right. What ensures that the defendant does not incur an excessive amount of punitive damages across the range of cases?

According to a line of relatively recent cases decided by the U.S. Supreme Court, defendants are protected against excessively high punitive damage awards by the Due Process Clause of the U.S. Constitution.[50] To determine whether a punitive damages award satisfies due process, judges must evaluate the award in terms of three factors: "(1) the degree of reprehensibility of the defendant's misconduct; (2) the disparity between the actual or potential harm suffered by the plaintiff and the punitive damages award; and (3) the difference between the punitive damages awarded by the jury and the civil penalties authorized or imposed in comparable cases."[51] In elaborating upon this inquiry, the Court has held "that, in practice, few awards exceeding a single-digit ratio between punitive and compensatory damages, to a significant degree, will satisfy due process."[52]

50. In 1989, the Court left open the question "whether due process acts as a check on undue jury discretion to award punitive damages in the absence of any express statutory limit." Browning–Ferris Indus. v. Kelco Disposal, Inc., 492 U.S. 257, 277 (1989). A decisive, affirmative answer to that question was provided by the Court a few years later in BMW of North America v. Gore, 517 U.S. 559 (1996).

51. *State Farm*, 538 U.S. at 418.

52. *Id.* at 425.

The due process inquiry is still rather new, making it difficult to determine how it will affect the role of punitive damages in product cases. The Court has recognized that a punitive damages award for an individual consumer can be based upon similar rights violations that the manufacturer's course of conduct has inflicted upon other consumers in the market.[53] Whether due process permits the amount of awards required for market-based deterrence accordingly depends on whether such awards can satisfy the presumptive, single-digit ratio between compensatory and punitive damages.

The single-digit ratio enables the plaintiff to recover up to $9 of punitive damages for each $1 of compensatory damages. A punitive damages multiplier of 9 would fully offset the deterrence problem created by a product market in which only 1 of 9 consumers with valid claims actually sue the manufacturer. The single-digit ratio would yield inadequate awards if a lower proportion of consumers with valid claims actually sue, but in these cases, the presumptive ratio need not apply. The Court has departed from the presumptive ratio when doing so is required in order to eliminate the benefit that the defendant had expected to derive from violating the plaintiff's right.[54] This justification would seem to apply if only 1 percent of all consumers with valid claims actually seek recovery, since the punitive damages multiplier must be 100 in order to eliminate the benefit that the manufacturer expected to derive by selling the defective product in violation of the plaintiff's right. The presumptive, single-digit ratio does not necessarily bar larger awards of punitive damages when doing so is required for purposes of market-based deterrence and the circumstances make it highly unlikely that the defendant will incur excessive liability across cases. At the time of the punitive damages award, for example, the statute of limitations may bar future claims, effectively limiting the defendant's liability to the case at hand. Applied in this manner, the requirements of due process allow punitive damages to promote

53. *See* BMW, 517 U.S. at 572–74. In another case, the Court arguably rejected the type of market-based deterrence argument supporting punitive damages, but the award in question was only justified in deterrence terms and not the plaintiff's underlying right. *See State Farm*, 538 U.S. at 427 (rejecting plaintiffs' argument that a punitive damages award set at a multiple of 50,000 times the compensatory award could be justified by a 1 in 50,000 chance that the defendant would be sued, because such an award "ha[s] little to do with the actual harm sustained by [plaintiffs]").

54. *See* TXO Production Corp. v. Alliance Resources Corp., 509 U.S. 443, 460 (1993) (upholding a punitive damages award of $10 million in a case involving $19,000 of compensatory damages because the relevant disparity involves the potential loss to the rightholder that could have occurred if the defendant had fully succeeded in its wrongful scheme).

deterrence while coordinating the damages across cases in order to protect the defendant from excessive liability.[55]

Nevertheless, other practical problems remain. The first involves the way in which the traditional legal standard for punitive damages affects the application of the risk-utility test in the courtroom.

The early common-law awards of punitive damages involved intentional torts, resulting in a legal standard that can produce perverse results in product cases. For example, the pattern jury instructions in California entitle the plaintiff to punitive damages when the defendant was "aware of the probable dangerous consequences of [its] conduct and willfully and deliberately fail[ed] to avoid those consequences."[56] The instruction works well for the intentional torts—it tells jurors to impose punitive damages upon a defendant who punched the plaintiff in the nose—but not for cases involving defective product design. If hindsight shows that the manufacturer erred in concluding that the cost of a safety improvement outweighed the benefit of risk reduction, then even if the manufacturer truly thought the product was not defectively designed, the legal standard for punitive damages apparently is satisfied. By foregoing a safety investment on the basis of cost considerations, the manufacturer was necessarily "aware of the probable dangerous consequences of [its] conduct and willfully and deliberately fail[ed] to avoid those consequences." Any type of cost-benefit balancing involving the risk of bodily injury can expose the manufacturer to liability for punitive damages, as it did in the highly publicized cases involving the Ford Pinto.[57] Consequently, manufac-

---

55. An alternative approach relies upon aggregating individual punitive claims in a class action. For good discussion of such an approach and other alternatives, see Catherine M. Sharkey, *Punitive Damages as Societal Damages*, 113 Yale L.J. 347 (2003).

56. California Jury Instructions—Civil, BAJI 14.71 (2005).

57. *See* Grimshaw v. Ford Motor Co., 119 Cal.App.3d 757, 813 (1981) (affirming punitive damages award on ground that "[Ford] decided to defer correction of the [Pinto's] shortcomings by engaging in cost-benefit analysis balancing human lives and limbs against corporate profits.... There was substantial evidence that Ford's conduct constituted 'conscious disregard' of the probability of injury to members of the consuming public."). In an exhaustive review of this case, Professor Gary Schwartz concluded that "because of [monetary cost concerns], Ford decided not to improve the Pinto's design, knowing that its decision would increase the chances of the loss of consumer life." Gary T. Schwartz, *The Myth of the Ford Pinto Case*, 43 Rutgers L. Rev. 1013,1034–35 (1991). This conduct, however, presumably occurs whenever a manufacturer decides to forego a safety investment. Schwartz saw "no evidence indicating that Ford's top officers ever acknowledged that the company would lose these lawsuits—that the Pinto's design was in fact defective." *Id.* at 1022 n. 29. The Pinto's record in rear-end fire fatalities "was apparently somewhat worse than the record of most (though not all) of its subcompact competitors." *Id.* at 1033. The safety record, though disappointing, does not support

turers in design-defect cases often are unwilling to admit that they made safety decisions on the basis of cost considerations.[58] This is a perverse result, given that the legal standard for design defects permits the seller to forego a safety investment if the cost or disutility is too high.

When a defendant manufacturer cannot fully defend its design decisions, there is an increased likelihood of an erroneous finding of defective design. On the basis of an incomplete evidentiary record, the court could find the design to be defective. Had the same court been provided with the complete evidentiary record, it might have found that the design passes the risk-utility test. By undermining the ability of manufacturers to rely upon cost considerations, the legal standard for punitive damages increases the likelihood of erroneous determinations of defective product design.

This problem could be addressed if the legal standard governing punitive damages were more sensitive to the nature of the consumer's tort right. The manufacturer "consciously disregarded" the consumer's tort right only if it sold a product that it knew was defective. Proof that the manufacturer sold a defective product does not show that it knew the product was defective at the time of sale. And even if the manufacturer deliberately chose not to eliminate a product risk, it may still not have known that the product was defective at the time of sale. As the risk-utility test establishes, the manufacturer could have justifiably foregone the safety improvements out of cost concerns. The jury, therefore, should be instructed that punitive damages require proof that the defendant knew the product was defective at the time of sale. Prior cases have shown that plaintiffs can procure evidence of this type.[59] When

the notoriety of the Pinto in this respect.

58. *See* Schwartz, *supra* note 57, at 1038 (summarizing the concern of defense lawyers in product cases that if you "argue that the manufacturer deliberately included a dangerous feature in the product's design because of the high monetary cost [of the alternative]," then "you're almost certain to lose on liability, and you can expose yourself to punitive damages as well."); *see also* W. Kip Viscusi, *Corporate Risk Analysis: A Reckless Act?*, 52 Stan. L. Rev. 547, 588 (2000) (analyzing results of a mock juror study and finding that the "most consistent result across the different scenarios was that undertaking any type of risk analysis was harmful to the corpora-

tion's prospects both with respect to the probability of punitive damages and, more importantly, with respect to the magnitude of the award.").

59. *See, e.g.,* Ford Motor Co. v. Ammerman, 705 N.E.2d 539, 562 (Ind. Ct. App. 1999) (upholding punitive damages award after finding that "Ford was motivated by profits rather than safety when it put into the stream of commerce a vehicle which it knew was dangerous and defective"); Tetuan v. A.H. Robins Co., 738 P.2d 1210, 1225 (Kan. 1987) (upholding punitive damages award levied against the manufacturer of the Dalkon Shield birth-control device on the ground that the "great weight of evidence at trial was that it was neither ['safe nor effective' as advertised by de-

formulated in this manner, the instructions would make clear that punitive damages are not warranted merely because the manufacturer was "aware of the probable dangerous consequences of [its] conduct and willfully and deliberately fail[ed] to avoid those consequences," the current standard for punitive damages in California and other jurisdictions.

Even if jury instructions are improved, punitive damages will continue to pose another problem that can be illustrated by the highly publicized hot-coffee cases. The most notorious case, *Liebeck v. McDonald's Restaurant*,[60] involved facts that are worth repeating at some length, in part to show how the media presentation of a case affects public perceptions of the tort system. As commonly understood, the case involved a plaintiff who spilled scalding coffee on her lap, shamelessly blamed McDonald's instead of herself, and recovered $2.9 million in punitive damages from an equally shameless jury.[61] The fact that someone is burned by hot coffee surely doesn't warrant punitive damages, much less compensatory damages. In other hot-coffee cases, the courts have summarily found in favor of defendants.[62] The facts in the McDonald's case, though, were significantly different, and that is the source of another practical problem created by punitive damages.

Contrary to popular perception, the facts in the McDonald's case present a compelling case for punitive damages.[63] The plaintiff bought the coffee from a McDonald's restaurant in New Mexico, which followed corporate policy by serving coffee at a temperature of 180 to 190 degrees Fahrenheit. The plaintiff's evidence showed that the industry average was less than 148 degrees, and that the temperature achieved by a typical home brewer ranges from 140 to 150 degrees. Based on this evidence, the higher temperature of the McDonald's coffee mattered a great deal. As the plaintiff further established, coffee served at that temperature will immediately burn human skin before anything can be done. There is no margin

fendant A.H. Robbins], and that Robins was aware it was not").

60. 1995 WL 360309 (N.M. Dist. 1994).

61. *See, e.g.*, Debra J. Saunders, *On the Docket: Americans vs. Themselves*, Detroit Free Press, Sept. 9, 1994, at 11-A ("There was a time when only the rare American would be so shameless as to sue McDonald's if her negligence contributed to a scalding.... Those days are long gone. America has devolved from a country of pioneers to a nation of plaintiffs.").

62. *See* McMahon v. Bunn–O–Matic Corp., 150 F.3d 651, 654 (7th Cir. 1998) (citing five hot-coffee cases that were summarily dismissed by the court, and two, including the McDonald's case, holding that a claim of this sort is triable).

63. The factual description of the case was generously provided to me by (then) Chief Justice Stanley Feldman of the Arizona Supreme Court, who in 1995 had his law clerk, Dave Abney, collect the information by interviewing lawyers involved in the case.

for error. The third-degree burns suffered by the plaintiff were so severe that she was hospitalized for eight days and endured excruciating skin grafts to help repair the wounds. The industry average temperature for serving coffee, by contrast, made it far less likely that a spill would cause any burn. Why, then, did McDonald's sell such hot coffee? It said a coffee consultant had once suggested that coffee tastes best that way, a claim that was contradicted by the plaintiff's evidence regarding industry practice. McDonald's also admitted that the temperature at which it sold coffee was unfit for human consumption and that corporate officials had received over 700 reports of coffee scalds in the past 10 years. Nevertheless, McDonald's refused to consult a burn doctor to assess the risks, refused to turn down the coffee brewer thermostats, and refused to print any warning label on the coffee cups.

On these facts, the jury could defensibly conclude that the temperature of McDonald's coffee was much greater than the temperature expected by the ordinary consumer, requiring a warning about the unanticipated, heightened risk of a scalding-burn injury. The jury accordingly awarded plaintiff $200,000 in compensatory damages, which was then reduced by 20 percent due to the plaintiff's contributory negligence. These facts also support the conclusion that McDonald's knew of the defect and failed to take corrective actions, despite repeated complaints by consumers who presumably had been surprised by the severity of their burn injuries. To jolt McDonald's from its corporate complacency, the jury awarded plaintiff $2.9 million in punitive damages, an amount representing the value of about two days of corporate coffee sales for McDonald's. (The trial judge subsequently reduced the award to $640,000.)

The McDonald's case only becomes troubling when considered in relation to other hot-coffee cases. Particularly instructive is *MacMahon v. Bunn–O–Matic Corporation*, which involved allegations that a coffeemaker manufactured by the defendant was defective for brewing coffee at 195 degrees Fahrenheit during the brewing cycle and 179 degrees Fahrenheit as the holding temperature of a carafe on its hotplate.[64] The alleged temperatures are within the range of those at issue in the McDonald's case. Nevertheless, the plaintiff's case in *Bunn-O–Matic* was dismissed by the U.S. Court of Appeals for the Seventh Circuit. As Judge Frank Easterbrook explained:

> Warning consumers about a surprising feature that is potentially dangerous yet hard to observe could be useful, but the

64. *McMahon*, 150 F.3d at 653.

record lacks any evidence that 179° F is unusually hot for coffee.... [In two earlier cases,] the courts reported that the industry-standard serving temperature is between 175° and 185° F, and if this is so then the [plaintiffs'] coffee held no surprises. What is more, most consumers prepare and consume hotter beverages at home.... Until 20 years ago most home coffee was made in percolators, where the water boiled during the brewing cycle and took some time to cool below 180°. Apparently the [plaintiffs] believe that home drip brewing machines now in common use are much cooler, but the record does not support this, and a little digging on our own part turned up [the following standard adopted by the American National Standards Institute for home coffeemakers]: "On completion of the brewing cycle and within a 2 minute interval, the beverage temperature in the dispensing vessel of the coffee maker while stirring should be between the limits of 170° F and 205° F. The upper finished brew temperature limit assures that the coffee does not reach the boiling point which can affect the taste and aroma. The lower temperature limit assures generally acceptable drinking temperature when pouring into a cold cup, adding cream, sugar and spoon."

... Coffee served at 180° by a roadside vendor, which doubtless expects that it will cool during the longer interval before consumption, does not seem so abnormal as to require a heads-up warning.[65]

In light of these facts, the justification for any liability, much less punitive damages, is less clear than it appeared to be in the McDonald's case. The comparison of the two cases does not imply that the McDonald's case was wrongly decided. On its facts, the McDonald's case was rightly decided. Comparing the two cases illustrates instead how a court's decision can critically depend upon the litigation strategies of the parties and the evidence upon which the decision is based. Differences in litigation strategies and evidence can produce different outcomes in cases that otherwise involve comparable allegations of defect. The McDonald's jury found that the coffee required a warning, whereas the court in *Bunn-O-Matic* held as a matter of law that the coffee required no such warning. Occasional differences like this are to be expected in the case law, but they are made much more problematic by punitive damages.

Suppose the court in *Bunn-O-Matic* correctly decided that no warning is required, and that if the same evidence had been given

65. *Id*. at 655.

to the court in the McDonald's case, it too would have found that the coffee did not require a warning. In these circumstances, even though the court in the McDonald's case reached the right result based on the evidence before it, the result is erroneous when evaluated by reference to a more complete evidentiary record. The error is then compounded by the award of punitive damages, since the award was designed to give McDonald's an incentive to change its behavior, as, in fact, it did.

Mistakes are inevitable for any form of products liability or any other form of safety regulation, including those promulgated by administrative agencies. Yet the problem is particularly pronounced for punitive damages. The mere prospect of punitive damages has limited the types of evidence that manufacturers can rely upon to defend the product design. The limited evidence increases the likelihood that the court will erroneously conclude that the design is defective. The rationale for punitive damages, however, critically depends upon a correct finding of defect. When the court mistakenly concludes that the product is defective, an award of punitive damages then exacerbates the error. The manufacturer is effectively forced to make a safety change that is not in the best interests of consumers or, in some cases, to forego making the product. Punitive damages can increase the likelihood of legal mistake while compounding the resultant cost. These problems help to explain why punitive damages have been a focal point in the debate over tort reform, despite the relative infrequency and undeniable benefits of these awards.

Chapter 10

DEFENSES BASED ON CONSUMER CONDUCT

Even if the plaintiff proves all of the elements necessary for tort liability, the defendant product seller may be able to avoid or reduce its liability by establishing an affirmative defense. Each defense—the contractual disclaimer or waiver of liability, assumption of risk, and contributory negligence or product misuse—involves different types of consumer conduct, requiring consideration of the appropriate interplay between consumer choice and tort liability.

I. Contractual Disclaimers or Waivers of Liability

The product seller may attempt to limit its liability by inserting a provision in the sales agreement that disclaims tort liability for any injuries caused by a defect in the product. A similar limitation of liability occurs when the sales agreement contains a provision pursuant to which the consumer waives any tort right to recover for injuries caused by product defects.

According to the *Restatement (Third)*, disclaimers and waivers "do not bar or reduce otherwise valid products liability claims against sellers or other distributors of new products for harm to persons."[1] A disclaimer or waiver operates against an existing tort duty—the contractual provision attempts to limit the tort liability that would otherwise be incurred by the product seller. The tort duty is predicated on the assumption that the ordinary consumer does not have sufficient information about product risk, creating a contracting problem that predictably produces unreasonably unsafe products.[2] This same informational problem seems to imply that the ordinary consumer would also make contractual decisions regarding disclaimers or waivers that predictably lead to unreasonably unsafe products. The rationale for the tort duty apparently explains why the contractual disclaimer or waiver of the duty should not be enforceable, enabling the *Restatement (Third)* to justify this rule on the ground that "[i]t is presumed that the ordinary product user or consumer lacks sufficient information and

---

1. Restatement (Third) § 18. **2.** *See* Chapter 2, section II.B.

227

bargaining power to execute a fair contractual limitation of rights to recover."[3]

However, the informational problem that justifies the tort duty does not necessarily mean that waivers should be unenforceable. The waiver transaction can be structured in a manner that increases the ordinary consumer's knowledge of product risk. For example, the enforceability of a waiver could be conditioned on the requirement that the seller provides a separate price quotation of its liability costs, so that the consumer could agree to the limitation of liability in exchange for a price reduction.[4] The amount of the price reduction tells consumers something about the product's safety and helps them to compare safety across brands. Even if two brands otherwise appear to be equally safe, consumers could infer that the brand with the larger price reduction (due to the larger amount of disclaimed liability costs) must be less safe (the reason for the high liability costs). Consequently, the informational problem that justifies the duty does not necessarily apply to the waiver transaction.

Possibilities like this explain why the *Restatement (Third)* limits the rule of nonenforceability to cases in which "commercial product sellers attempt *unfairly* to disclaim or otherwise limit their liability to the majority of users and consumers who are presumed to lack information and bargaining power adequate to protect their interests." The *Restatement (Third)* simply "does not address" the issue of whether consumers can ever enter into fair agreements limiting the liability of commercial product sellers.[5]

Upon further analysis, it turns out that the same informational problem that justifies the tort duty also makes it unlikely that the waiver transaction, however structured, would fairly limit the seller's tort liability. When the ordinary consumer underestimates product risk—the behavior assumed by the tort duty—she would underestimate the injury costs she can expect to incur by waiving liability, resulting in unfair waiver transactions. To ensure that sellers cannot excessively limit their liability and sell insufficiently safe products with impunity, disclaimers and waivers of liability must not be enforceable.[6]

---

3. Restatement (Third) § 18 cmt. a.

4. For proposals of this type, see Mark Geistfeld, *Imperfect Information, the Pricing Mechanism, and Products Liability*, 88 Colum. L. Rev. 1057 (1988); Alan Schwartz, *Proposals for Products Liability Reform: A Theoretical Synthesis*, 97 Yale L.J. 353 (1988).

5. Restatement (Third) § 18 cmt. d (emphasis added).

6. For more extensive analysis supporting this conclusion, see Mark Geistfeld, *The Political Economy of Neocontractual Proposals for Products Liability Reform*, 72 Tex. L. Rev. 803, 819–33 (1994).

This conclusion can be squared with the two important exceptions to the rule of nonenforceability. Many courts enforce disclaimers or waivers governing the seller of a used product, as when the merchant sells the used good "as is."[7] At first glance, this exception appears to be puzzling. Even though someone else has used the product, the consumer does not necessarily have good information about the product risk. The purchaser of a used automobile, for example, does not plausibly have better knowledge of product risk than the purchaser of a new automobile. Why, then, should the disclaimer be effective against the one consumer but not the other? The reason is that the disclaimer only applies to the retailer of the used car and not to the manufacturer—the seller of a new product. By enforcing disclaimers made by the sellers of used goods, courts typically are doing nothing more than limiting the liability of a nonmanufacturing retailer. As we will find later, such a limitation of liability does not usually create a safety problem.[8] The waiver of liability does not undermine the safety rationale for the tort duty, making these cases consistent with the general rule that safety concerns render disclaimers and waivers unenforceable.

Courts also enforce disclaimers or waivers of liability for pure economic loss, the type of loss that occurs when the defect causes damage only to the product itself in addition to intangible economic harms, such as lost profits. Recall that the risk of pure economic loss is not ordinarily encompassed within the tort duty. As we have found, this limitation of the tort duty does not pose a safety problem, because the ordinary consumer has good information about the risk of pure economic loss and can adequately protect this interest by contracting.[9] Having been excluded from the tort duty, the risk of pure economic loss is governed by the implied warranty provisions in the Uniform Commercial Code. A defective product usually breaches the implied warranty, but a seller can limit its liability under the implied warranty as long as the contractual limitation of liability satisfies certain requirements.[10]

When the tort claim is based upon negligence liability, there is some authority supporting the proposition that courts are more willing to enforce waivers or disclaimers for any type of injury and any type of seller.[11] The enforcement of the disclaimer or waiver,

---

7. Restatement (Third) § 8 cmt. k.

8. *See* Chapter 11.

9. *See* Chapter 9, section I.

10. *See* 1 Madden & Owen on Products Liability §§ 4:14–19 (describing requirements).

11. *See* 2 Madden & Owen on Products Liability § 14:3 ("In negligence, the products liability cases parallel the general tort law principles: a disclaimer is effective only if it clearly and unequivocally relieves the defendant of responsi-

however, should not depend upon whether the claim is based upon negligence or strict products liability. Negligence liability also requires a tort duty, which can be justified only if informational problems cause the ordinary consumer to make contractual choices resulting in overly unsafe products. Without that informational problem, there is no safety rationale for regulating the contractual relationship with tort law, whether in the form of negligence or strict liability. The informational problem disables consumers from entering into fair agreements that limit the negligence liability of product sellers. The only exceptions are for transactions involving used products and waivers of pure economic loss, because in these transactions, the ordinary consumer will not make contracting choices that result in unreasonably unsafe products.

II. Assumption of Risk

To establish assumption of risk, the defendant must prove that the plaintiff *voluntarily* chose to face a *known* risk that subsequently caused the injury for which she seeks compensation. Having assumed the risk, the plaintiff incurs a responsibility for that risk that justifies a limitation of the defendant's liability.

The knowledge requirement is not satisfied by the plaintiff's awareness that the product might be defective. That degree of knowledge could be imputed to any consumer who agreed to a contractual disclaimer or waiver of liability, as there would be no need for such a limitation of liability unless there was some possibility of defect. These contractual limitations of liability are not ordinarily enforceable, implying that the defendant's liability cannot be limited merely because the plaintiff chose to use the product while knowing that the product might be defective in some respect. The plaintiff must have more particularized knowledge.

Despite general agreement on this requirement, courts have not agreed upon its meaning. One court, for example, has said that "the defendant must show that the plaintiff knew of the specific defect in the product and was aware of the danger arising from it," whereas another has said that "the assumption of risk defense is premised upon knowledge of the dangerous condition of a product rather than recognition of its defectiveness."[12] The courts disagree about whether the plaintiff must know of the defect or only of the danger.

bility for harm caused by the defendant's negligence.").

12. Warner Fruehauf Trailer Co., Inc. v. Boston, 654 A.2d 1272, 1275 (D.C. 1995); Heil Co. v. Grant, 534 S.W.2d 916, 921 (Tex. Civ. App. 1976), writ refused n.r.e. (June 16, 1976).

Similarly, courts have differing interpretations of the requirement that the plaintiff must have voluntarily faced the risk. In many jurisdictions, the requirement is satisfied if the plaintiff made some choice to use the defective product. For example, even if the plaintiff claims that she would have lost her job by refusing to use the defective product, some courts have found that the plaintiff assumed the risk.[13] The plaintiff, after all, could have quit the job rather than face the risk, thereby establishing the existence of choice as required by the defense. By contrast, other courts have found that employees do not voluntarily expose themselves to product defects in the workplace.[14] For these courts, the issue is not whether the plaintiff made some choice to use the defective product, but whether the plaintiff had a reasonable option to do otherwise. Lacking a reasonable alternative, the plaintiff does not voluntarily choose to face the risk by using the defective product. The courts disagree about whether voluntariness merely requires some choice or must involve a reasonable alternative.

To evaluate these issues, we can get guidance from the other doctrines that depend upon consumer choice. As we found earlier, if the ordinary consumer can make an informed safety choice, the risk in question is excluded from the tort duty.[15] As we then found, this principle of consumer choice explains a number of important doctrines, including the general rule immunizing product sellers from categorical liability.[16] These doctrines govern cases in which the ordinary consumer is offered safety alternatives, such as the choice of products in different categories (like a microbus or standard passenger car). In making these choices, the ordinary consumer faces low information costs, enabling her to make an adequately informed risk-utility decision. Having chosen a less safe alternative (a microbus), the ordinary consumer does not reasonably expect the greater safety offered by the product configuration she decided not to purchase (the standard passenger car). The satisfaction of actual consumer expectations explains why this form of consumer choice appropriately limits the seller's duty. Since an adequately informed risk-utility choice by the *ordinary* consumer limits liability, an adequately informed risk-utility choice by an *individual* consumer—the plaintiff—can also limit liability. This principle is sufficient

---

13. *E.g.*, Orfield v. International Harvester Co., 535 F.2d 959, 964 (6th Cir. 1976).

14. *E.g.*, Cremeans v. Willmar Henderson Mfg. Co., 566 N.E.2d 1203 (Ohio 1991) (eliminating defense of assumption of risk for workplace injuries caused by defective products); Rhoads v. Service Mach. Co., 329 F.Supp. 367, 381 (E.D. Ark. 1971) ("The 'voluntariness' with which a worker assigned to a dangerous machine in a factory 'assumes the risk of injury' from the machine is illusory.").

15. *See* Chapter 2, section II.B.

16. *See* Chapter 6, section III.

for resolving the issues that have caused disagreement among courts.

Consider a machine that is defective for not having a guard that would protect users from the exposed moving parts. The design is defective because the cost of the guard is less than the safety benefit of eliminating the risk posed by the exposed moving parts: $B_{guard} < PL$. Suppose the plaintiff is a worker who either had to use the defective machine or quit the job. In making this decision, the plaintiff presumably considered the cost or burden of quitting the job as compared to the risk of being harmed by the exposed moving parts. Since the cost of changing jobs is quite high, the plaintiff decided to face the risk: $B_{quit} > PL$. The plaintiff's risk-utility decision differs from the risk-utility evaluation of the product design. The plaintiff can consistently maintain that the product should be redesigned ($B_{guard} < PL$), even though she made a choice to face the risk ($B_{quit} > PL$). The plaintiff's decision to continue working does not undermine her claim that she is entitled to compensation for the injuries caused by the defect.

The same outcome occurs if the plaintiff had to choose between using the defective product or not using the product at all. To eliminate the risk posed by the defect, the plaintiff must incur the burden of lost product use. By deciding to use the defective product, the plaintiff has concluded that the total benefit of using the product exceeds the injury costs she can expect to incur because of the defect. The plaintiff's decision to use the defective product ($B_{lost\ use} > PL$) does not undermine her claim that the product should be redesigned to eliminate the defect ($B_{precaution} < PL$).

In making a Hobson's choice to use a defective product, the plaintiff has not acted in a manner that persuasively justifies a limitation of liability. If such a choice were sufficient for establishing assumption of risk, then manufacturers would be absolved of liability for defects posing open and obvious dangers or any other risks readily known by product users. The decision to use a product (voluntariness) with an obvious defect (knowledge) would constitute assumption of risk, and the resultant limitation of liability would effectively revitalize the patent danger rule. Such a limitation of liability would be troubling, given the widespread rejection of that rule. To avoid that problem, assumption of risk cannot depend upon any choice to use the defective product. The defense must instead depend upon the right type of choice.

Now suppose that the plaintiff could have used the machine with a guard, but chose not to do so. By deciding to forego that reasonable safety option, the plaintiff presumably concluded that the precaution did not make sense for her. As long as the plaintiff made this decision with sufficient knowledge of the risk-utility factors, her choice to face the risk ($B_{guard} > PL$) is inconsistent with her claim that the defendant has wronged her by selling the defectively designed product ($B_{guard} < PL$). In these circumstances, the plaintiff's choice to use the defective product undermines her claim for compensation, justifying a limitation of liability.

As this analysis shows, the choice can be voluntary only if the plaintiff had a reasonable alternative to using the defective product. For purposes of products liability, reasonableness is defined by the risk-utility test or the equivalent concept of reasonable consumer expectations. The plaintiff therefore can only face a reasonable alternative if she had the option of using a nondefective version of the product, like the guarded machine in the previous example.[17] Having made a well-informed choice to forego this reasonable alternative, the plaintiff assumed the risk. This reasoning explains why "courts are likely to be sympathetic to defendants offering the assumption of risk defense ... when the plaintiff does not use a readily available safety device."[18]

The plaintiff can assume the risk only when she has good information about all of the risk-utility factors that are implicated by the alleged defect. A plaintiff who knows of the danger or risk, *PL*, cannot necessarily make a well-informed risk-utility decision. The plaintiff must know both the risk *PL* and the associated disutility or burden *B* of the safety device, the absence of which renders the product defective. This requirement is consistent with the case law stating that the plaintiff must know of the specific defect rather than only the danger posed by the defect.[19]

Once the defendant has proven that the plaintiff assumed the risk, the next issue involves the impact of this defense on liability. Under the *Restatement (Second)* rule of strict products liability, "the form of contributory negligence which consists in voluntarily and unreasonably proceeding to encounter a known danger, and commonly passes under the name of assumption of risk, is a

17. For further justification of this requirement, see Kenneth W. Simons, *Assumption of Risk and Consent in the Law of Torts: A Theory of Full Preference*, 67 B.U. L. Rev. 213, 238 (1987) (showing why assumption of risk should only apply when the plaintiff's "chosen course of action was based on a full and true preference, i.e., made with knowledge of all the alternatives that defendant had a duty to offer, including that alternative which plaintiff claims defendant tortiously failed to offer.").

18. Shapo, 2 Law of Products Liability ¶ 20.03[7][a], at 11,066.

19. This requirement is also consistent with the rejection of the patent danger rule. *See* Chapter 2, section II.B (explaining why the plaintiff's mere awareness of risk is not a sufficient reason for limiting the seller's duty with respect to open and obvious dangers).

defense" barring the plaintiff from recovery.[20] Today, only some courts bar recovery in these circumstances. Most courts now treat assumption of risk as a form of consumer misconduct that justifies the reduction of liability under principles of comparative responsibility, which is the rule adopted by the *Restatement (Third)*.[21]

Despite their apparent difference, the rules in the *Restatement (Second)* and *Restatement (Third)* can be harmonized. The *Restatement (Second)* characterizes assumption of risk as a form of contributory negligence, and at the time when the *Restatement (Second)* was promulgated, contributory negligence was a complete bar to recovery, explaining why the *Restatement (Second)* treats the defense in this way. In the ensuing decades, the doctrine of comparative responsibility was widely adopted in the U.S., and contributory negligence no longer necessarily barred the plaintiff from recovery. Insofar as assumption of risk is merely one form of contributory negligence—the rule in the *Restatement (Second)*—then the defense only justifies the reduction of liability under the principles of comparative responsibility—the rule in the *Restatement (Third)*.[22]

This treatment of the defense requires justification. There has long been controversy over the issue of whether assumption of risk is a form of contributory negligence. The issue is often framed in terms of the following distinction. In a case involving *primary assumption of risk*, the plaintiff's consent relieves the defendant of the associated duty, thereby barring the plaintiff from recovery altogether, even within a system of comparative responsibility. In a case involving *secondary assumption of risk*, the defendant first breaches an existing duty to the plaintiff, and the plaintiff then assumes the risk. If the plaintiff's choice to face the risk was unreasonable, the conduct is a form of contributory negligence that can reduce the plaintiff's recovery within a system of comparative responsibility. Whether assumption of risk should bar or only reduce recovery accordingly depends upon whether product cases involve primary or secondary assumption of risk, an issue that depends upon the nature of the duty owed by the defendant to the plaintiff.

Duty can be formulated in a manner that excludes the well-informed risk choices made by an individual consumer—the plaintiff. Even if the plaintiff had already been exposed to the risk of

---

20. Restatement (Second) § 402A cmt. n.

21. Restatement (Third) § 17 cmt. d.

22. *See also* Restatement (Third) of Torts: Apportionment of Liability §§ 2

cmt. i, 3 cmt. c (2000) (treating implied or noncontractual assumption of risk as a form of plaintiff negligence governed by comparative responsibility).

being injured by the product defect, her assumption of risk would eliminate the duty before the injury occurred. Lacking the element of duty, the defendant cannot be liable for the subsequently occurring injury. The plaintiff always primarily assumes the risk, then, if her informed risk-utility choices can limit duty.

A different result occurs if the only informed risk choices that can limit duty are those made by the ordinary consumer. When the ordinary consumer cannot make an informed risk-utility decision, the risk is included within the duty, regardless of whether the plaintiff had made an informed choice to face the risk. By selling the defective product that proximately caused the plaintiff's injury, the defendant breached this duty and can be subject to liability. The risk of defect could have been assumed by the plaintiff only if she had decided not to use an available, nondefective version of the product. The plaintiff's choice not to use the nondefective product was objectively unreasonable, since that version of the product, unlike the defective one used by the plaintiff, satisfies the reasonable safety expectations of the ordinary consumer. The plaintiff always secondarily assumes the risk, then, if the only informed risk-utility decisions that can limit duty are those made by the ordinary consumer.

In comparing these two formulations of duty, the analytics favor the formulation that allows for primary assumption of risk, barring the plaintiff from recovery. To repeat an earlier point, the plaintiff's well-informed risk-utility choice to face the risk ($B_{precaution}$ > PL) is inconsistent with her claim that the defendant has wronged her by selling the product that is defective when evaluated in terms of the same risk-utility factors ($B_{precaution}$ < PL). Lacking any wrongdoing, the plaintiff is not entitled to recover from the defendant.

Raw analytics are not necessarily decisive, however. Practical concerns must be considered as well. The difficulty of determining whether an individual plaintiff truly assumed the risk could justify a duty that can be limited only by the informed risk-utility choices of the ordinary consumer, turning assumption of risk into a form of contributory negligence that reduces the plaintiff's recovery under comparative responsibility—the rule adopted by the majority of courts and the *Restatement (Third)*.

To evaluate this rationale, we need to consider more closely the circumstances in which the plaintiff can properly assume the risk. The plaintiff can assume the risk only by making a well-informed choice to use the defective product, despite having had the option of using a nondefective version of the product. This behavior differs from the behavior of the ordinary consumer in every relevant respect. Unlike the plaintiff, the ordinary consumer is unable to make a well-informed choice to face the risk, for otherwise the defendant would owe no duty with respect to that risk, making the plaintiff's conduct irrelevant. And even if the ordinary consumer were well-informed, she would use the nondefective version of the product, unlike the plaintiff who selected the defective version. Assumption of risk therefore requires proof that the plaintiff had better information than the ordinary consumer, and that the plaintiff also had reasons to act differently than the ordinary consumer by using the defective product, despite having had the opportunity to use the nondefective version of the product.

The plaintiff's expertise or prior experience with the product would seem to be probative of these issues, and the courts regularly rely upon these factors to determine whether the plaintiff assumed the risk.[23] This evidence, though, does not reliably show that the plaintiff had better information than the ordinary consumer, or that the plaintiff had reasons to act differently than the ordinary consumer by using the defective product.

Even if the plaintiff has had extensive experience with the product, she might still not adequately appreciate the risk. As long as the plaintiff has not experienced or observed any injuries caused by this particular form of product use, the representative product experience is one of safety rather than risk. When evaluating risk, individuals tend to base their decisions on their representative experiences.[24] Consequently, a consumer who has had extensive experience with a product will often choose to use the defective product by relying upon her representative experience of safety. But if the consumer had not merely relied upon her representative experience and instead fully appreciated the risk, she could easily have chosen otherwise and acted like the ordinary consumer. The plaintiff's extensive experience with the product does not provide a reliable basis for concluding that she made an informed choice to use the defective product.

Individuals also tend to overestimate their abilities.[25] This bias is sometimes called the Lake Woebegone effect, in reference to the

---

23. For a discussion of cases "illustrating generally that plaintiffs are vulnerable to assumption of risk in proportion to their familiarity with products," see Shapo, 2 Law of Products Liability ¶ 20.03[5][b][i].

24. Cognitive psychologists call this the *availability heuristic*, which is based upon the notion that "[f]requently occurring events are generally easier to

imagine and recall than rare events." Studies have found that individuals often rely on this heuristic, which can make them complacent about risk. In effect, what is "out of sight" (the rarely occurring injury) is "out of mind." Paul Slovic, The Perception of Risk 104, 105–09 (2000).

25. "Although psychologists debate the underlying cause of the self-serving

fictional Midwestern town where every child is above average. The bias can cause an experienced user of a machine to remove the guard after concluding that she could always avoid the exposed moving parts, something the ordinary consumer is unable to do. Rather than making an informed decision, the experienced user may be overestimating her ability to avoid inadvertent contact with the machine. Once again, the plaintiff's experience or expertise does not reliably show that she made an informed decision to use the defective (unguarded) machine.

Finally, the plaintiff's experience or expertise with the product does not typically provide any reason for using the defective product rather than its nondefective version. The ordinary consumer, upon being informed of the risk-utility factors, would not choose to use the defective product, so what explains why the plaintiff made that choice? The plaintiff must have a preference for the defective product that is not shared by the ordinary consumer. "Unless we provide our consumer with a questionnaire or otherwise directly inquire as to her preferences, the only signs we will see of her preferences are the choices she makes."[26] The actual choice made by the plaintiff, though, does not imply that she truly preferred the defective product. The plaintiff's choice could easily have been the result of a poorly informed decision rather than a well-informed preference for using the product in its defective condition. What, then, is the evidentiary basis for concluding that the plaintiff had good reasons for using the defective product when the ordinary consumer would make an informed choice to do otherwise?

Since the plaintiff's experience or expertise does not provide a reliable basis for establishing assumption of risk, the court will have a hard time determining whether the plaintiff truly assumed the risk and properly absolved the defendant of any responsibility for the injury. At best, the court can only evaluate the plaintiff's conduct relative to the conduct of the ordinary consumer. The ordinary consumer, upon being informed of the risk, would choose not to face the risk by using the defective product. Insofar as this is the sole reliable evidence, it only supports the conclusion that the plaintiff's decision to face the risk—to use the defective product rather than the nondefective alternative—was an unreasonable

bias, its existence is rarely questioned. The self-serving bias is evident in the 'above average' effect, whereby well over half of survey respondents typically rate themselves in the top 50 percent of drivers, ethics, managerial prowess, productivity, health, and a variety of other desirable skills." Linda Babcock &

George Lowenstein, *Explaining Bargaining Impasse: The Role of Self-serving Biases* in Behavioral Law & Economics 355, 356 (Cass Sunstein ed., 2000) (citations omitted).

26. David M. Kreps, A Course in Microeconomic Theory 26 (1990).

form of product misuse. Evidentiary limitations, therefore, explain why courts can defensibly treat assumption of risk as a form of contributory negligence, with the associated implication that product cases only involve secondary assumption of risk.

Although it does not rely upon these doctrinal labels, this rule has been adopted by the *Restatement (Third)*:

> A plaintiff's recovery of damages for harm caused by a product defect may be reduced if the conduct of the plaintiff combines with the product defect to cause the harm and the plaintiff's conduct fails to conform to generally applicable rules establishing appropriate standards of care.[27]

Under this rule, consumer choice still determines the appropriateness of liability, with the relevant form of consumer choice involving the ordinary consumer. If the ordinary consumer can make a well-informed risk-utility decision, the seller owes no duty and the product cannot be defective in that respect.[28] But if the ordinary consumer is not well informed and would not knowingly face the risk, then these consumer choices define the "generally applicable rules establishing appropriate standards of care." A plaintiff who chose to use a defective product rather than a nondefective alternative has acted unreasonably, making assumption of risk a form of contributory negligence or product misuse.

III. Contributory Negligence and Product Misuse

The defense of contributory negligence could encompass any unreasonable conduct by the plaintiff that proximately caused the injury for which she seeks compensation. The defense operates in this manner when applied to negligence claims, but not when applied to the rule of strict products liability in the *Restatement (Second)*. Under that rule, the only form of contributory negligence involves the plaintiff's "voluntarily and unreasonably proceeding to encounter a known danger," a form of consumer conduct that "commonly passes under the name of assumption of risk." Contributory negligence is not a defense "when such negligence consists merely in a failure to discover the defect in the product, or to guard against its existence."[29] These provisions have been widely

---

27. Restatement (Third) § 17(a).

28. *See* Chapter 6, section III (discussing application of this principle with respect to categorical liability and related doctrines).

29. Restatement (Second) § 402A cmt. n.

adopted.[30]

By absolving the consumer of any duty to discover product defects, the *Restatement (Second)* affirms that the rule of strict products liability is formulated to protect reasonable consumer expectations of safety. The liability rule makes it reasonable for the consumer to assume that the product is not defective, relieving her of any obligation to discover defects. As one court observed, to impose such an obligation on the consumer "would contradict this normal expectation of product safety."[31]

This form of contributory negligence requires an *unreasonable, voluntary* choice to face a *known* risk. For reasons discussed in the last section, the choice can be voluntary only if the plaintiff had a reasonable alternative to using the defective product. Consequently, the plaintiff would be contributorily negligent for using the defective product after having made an informed decision not to use an available nondefective version of the product. In other circumstances, the plaintiff can make a reasonable choice to use a defective product.

Consider an automobile that is defective for not having airbags. To eliminate the risk posed by the defect, the consumer would have to stop using the car. The ordinary consumer is likely to incur a burden of lost product use that is substantially greater than the risk posed by the defect: $B_{lost\ use} > PL$. In these circumstances, the plaintiff's decision to continue using the defective car is objectively reasonable. The plaintiff is not contributorily negligent.

Frequently, the consumer has the option of repairing the product to eliminate the defect. As long as the defect has not caused physical harm, the repair costs involve pure economic loss that is excluded from the seller's tort duty in most jurisdictions.[32] The consumer is responsible for these costs and can act unreasonably by not repairing the defect. The issue depends upon the magnitude of the repair costs. For example, if the cost of installing airbags in the defective automobile would be too expensive ($B_{repair} > PL$), then repair is not a reasonable alternative. The plaintiff is not contributorily negligent for failing to repair the defect. But when the cost of repair is reasonable ($B_{repair} < PL$), and the plaintiff knew of the defect, she could be contributorily negligent for using the defective product rather than repairing it.[33]

30. 2 Madden & Owen on Products Liability § 14:2.

31. McCown v. International Harvester Co., 342 A.2d 381, 382 (Pa. 1975).

32. *See* Chapter 9, section I.

33. Contributory negligence cannot depend upon the plaintiff's constructive knowledge of the defect—that is, knowledge of the defect that the plaintiff did not have but should have had—since the

The *Restatement (Second)* formulation of contributory negligence therefore applies to cases in which (1) the plaintiff secondarily assumed the risk by unreasonably choosing to use the defective product, despite having had the option of using a nondefective version of the product; (2) the plaintiff should not have used the product at all ($B_{lost\ use} < PL$); or (3) the plaintiff should have repaired the defect ($B_{repair} < PL$).

This formulation of contributory negligence does not include an important class of consumer misconduct. For example, suppose a car is defective for having tires that explode once the car is driven at least five miles per hour above the speed limit. Anyone who drives the car at such a speed is acting unreasonably by driving in excess of the legal speed limit. This form of unreasonable consumer behavior is not a cognizable defense under the *Restatement (Second)*, assuming that the plaintiff who was injured by the exploding tire was unaware of the defect. Why did the *Restatement (Second)* limit contributory negligence in this respect?

At the time when the *Restatement (Second)* was promulgated, a contributorily negligent plaintiff was barred from any recovery. This limitation of liability was particularly problematic for defects involving reasonably foreseeable product misuse. Drivers regularly exceed the speed limit, making this form of product misuse a reasonably foreseeable risk that is encompassed by the manufacturer's duty. But if the plaintiff's speeding established contributory negligence and barred the plaintiff from recovery, the car manufacturer would never be liable for defects involving the risk of speeding, like the exploding tire. To avoid this problem, the plaintiff's reasonably foreseeable misuse of the product cannot be contributory negligence. As one court put it, "The asserted negligence of the plaintiff ... was the very eventuality the safety devices were designed to guard against. It would be anomalous to hold that defendant has a duty to install safety devices but a breach of that duty results in no liability for the very injury the duty was meant to protect against."[34] The *Restatement (Second)* had to limit the de-

---

plaintiff as consumer has no duty to discover the defect. The plaintiff must know of the defect. Consequently, the plaintiff may not even be contributorily negligent for failing to repair a known defect, since she has no duty to "guard against [the defect's] existence" under the *Restatement (Second)* rule of strict products liability. The issue is arguable because the language is ambiguous. Does it refer to the plaintiff's need to guard against the possibility a defect exists, or to guard against a known defect by making reasonable repairs? If the plaintiff has no duty to repair, then the cost of repair must be included within the seller's duty, the result achieved by the intermediate rule on economic loss. *See* Chapter 9, section I.

34. Bexiga v. Havir Mfg. Corp., 290 A.2d 281, 286 (N.J. 1972).

fense of contributory negligence in order to retain the necessary safety incentives for product sellers.

Now that comparative responsibility has been widely adopted, the situation has changed. A driver who foreseeably misuses the car by exceeding the speed limit is no longer necessarily barred from recovery. The prospect of at least some recovery means that contributory negligence no longer has to exclude foreseeable product misuse. A plaintiff who foreseeably misused a product can still recover, and the resultant liability can be sufficient to ensure that product sellers comply with the duty regarding foreseeable product misuse. As long as the plaintiff can recover some compensatory damages, she also is entitled to punitive damages in the event that the product seller knew that the product was defective at the time of sale.[35] The threat of punitive damages can give manufacturers the incentive to provide nondefective products involving the risk of foreseeable product misuse. The rationale for excluding product misuse from the rule of contributory negligence no longer applies in a world of comparative responsibility, although there still must be some affirmative reason for treating product misuse as a form of contributory negligence that reduces the plaintiff's recovery.

The reason does not plausibly depend upon safety concerns. The victim of a product accident ordinarily cannot expect to be fully compensated for her injuries. The plaintiff's compensatory damages are reduced by legal fees, typically at least one-third of the damages, and a monetary damages award does not realistically make the victim "whole" for serious physical injuries. From the consumer's perspective, tort damages are not fully compensatory, giving her a sufficient incentive to exercise reasonable care regardless of how liability is apportioned in cases of contributory negligence. After all, how plausible is it that someone would decide to misuse a product and risk injury after reasoning that such behavior would not limit recovery in a tort suit?

A more persuasive reason for limiting the recovery in cases of contributory negligence is one of fairness across consumers. The seller's liability costs are spread among all consumers of the product, and so the cost of product misuse is partially incurred by careful consumers. A "major policy reason which courts articulate for accepting comparative responsibility is that allowing a victim's negligence to be irrelevant to her recovery is unfair because it makes careful product users bear the costs created by the careless users of products."[36]

---

35. *See* Chapter 9, section III.

36. William J. McNichols, *The Relevance of the Plaintiff's Misconduct in*

For good reasons, the courts decided that comparative responsibility applies to product misuse, which is why the *Restatement (Third)* adopts a more expansive conception of contributory negligence than the *Restatement (Second)*. The particular label for the defense no longer matters, however. Under the *Restatement (Third)*, the plaintiff's recovery can be reduced by any form of conduct that "fails to conform to generally applicable rules establishing appropriate standards of care."[37] By definition, product misuse does not conform to the appropriate standard of care, making this form of consumer misconduct an important limitation liability.

Product misuse can limit liability in different ways. The courts have not always been careful to draw these distinctions, making the "relevance of plaintiff's conduct to the plaintiff's recovery in strict tort products liability ... one of the most confusing and perplexing areas of products liability doctrine."[38] Once the relevant distinctions are drawn, however, the appropriate role of product misuse in any given case becomes clear:

1. The tort duty excludes unforeseeable risks. Consequently, if the risk posed by the alleged defect only involves unforeseeable product misuse, the seller has no duty with respect to such product use and the product cannot be defective in that respect.[39] This form of product misuse pertains to the element of duty and is not an affirmative defense based on consumer misconduct.

2. Even if the product is defective with respect to a foreseeable risk of misuse, the plaintiff's unforeseeable misuse can still bar recovery as a matter of proximate cause. In most jurisdictions, the element of proximate cause requires that the plaintiff's injury must be a foreseeable result of the defect.[40] When the plaintiff's unforeseeable misuse is a cause of the injury, most courts conclude that the misuse is a superseding cause of the injury that absolves the defendant of liability.[41] This form of product misuse pertains to the element of proximate cause and is not an affirmative defense based on consumer misconduct.

Strict Tort Products Liability, the Advent of Comparative Responsibility, and the Proposed Restatement (Third) of Torts, 47 Okla. L. Rev. 201, 242 (1994).

37. Restatement (Third) § 17(a).

38. McNichols, *supra* note 36, at 203. Professor McNichols nicely illustrates the confusion that can be engendered by product misuse in his discussion of the Oklahoma cases. *See id.* at 215–229.

39. Restatement (Third) § 2 cmt. p.

40. *See* Chapter 8, section II.

41. *See* 2 Madden & Owen on Products Liability § 14:5.

3. If the product is defective with respect to a foreseeable risk of misuse, and the plaintiff misused the product in a foreseeable manner, the plaintiff is not barred from recovery. The plaintiff's unreasonable behavior provides a defense that must be affirmatively proven by the defendant.

Since the product misuse must be reasonably foreseeable in order for it to be relevant to contributory negligence, the issue of foreseeability is an important aspect of the defense. The issue depends upon consumer expectations. For many products, the consumer can expect to misuse the product in certain circumstances. Virtually all drivers expect that at some time they will exceed the speed limit on a highway, and so the ordinary consumer reasonably expects the car manufacturer to consider the risk of speeding while making safety decisions. Foreseeability accordingly depends upon the likelihood that a consumer will misuse the product in a particular manner. Frequent forms of product misuse are foreseeable, and as the misuse becomes more infrequent, it is more likely to be unforeseeable. As one court put it, such a "use or handling [is] so unusual that the average consumer could not reasonably expect the product to be designed and manufactured to withstand it—a use which the seller, therefore, need not anticipate and provide for."[42] *A form of product misuse is foreseeable if the ordinary consumer would want the product seller to consider the risk while making safety decisions.*

Framed in this manner, the foreseeability inquiry regarding product misuse is identical to the foreseeability inquiry regarding duty and proximate cause.[43] Consequently, an unforeseeable form of product misuse is either outside of the defendant's duty or a superseding cause of the injury that absolves the defendant of liability (points 1 and 2 above). The elements of duty and proximate cause are part of the plaintiff's prima facie case, and so the plaintiff bears the burden of proving that the product use was foreseeable. An unforeseeable product use is not an affirmative defense based on consumer misconduct. Once the plaintiff has proven foreseeability the defendant must prove that the product use in question was unreasonable.

42. Findlay v. Copeland Lumber Co., 509 P.2d 28, 31 (Or. 1973).

43. *See* Chapter 8, section II.

Chapter 11

DISTRIBUTOR AND RETAILER LIABILITY

The rule of strict products liability in the *Restatement (Second)* applies both to the manufacturer of the defective product and "to any wholesale or retail dealer or distributor, and to the operator of a restaurant."[1] The courts "with little dissent ... quite quickly applied the strict tort doctrine to retailers and other nonmanufacturing distributors of defective products."[2]

In these cases, the rule truly is one of strict liability. "Liability attaches even when ... nonmanufacturing sellers or distributors [of defective products] do not themselves render the products defective and regardless of whether they are in a position to prevent defects from occurring."[3]

To be consistent with the requirement of defect, the rule of strict liability for nonmanufacturing sellers and distributors must be based upon a safety rationale. The requirement of defect implies that tort liability can be justified only when it gives product sellers an incentive to supply nondefective products.[4] Otherwise, liability only makes the seller an "insurer" of the product, an outcome the courts routinely reject.

In the landmark opinion that first applied strict products liability to nonmanufacturing retailers and distributors, the California Supreme Court justified strict liability in terms of its ability to promote product safety:

> In some cases the retailer may be the only member of [the overall producing and marketing] enterprise reasonably available to the injured plaintiff. In other cases the retailer himself may play a substantial part in insuring that the product is safe or may be in a position to exert pressure on the manufacturer to that end; the retailer's strict liability thus serves as an added incentive to safety.[5]

Once the retailer has incurred liability for the product defect, it can be indemnified by other product sellers further up the distribu-

---

1. Restatement (Second) § 402A cmt. f.

2. 2 Madden & Owen on Products Liability § 19:1, at 345 (citations omitted).

3. Restatement (Third) § 1 cmt. e.

4. *See* Chapter 3, section III.

5. Vandermark v. Ford Motor Co., 391 P.2d 168, 171–72 (Cal. 1964) (Traynor, J.).

tion chain.[6] When all members of the producing and marketing enterprise are solvent, the indemnity actions will pass liability along to the party responsible for the defect, thereby creating the correct safety incentives. Of course, an upstream distributor or the manufacturer can be insolvent, leaving a nonmanufacturing seller without recourse. That prospect, however, gives sellers an incentive to deal with financially sound distributors and manufacturers. And to the extent that a seller is concerned about liability, it has an incentive to engage in independent product testing, a practice that is increasingly being adopted by large retailers of products manufactured by foreign firms.[7]

Although the rule of strict liability for nonmanufacturing retailers and distributors can promote product safety, this justification is problematic in some respects. Even if the retailer can be indemnified, it must incur substantial legal costs to achieve this outcome. Why permit the plaintiff to sue the retailer when recovery is available from the manufacturer? Inclusion of the retailer in the suit merely raises the cost of distribution (and product price) without providing any safety benefit. Moreover, a small business like the corner deli can sell hundreds of products from different manufacturers and distributors. Does a small business really have the ability to exert any pressure on its upstream distributors and manufacturers with respect to issues of product safety?

Due to these problems, at least 17 states have enacted tort-reform statutes limiting the liability of nonmanufacturing product sellers. "[T]he statutes generally provide that the nonmanufacturing seller or distributor is immunized from strict liability only if: (1) the manufacturer is subject to the jurisdiction of the court of plaintiff's domicile; and (2) the manufacturer is not, nor is likely to become, insolvent."[8] In these circumstances, the plaintiff can obtain full recovery from the manufacturer under strict products liability, so she ordinarily has no reason for attempting to establish negligence liability against a nonmanufacturing seller.[9] Absent a contractual right to indemnification, the manufacturer can receive indemnification from a nonmanufacturing seller only by proving

6. *See, e.g.*, Godoy v. Abamaster of Miami, Inc., 302 A.D.2d 57, 62–63, 754 N.Y.S.2d 301 (N.Y. App. Div. 2d Dept. 2003) (holding that retailers and distributors have actions for indemnity against parties further up the distribution chain).

7. *See* Matt Pottinger, *Outsourcing Safety Tests*, Wall St. J., Nov. 26, 2004, at B1.

8. Restatement (Third) § 1 cmt. e.

9. The seller of an item manufactured by a third party is not subject to negligence liability for harm caused by the "dangerous character or condition" of the item if the seller "neither knows nor has reason to know that it is, or is likely to be, dangerous." Restatement (Second) § 402.

negligence. For cases in which none of the nonmanufacturing sellers were negligent, the manufacturer bears full liability for the defect—the proper result for safety purposes—and the nonmanufacturing sellers typically avoid the unnecessary legal expenses they would otherwise incur if they were subject to strict liability.

The courts have also limited the rule of strict liability, most notably with respect to the sale of used products. Whether strict liability should apply to these transactions has been called "[t]he big question in modern products liability litigation."[10] The issue might seem to be fairly simple—the rule of strict liability in the *Restatement (Second)* expressly applies to "[o]ne who sells *any* product in a defective condition," a provision not limited to new products.[11] Nevertheless, the decisions are "severely split," with "a majority of courts" holding that "strict liability in tort does *not* ordinarily apply to the sale of used products."[12]

The most influential case addressing this issue is *Tillman v. Vance Equipment Company*, which held that the seller of a used crane on an "as is" basis was not subject to strict liability.[13] The Oregon Supreme Court concluded that strict liability would not sufficiently improve product safety:

> As to the risk-reduction aspect of strict products liability, the position of the used-goods dealer is normally entirely outside the original chain of distribution of the product. As a consequence, we conclude, any risk reduction which would be accomplished by imposing strict liability on the dealer in used goods would not be significant enough to justify our taking that step. The dealer in used goods generally has no direct relationship with either manufacturers or distributors. Thus, there is no ready channel of communication by which the dealer and the manufacturer can exchange information about possible dangerous defects in particular product lines or about actual and potential liability claims.

> In theory, a dealer in used goods who is held liable for injuries caused by a design defect or manufacturing flaw could obtain indemnity from the manufacturer. This possibility supports the argument that permitting strict liability claims against dealers in used goods will add to the financial incentive for manufac-

---

10. 2 Madden & Owen on Products Liability § 20:5, at 460.

11. Restatement (Second) § 402A (emphasis added).

12. 2 Madden & Owen on Products Liability § 20:5, at 460–61.

13. 596 P.2d 1299, 1303 (Or. 1979). This is "[p]erhaps the most oft-cited case" addressing the issue. Restatement (Third) § 8 cmt. b Rptrs' Note at 182.

turers to design and build safe products. We believe, however, that the influence of this possibility as a practical factor in risk prevention is considerably diluted where used goods are involved due to such problems as statutes of limitation and the increasing difficulty as time passes of locating a still existing and solvent manufacturer.

Both of these considerations, of course, are also obstacles to injured parties attempting to recover directly from the manufacturer. However, although the provision of an adequate remedy for persons injured by defective products has been the major impetus to the development of strict product liability, it cannot provide the sole justification for imposing liability without fault on a particular class of defendants.[14]

Having rejected strict liability for the reason that it does not sufficiently promote product safety, the *Tillman* court also concluded that the seller of the used crane did not make any safety representations that could have created the type of consumer expectation required by strict liability. This aspect of the opinion is emphasized by the *Restatement (Third)*, which maintains that consumer expectations are the reason why strict liability does not ordinarily apply to the sale of used products.[15]

The safety expectations of the ordinary consumer undoubtedly depend upon whether the product is new or used. As a result of deterioration and other factors, a used product ordinarily is less safe than a new one. This safety difference influences consumer expectations, but it does not justify a special rule limiting the liability of used-good sellers. Product age or usage is a factor that limits liability for *any* product seller.[16] Since this factor already limits liability, it does not persuasively justify a further limitation of liability for a seller of used products.

Consumer expectations instead provide a different explanation for the limitation of strict liability. The ordinary consumer does not

---

14. 596 P.2d at 1304.

15. Restatement (Third) § 8 cmt. b. The seller of a used product is subject to the same liability as the seller of a new product if the "seller's marketing of the [used] product would cause a reasonable person in the position of the buyer to expect the used product to present no greater risk of defect than if the product were new" or if the used product had been "remanufactured by the seller or a predecessor in the commercial chain of distribution of the used product." *Id.* § 8(b)-(c).

16. A manufacturer does not have a duty to provide products that last forever. Consequently, "as products age, responsibility for accident prevention shifts incrementally from the manufacturer to the user.... As a product ages, the user's responsibility is to use and maintain the product properly, to inspect the product for the possibility of wear, and to replace such parts as prudence dictates." 1 Madden & Owen on Products Liability § 10:9, at 673–75.

reasonably expect the seller to be a mere "insurer" of the product. Rather, the ordinary consumer expects the seller of a used product to incur responsibility for a product defect only when doing so promotes product safety. As the *Tillman* court explained, the rule of strict liability when applied to used-product sellers is unlikely to reduce risk. Other courts have immunized the sellers of used goods from strict liability for the same reason.[17] The used-product cases further illustrate how strict liability requires a safety rationale.

The safety rationale also means that nonmanufacturing product sellers should not be subject to strict liability when it would disrupt the product market in a manner that would be harmful to public health and safety. This safety concern underlies the limitation of strict liability provided by comment *k* of the *Restatement (Second)* rule of strict products liability.[18]

Rather than expressly relying upon comment *k*, the courts in a number of cases have limited liability by determining that the transaction involved the sale of a service not governed by the rule of strict *products* liability. The product/service distinction developed by the courts, however, often makes little sense unless understood as a means of limiting strict liability in accordance with the policy reasons identified by comment *k*.

Transactions frequently involve both the provision of a service and the sale of a product. A doctor who implants a medical device provides medical services, while charging the patient for the device. In the event that the medical device is defective, most courts have concluded that the doctor did not sell a product that would subject her to strict liability, with the typical reason being that the sale of the medical device was "incidental" or "ancillary" to the transaction.[19] To determine whether the transaction involved a product or service, most courts look to the essence of the transaction. "The determinative question becomes not what is being charged, but what is being done."[20]

This inquiry is puzzling. Why does it matter whether the essence of the transaction involves the provision of a service or sale of a product? According to the *Restatement (Second)*, "[i]t is not necessary that the seller be engaged solely in the business of selling such products. Thus the rule [of strict liability] applies to the owner of a motion picture theatre who sells popcorn or ice cream, either

17. *E.g.*, Peterson v. Superior Court, 899 P.2d 905, 915 (Cal. 1995) (emphasizing the absence of "risk reduction" as the reason for ordinarily immunizing the seller of used goods from strict liability).

18. *See* Chapter 5, section II.

19. *See, e.g.*, Cafazzo v. Central Medical Health Services, Inc., 668 A.2d 521 (Pa. 1995).

20. *Id.* at 524.

for consumption on the premises or in packages to be taken home."[21] The popcorn might be quite tasty, but it is not the essence of the movie-going experience for the consumer. Nevertheless, the owner of the movie theater is subject to the rule of strict liability under both the *Restatement (Second)* and the *Restatement (Third)*.[22] Since the essence of the movie transaction does not determine whether the theater's sale of popcorn is governed by strict liability, why should the essence of the medical transaction determine whether the doctor's sale of the medical device is governed by strict liability?[23]

According to a leading treatise, the judicial inquiry in these cases does not really depend upon the essence of the transaction, but instead takes the following form:

> In the final analysis, courts often appropriately return to boundary definitions that distinguish products liability from other types of cases—whether the defendant was instrumental in moving a harm-producing "product" through the stream of commerce and whether the chain of distribution ended effectively with the defendant who was more of a product user than supplier.[24]

This interpretation of the judicial inquiry still does not satisfactorily explain the case law. After all, the surgeon who implants the medical device is instrumental in moving the product through the stream of commerce. Unless the device is surgically implanted, it has no commercial value. The surgeon also is not the user of a product like a heart valve; the patient is. The "boundary definitions that distinguish products liability from other types of cases" do not explain why courts have concluded that the surgeon sold a service rather than a product.

Many courts have recognized that the product/service inquiry requires a policy analysis to determine whether the transaction is appropriately governed by strict products liability.[25] Of course,

---

21. Restatement (Second) § 402A cmt. f.

22. *See* Restatement (Third) § 1 cmt. c ("[T]he rule applies to a motion-picture theater's routine sales of popcorn or ice cream, either for consumption on the premises or in packages to be taken home.").

23. To be sure, one might try to separate the popcorn transaction from the movie-ticket transaction. But the provision of health care and a medical device can also be split in this manner, as each involves a separate cost that is charged to the consumer. Moreover, the popcorn transaction depends upon the movie-ticket transaction (the consumer otherwise wouldn't be buying the popcorn), so the fact that the medical-device transaction depends upon the provision of health care does not distinguish the cases.

24. 2 Madden & Owen on Products Liability § 20:3, at 445.

25. *E.g.*, Cafazzo, 668 A.2d at 525–27.

policy analysis can be mushy and unhelpful, but the courts can derive the relevant guidance from comment *k*. The rule of strict products liability is limited for the policy reasons identified by comment *k,* implying that the rule of strict products liability for nonmanufacturing sellers can be limited for these same reasons.

For example, many courts have concluded that pharmaceuticals and other medical products are "unavoidably unsafe" products under comment *k* that are not subject to strict liability.[26] This conclusion implies that the nonmanufacturing sellers of such products are also exempt from strict liability. Consistently with this reasoning, most courts have concluded that medical professionals and even pharmacies sell services and not products. This limitation of strict liability, however, is based on the product/service distinction rather than comment *k*.[27]

By expressly relying upon comment *k*, the courts could provide better-reasoned results in these cases. A good illustration is provided by a pair of cases decided by the New Jersey Supreme Court. In *Magrine v. Spector*, the court held that a dentist was not the seller of a defective syringe needle because he was providing a service to the plaintiff.[28] Thereafter, the court was confronted by a case in which the plaintiff sought to impose strict liability on a beauty parlor for applying a defective permanent wave solution to her hair, causing it to fall out. Like a dentist or doctor, the beauty parlor provided a service requiring the use of a product for which it did not separately charge the customer. Nevertheless, the court applied strict liability to the beauty parlor:

> The beautician is engaged in a commercial enterprise; the dentist and doctor in a profession. The former caters publicly not to a need but to a form of aesthetic convenience or luxury, involving the rendition of non-professional services and the application of products for which a charge is made.... [Dentists and doctors] must be deemed to have a special and essential role in our society, that of studying our physical and mental ills and ways to alleviate or cure them, and that of applying their knowledge, empirical judgment and skill in an effort to diagnose and then to relieve or to cure the ailment of a particular patient. Thus their paramount function—the essence of their function—ought to be regarded as the furnishing of opinions and services. Their unique status and the rendition

26. *See* Chapter 5, section III.

27. *E.g.,* Murphy v. E.R. Squibb & Sons, Inc., 710 P.2d 247 (Cal. 1985) (holding that pharmacy was engaged in the business of supplying a service that was not subject to strict products liability).

28. 250 A.2d 129 (N.J. 1969).

of these sui generis services bear such a necessary and intimate relationship to public health and welfare that their obligation ought to be grounded and expressed in a duty to exercise reasonable competence and care toward their patients. In our judgment, the nature of the services, the utility of and the need for them, involving as they do, the health and even survival of many people, are so important to the general welfare as to outweigh in the policy scale any need for the imposition on dentists and doctors of the rules of strict liability in tort.[29]

The court emphasizes that the essence of the transaction for medical professionals involves the "furnishing of opinions and services," but the reason for exempting these individuals from strict liability involves the importance of the transaction for "the health and even survival of many people." As comment *k* establishes, these transactions should be exempt from strict liability due to the way in which that liability rule can disrupt a market essential to public health and safety. Had the court expressly relied upon the policy reasons in comment *k* to exempt medical professionals from strict liability, it could have avoided the unnecessary disparagement of beauticians. One can accept that beauty parlors are properly subject to strict liability because they provide a product/service hybrid that is not essential to public health and safety. That conclusion does not require assertions about the professionalism of beauticians. But when the decision instead depends upon the essence of the transaction, the courts end up making an "elitist distinction" between professionals and nonprofessionals.[30] This problem could be avoided if courts relied upon the policy reasons in comment *k* to determine whether a nonmanufacturing seller should be subject to strict liability.

As illustrated by this issue and others involving the liability of nonmanufacturing distributors and retailers, courts tend to reach the right results in these cases, although their failure to rely exclusively upon the safety rationale for strict products liability has produced confusing opinions and some severe splits in the case law. By analyzing these issues in terms of safety or risk reduction, courts could more persuasively justify a number of doctrines that have otherwise eluded satisfactory explanation.

29. Newmark v. Gimbel's Inc., 258 A.2d 697, 702–03 (N.J. 1969).

30. *Murphy*, 710 P.2d at 258 (Bird, J., dissenting).

Chapter 12

BYSTANDER INJURIES

By focusing almost exclusively on the consumer—the purchaser or user of the product—our approach so far reflects the orientation of products liability. The consumerist orientation comes from the implied warranty, which is the primary rationale for strict products liability in the *Restatement (Second)*.[1] One who offers a product for sale implicitly represents that the product can safely perform its intended function. The implied warranty accordingly protects the consumer's reasonable expectation that the seller has provided a nondefective product, and the frustration of this safety expectation justifies holding the seller strictly liable for the defect. The product transaction does not create an implied representation of safety for a bystander. Consequently, the *Restatement (Second)* "expresses no opinion" whether strict products liability applies "to harm to persons other than users or consumers."[2]

After the courts adopted the *Restatement (Second)* rule of strict products liability, subsequent decisions "almost unanimously allowed foreseeable bystanders, including rescuers, to recover for their injuries caused by defective products."[3] The courts had already held that the implied warranty is not limited by the requirement of privity—one who buys a product has the same safety expectations as one who uses the product—and "the same precautions required to protect the buyer or user would generally do the same for the bystander."[4] Thus, the "prevailing reason for the extension [was] the feeling that there is no essential difference between the injured user or consumer and the injured bystander."[5]

In one of the first cases posing this issue, the drive shaft in a new automobile buckled, causing the driver to lose control of the car on the highway and crash into an oncoming automobile driven by the plaintiff. The California Supreme Court decided that the plaintiff could recover under strict products liability: "An automobile with a defectively connected drive shaft constitutes a substantial hazard on the highway not only to the driver and passenger of the car but also to pedestrians and other drivers. The public policy

---

1. *See* Chapter 1, section I.

2. Restatement (Second) § 402A, caveat (1).

3. 1 Madden & Owen on Products Liability § 5:3, at 269.

4. Giberson v. Ford Motor Co., 504 S.W.2d 8, 12 (Mo. 1974).

5. *Id.* at 11.

which protects the driver and passenger of the car should also protect the bystander...."[6] Since the defect threatened both consumers and bystanders, the court—like others—could easily conclude that bystanders are protected by strict products liability.

This extension of strict products liability has masked an important difference between bystanders and consumers. Unlike bystanders, the consumer has the opportunity to make product choices. When the ordinary consumer makes well-informed safety choices, the resultant satisfaction of consumer expectations eliminates the rationale for the tort duty. This limitation of liability finds expression in many doctrines, including the general rule against categorical liability, which are formulated to ensure that tort liability does not unduly restrict consumer choice.[7] These consumer-choice doctrines should not necessarily limit the liability of product sellers with respect to third-party harms. Consumers can make product choices that create unreasonable risks for bystanders, a good example being provided by a case we considered earlier in which the consumer purchased an ornamental hubcap for an automobile with "protruding spinning blades" that severely injured a motorcycle rider.[8] The hubcap did not frustrate the consumer's expectations of safety, but it did create an unreasonable risk of harm for the plaintiff motorcycle rider—a bystander—who was badly injured by the hubcap. In these circumstances, the satisfaction of consumer expectations does not justify a limitation of the manufacturer's liability, although courts have often made this mistake by not distinguishing between bystanders and consumers.

A good example involves the wrongful death actions filed against the manufacturer of Black Talon bullets. Upon impact, the bullets expose razor-sharp edges at a 90–degree angle to the bullet, substantially increasing the wounding power of the bullet. A number of third-party victims were injured or killed by these bullets when Colin Ferguson went on a shooting rampage on the Long Island Railroad. The plaintiffs claimed the design was defective, with the alleged reasonable alternative design being an "ordinary" bullet. In dismissing these claims, the federal appellate court concluded that "[t]here is no reason to search for an alternative safer design where the product's sole utility is to kill and maim."[9] In dissent, Judge Guido Calabresi argued that the design could be defective for having a low social utility that was outweighed by the

---

6. Elmore v. American Motors Corp., 451 P.2d 84, 89 (Cal. 1969).

7. *See* Chapter 6, section III.

8. Passwaters v. General Motors Corp., 454 F.2d 1270 (8th Cir. 1972)

(applying Iowa law). The case is discussed in Chapter 6, section III.

9. McCarthy v. Olin Corp., 119 F.3d 148, 155 (2d Cir. 1997) (applying New York law).

great danger posed by the bullets.[10] Judge Calabresi was correct, although he failed to persuade the majority. His dissenting opinion never identified how the majority's ruling inappropriately relied upon consumer-choice doctrines to resolve tort claims that did not involve any injured consumers.

Consumer-choice doctrines are obviously relevant for cases involving injured consumers. A consumer presumably purchases the Black Talon bullet because of its enhanced wounding capabilities. This informed consumer choice to forego a safer alternative (ordinary bullets) ordinarily should absolve the manufacturer of liability for defective design.[11] However, a consumer-choice doctrine should not limit the manufacturer's liability in cases involving third-party harms. The consumer who is attracted by the ability of the Black Talon bullets to "maim and kill" may not sufficiently account for this impact on innocent third parties. Indeed, the self-interested consumer would ignore these third-party harms altogether. The tort question accordingly depends upon the issue of whether the Black Talon bullets present an unreasonable risk of harm to bystanders. The reasonableness inquiry would determine whether ordinary bullets adequately "maim and kill" for purposes of self-defense, which presumably is the only legitimate consumer interest involved in the bullet design. If ordinary bullets are sufficient for purposes of self-defense, then the Black Talon bullets would create an unreasonable risk for innocent third parties. Even though the sole utility of the Black Talon bullets is to "maim and kill," as the majority held, that is not a sufficient reason for summarily rejecting the reasonable alternative design proposed by the bystander plaintiffs.

The majority's reasoning in the Black Talon case is reflective of the approach taken by courts in other tort cases involving gun manufacturers. As a product category, guns impose substantial risks on third parties. In 1993, for example, criminals used guns in the commission of over one million murders, assaults, robberies and rapes.[12] The risk of criminal misuse becomes even higher when defined in terms of handguns rather than guns.[13] The products liability claims filed on behalf of gunshot victims against gun manufacturers have been uniformly rejected by courts because plaintiffs could not show that the handguns were defectively de-

---

10. *Id.* at 162 (Calabresi, J., dissenting).

11. *See* Chapter 6, section III.

12. Gary Kleck, Targeting Guns 24 (1997).

13. *See generally* Stephen P. Teret & Garen J. Wintemute, *Handgun Injuries: The Epidemiologic Evidence for Assessing Legal Responsibility*, 6 Hamline L. Rev. 341 (1983).

signed.[14] Absent an identifiable defect, the courts would have to impose categorical liability on handguns. The courts' resistance to categorical liability would be understandable for claims brought by consumers, since the general rule against categorical liability stems from the desirability of fostering consumer choice across product categories. But these cases typically involve bystander injuries, with the plaintiff alleging that consumers should not be given the choice to purchase the gun in question. By relying on the general rule against categorical liability to dismiss these claims, the courts have failed to recognize that products can be unreasonably dangerous for the innocent third parties who suffer the injurious consequences of consumer product choices.

To be sure, the courts could appropriately reject categorical liability in the gun cases for other reasons.[15] Regardless of the correct outcome, these cases show how courts routinely rely upon consumer-choice doctrines to dismiss tort claims involving bystanders, a predictable outcome of a tradition that treats bystanders and consumers as being "essentially similar" for purposes of products liability.

The problem may be even more acute for car accidents involving passenger vehicles and sport utility vehicles (SUVs).[16] According to one government study, SUV designs in 1999 were causing nearly 1,000 "unnecessary deaths a year in other vehicles."[17]

14. *See* Timothy D. Lytton, *Tort Claims Against Gun Manufacturers for Crime–Related Injuries: Defining a Suitable Role for the Tort System in Regulating the Firearms Industry*, 65 Mo. L. Rev. 1, 10–14 (2000).

15. If a gun is defective no matter how designed, then it will be driven from the market. Any seller that decided to continue marketing the gun would face punitive damages for selling a product known to be defective. *See* Chapter 9, section III. For this reason, a court could defensibly conclude that any ban of a gun is a matter for the legislature and not the courts.

This problem, though, does not foreclose other tort suits against the sellers of handguns. Once the bystander is adequately distinguished from the consumer for purposes of tort liability, then the evidentiary rationale for strict liability can justify a rule of strict liability for the abnormally dangerous activity of marketing and selling handguns. *See* Mark Geistfeld, *Tort Law and Criminal Be-havior (Guns)*, 43 Ariz. L. Rev. 311 (2001) (explaining why the only reason for not applying strict liability involves the gun owner's interest in self-defense).

16. This material is drawn from the eye-opening article by Howard Latin & Bobby Kasolas, *Bad Designs, Lethal Profits: The Duty to Protect Other Motorists Against SUV Collision Risks*, 82 B.U. L. Rev. 1161 (2002). The authors argue that the courts have erroneously failed to appreciate the duty that automobile manufacturers owe to bystanders. While agreeing with this conclusion, my claim is that the problem is attributable to the courts' general failure to recognize that consumer-choice limitations on duty do not apply to bystander claims.

17. *See* Keith Bradsher, *Carmakers to Alter S.U.V.'s to Reduce Risk to Other Autos*, N.Y. Times, March 21, 2000, at A1.

SUVs impose excessive collision damage because the height differential creates a mismatch between their structures and the protective structures of vehicles with lower ride-heights. In frontal collisions or collisions on a tangent, SUVs often override a passenger car's front bumper and frame, driving the engine or other relatively soft metal components into the passenger compartment. In frontal collisions between large SUVs and passenger cars, the SUV can ride up onto the car's hood and crush it, striking the base of the windshield and causing devastating damage to the car's passenger compartment and its occupants. This height differential is even more lethal in side-impact collisions.[18]

In the first reported case involving the allegation that a SUV design posed an unreasonable override risk for occupants of other cars, the plaintiff was injured when a Range Rover crashed into the side of her passenger vehicle and penetrated the passenger compartment.[19] The plaintiff's expert testified that the Range Rover could have been redesigned to reduce the likelihood that it would override another vehicle in a manner that would not have reduced the utility of a SUV. In support, the expert pointed to designs that SUV manufacturers had subsequently adopted to reduce the risk of override. After observing that the Range Rover's "bumper height, stiffness coefficient, and weight are comparable to similar SUV makes and models" that were manufactured in the same model year, the California Appellate Court affirmed dismissal of the plaintiff's claim for negligent design:

> The law does not impose an obligation on automobile manufacturers to make homogenous vehicles, but takes into account, in determining liability, the unique designs of a vehicle. For example, in *Dreisonstok v. Volkswagenwerk, A.G.,* . . . the Fourth Circuit considered the unique design of a minibus, concluding that the manufacturer did not violate a duty of care. While its minibus design did not afford the same protection to its passengers as compared with a conventional passenger car, it had the design advantage of maximizing cargo space. . . . Just as in *Dreisonstok*, accepting [plaintiff's] theory of liability fails to consider the unique features of a special

18. Latin & Kasolas, *supra* note 16, at 1201–02 (citations and paragraph structure omitted).

19. De Veer v. Land Rover North America, Inc., 2001 WL 34354946, slip op. (Cal. Ct. App. Aug. 14, 2001) (reprinted in Latin & Kasolas, *supra* note 16, at 1229–40). This was the only "pertinent" case that could be found by Latin & Kasolas.

class of vehicles that are designed to perform off road and carry more and heavier cargo.[20]

This case further illustrates how courts rely upon a consumer-choice doctrine to dismiss the tort claims of a bystander. As discussed earlier, the *Dreisenstok* case establishes that the consumer choice of a product category limits the duty of the product seller.[21] In the circumstances of the case, however, a consumer-choice doctrine does not provide an appropriate limitation of liability. A well-informed consumer choice of SUV design predictably leads to an "arms war" on the highway. To protect themselves from the increased override risk posed by SUVs, consumers rationally purchase an SUV for themselves. But as one empirical study has recently found, when "drivers shift from cars to light trucks or SUVs, each crash involving fatalities of light-truck or SUV occupants that is prevented comes at a cost of at least 4.3 additional crashes that involve deaths of car occupants, pedestrians, bicyclists, or motorcyclists."[22] The implications of these consumer choices have been summed up the Administrator of the National Highway Safety Administration: "The theory that I'm going to protect myself and my family even if it costs other people's lives has been the operative incentive for the design of these vehicles, and that's just wrong."[23] Consumer choices can create incentives for sellers to adopt product designs that are unreasonably dangerous for bystanders. To evaluate the bystander's allegation of wrongdoing, a court cannot summarily dismiss the design-defect claim by relying on consumer-choice doctrines. To do so merely enshrines the operative incentive that ignores bystander interests.

In extending strict products liability to bystanders, the California Supreme Court did not contemplate that bystanders would be treated in this manner:

> If anything, bystanders should be entitled to greater protection than the consumer or user where injury to bystanders from the defect is reasonably foreseeable. Consumers and users, at least, have the opportunity to inspect for defects and to limit their purchases to articles manufactured by reputable manufacturers and sold by reputable retailers, whereas the bystander ordinarily has no such opportunities. In short, the bystander is in

---

20. *De Veer*, 2001 WL 34354946 (reprinted in Latin & Kasolas, *supra* note 16, at 1239) (citation omitted).

21. *See* Chapter 6, section III.

22. Michelle J. White, *The "Arms Race" on American Roads: The Effect of Sport Utility Vehicles and Pickup Trucks*

on Traffic Safety, 47 J.L. & Econ. 333, 334 (2004).

23. Danny Hakim, *Regulators Seek to Make S.U.V.'s Safer*, N.Y. Times, Jan. 30, 2003, at C1 (quoting Dr. Jeffrey W. Runge).

greater need of protection from defective products which are dangerous, and if any distinction should be made between bystanders and users, it should be made ... to extend greater liability in favor of the bystanders.[24]

As a stranger to the product transaction, the bystander cannot protect herself by making the sort of choices available to consumers. Lacking this means of protection, the bystander should be afforded greater protection than the consumer. Bystanders could receive greater protection if their tort claims were not limited by consumer-choice doctrines, but the courts have not protected bystanders in this way. Instead, the courts typically treat the bystander as being essentially similar to the consumer.

By not distinguishing bystanders from consumers, the courts have failed to appreciate the distinctive characteristic of products liability. Unlike other tort doctrines, products liability involves a confluence of the implied warranty and general negligence principles. Each provides a sufficient justification for strict products liability, with the implied warranty yielding the consumer expectations test for liability, and negligence principles yielding the risk-utility test. As applied to the consumer, these two doctrines are substantively equivalent: The ordinary consumer reasonably expects the amount of product safety that maximizes consumer welfare, and that amount of safety is required by the risk-utility test.[25] The product transaction does not create any safety expectations for those who are complete strangers to the transacting parties. The implied warranty no longer applies, and the liability rule does not have to protect the reasonable safety expectations of the ordinary consumer. The distinctive feature of products liability is missing in cases involving bystanders, making it necessary to protect bystanders with a general rule of tort law, rather than any rule specific to products liability.

Tort law ordinarily mediates the risky interactions between strangers by the rule of negligence. As previously discussed, negligence principles can justify the rule of strict products liability. According to this justification, strict liability should apply to manufacturing defects, like a defective drive shaft in an automobile, because of the evidentiary difficulties that would be faced by a plaintiff who had to prove that the seller unreasonably failed to discover the defect.[26] These evidentiary difficulties are the same for all plaintiffs, whether a consumer or bystander. The evidentiary

24. *Elmore*, 451 P.2d at 89.
25. *See* Chapter 2, section II.A.
26. *See* Chapter 1, section II.

rationale for strict liability, therefore, justifies the extension of strict products liability to bystanders.

This extension does not imply that the bystander only merits the same degree of tort protection as a consumer. The bystander's tort rights do not have to be efficient or otherwise maximize the welfare of consumers. The consumer benefits from the product use, whereas the bystander merely faces the risk of injury. Unlike consumers, bystanders do not incur both the burdens and benefits of products liability, and so the fair protection of the bystander's tort right does not have to efficiently trade off these costs and benefits.[27] The tort issue no longer involves protecting consumer safety expectations with liability rules that maximize consumer welfare—the distinctive characteristic of products liability. These cases instead return us to the general study of tort law.

---

27. *See* Chapter 2, section I (explaining how the requirements of fairness correspond to the requirements of efficiency when the right-holder internalizes the costs and benefits of tort liability).

*

TABLE OF CASES

References are to Pages.

261

INDEX

References are to pages

†